African American Philosophers and Philosophy

African American Philosophers and Philosophy

An Introduction to the History, Concepts, and Contemporary Issues

John H. McClendon III and Stephen C. Ferguson II

BLOOMSBURY ACADEMIC
LONDON • NEW YORK • OXFORD • NEW DELHI • SYDNEY

BLOOMSBURY ACADEMIC
Bloomsbury Publishing Plc
50 Bedford Square, London, WC1B 3DP, UK
1385 Broadway, New York, NY 10018, USA
29 Earlsfort Terrace, Dublin 2, Ireland

BLOOMSBURY, BLOOMSBURY ACADEMIC and the Diana logo are trademarks of
Bloomsbury Publishing Plc

First published in Great Britain 2019
Reprinted 2019, 2020 (twice), 2021, 2022

Cover design by Maria Rajka
Cover illustration by Boaz Balachsan

A catalogue record for this book is available from the British Library.

A catalog record for this book is available from the Library of Congress.

ISBN: HB: 978-1-3500-5794-4
PB: 978-1-3500-5795-1
ePDF: 978-1-3500-5793-7
eBook: 978-1-3500-5797-5

Typeset by Deanta Global Publishing Services, Chennai, India
Printed and bound in Great Britain

To find out more about our authors and books visit www.bloomsbury.com
and sign up for our newsletters.

Contents

Tables

Acknowledgments

All intellectual work—like human labor—is social and collective. Work such as ours that has been percolating for over twenty years owes much to the support and assistance of a great many institutions and individuals. First and foremost, the completion of this book would not have been possible without the love, support, and assistance of our friends and families. John H. McClendon says this: I would like to thank a number of colleagues, family, and friends for valuable contributions in facilitating my research and substantive thinking on numerous topics pertaining to various aspects of the subject matter. Deborah L. McClendon, Pia Dara McClendon, Roger L. McClendon, Suzanne McClendon, Renee L. McClendon, Bob 'Big Cutty' Bass, Malik Simba, Keith Parker, and the late Terry Day have all assisted me and undoubtedly your personal encouragement has been priceless. Your enduring patience and support cannot be captured in words. My initial work in philosophy of science was considerably grounded on the insights gained from Roger L. McClendon, Wilson Jones, and Mr. Percy Jones. My grasp of philosophy of music is considerably aided by the astute knowledge provided by Bob 'Big Cutty' Bass and Renee L. McClendon. The late Drs. Francis A. Thomas and William R. Jones were my mentors in the history of African American philosophy, and they collectively paved the way for our text. Drs. John Mendez and Clanton C. W. Dawson offered room for my reflections in the philosophy of religion. Dr. Terry Day willingly gave his expertise in the field of psychology, while Dr. George Yancy and I have shared in numerous discussions on historic Black philosophers; such deliberations are greatly appreciated. My research efforts over the years gained financial support from Dr. Jill Reich, then vice president of Academic Affairs at Bates College and more recently from Dr. Matt McKeon, chair of the Department of Philosophy at Michigan State University. Dr. McKeon's support by way of a sabbatical leave in the spring semester of 2018 was an immeasurable contribution for granting me time in finishing our project. The Undergraduate Research Initiative grant from the MSU College of Arts and Letters in the academic year 2017–18 also provided for the services of Ramon Wright, and he did an exemplary job in uncovering needed resources. And to Deja, Maya, Marquis,

Jordan, and Shawntre, now you have a source for comprehending how Papa views the world of which you will shape its future. Lastly, to my cherished coauthor Dr. Stephen C. Ferguson, if we were playing the piano you would be my right hand that played the melody with brilliance and poise. Thanks for making this project the fruition of decades of hard work. This book is dedicated to my son Roger LaMonte McClendon and my daughter Pia Dara McClendon; thanks for your unconditional love.

Stephen C. Ferguson would like to thank his parents Nancy and Stephen Ferguson. He says this: I am grateful to a host of friends and colleagues, who provided assistance, support, or just a good laugh during the writing of this book: Tariq Al-Jamil, Jason Coupet, Greg Dawes, the late Terry Day, Michelle Eley, Barbara Foley, John Mendez, Gregory Meyerson, Anthony Neal, Antonie Rice, Dwayne Tunstall, and George Yancy. Each, in his or her own way, has gone beyond the call of duty to help us through this process. Olen Cole, as the former chair of History at North Carolina A&T, made me aware of Wayman B. McLaughlin. And I would like to thank my colleagues in the Department of Philosophy and Religious Studies, particularly Michael Pendelbury, for providing an academic home. And to my coauthor John McClendon, working with you is like composing a great jazz composition; our chemistry is like William "Billy" Strayhorn and Duke Ellington. Thank you for the many years of laughs, cigars, and political friendship. I would like to dedicate this book to the memory of my grandma Doris Handy and William R. Jones. Lastly, I want to acknowledge my son, Trey. While I worked away on this book, you have grown into a teenager and locked yourself away in your room. Please come out of your room and become a part of our intergenerational relay race. Take the baton and advance the struggle. As always, my son is responsible for the one or two mistakes you may find—if there are any mistakes at all.

Special thanks goes to Terry Day, Albert G. Mosley, Antonie Rice, Malik Simba, Robert Bass, and Brittany O'Neal who read portions of the manuscript in a spirit of constructive criticism.

Research often grows out of teaching. Many of the ideas for this book grew out of seminars and courses we have taught over the years dealing with African American philosophy. We would like to thank the following former students for their assistance and/or intellectual energy: both Victoria Holsey and Kelsey Overberg were not only outstanding students of McClendon at MSU which provided insights for our text but each also read portions of our manuscript and provided helpful suggestions. In addition, the following students were vital contributors as researchers: Gayla Aikens, Kimberly

Harris, Melissa Murdock, Brittany O'Neal, Swayzine Thompson, Andrew Woodson, Dwayne Freeman, Lorenzo Buchanan, Nanfeng Li, and Ramon Wright.

We wish to thank Philosophy Editor Colleen Coalter and her editorial assistants Helen Saunders and Becky Holland in addition to all of the other staff at Bloomsbury, particularly Leela Ulaganathan, for their tremendous efforts and hard work in helping to realize our vision for this book.

In our search to reconstruct the history of African American philosophers, we were provided with the invaluable assistance of archivists and research librarians, particularly the Inter-Library Loan staff at North Carolina State University and Michigan State University. We would like to thank the following archives, archivists, and reference librarians at the following colleges and universities: Ms. Gail Favors at North Carolina A&T State University; St. Augustine; Dr. Nikki Maggie at Olivet College; Ms. Kristen Chinery at Wayne State University; Ms. Diane Gallagher at Boston University; Ms. Rosemary Stevenson and Ms. Vera Mitchell at University of Illinois-Champaign; Dr. Linda Tang at Michigan State University; Ms. LeTisha Stacey at Philander Smith College; Ms. Lynn Ayers at Payne Theological Seminary; Ms. Jacqueline Brown at Wilberforce University; Ms. Francine B. Archer at Virginia State University; Ms. Andrea Twiss-Brooks at the University of Chicago; Ms. Stacy S. Jones at the Atlanta University Center; Dr. Alan Delozier at Seton Hall University; and Ms. Karen Klinkenberg at the University of Minnesota.

Lastly, we would like to thank the Institute for Race Relations for permission to reprint portions of the following article: John H. McClendon, "The Afro-American Philosopher and the Philosophy of the Black Experience: A Bibliographic Essay on a Neglected Topic in Philosophy and Black Studies," *Sage Race Relations Abstracts* 7(1) (1982), 1–51.

Biographical Information on Selected African American Philosophers

Chapter 1

1 **Henry T. Johnson** attended the University of South Carolina studying with Black philosopher Richard T. Greener. A student at the Historically Black University Colleges (HBCU) of Howard University and Lincoln University (PA), Johnson graduated from the latter with high honors in 1883. Johnson had the DD and PhD conferred. Among his many publications are *The Elements of Physic Philosophy* and *The Black Man's Burden*.

2 **William D. Johnson** graduated as valedictorian from Lincoln University (PA) in 1868. During his student years at Lincoln, he wrote a short history of the institution. Additionally, Johnson served as both commissioner and secretary of Education of the A.M.E. Church and was an ordained A.M.E minister. Lincoln conferred on Johnson both MA and DD.

3 Born in Williamsport, Pennsylvania, in 1864, **Charles Victor Roman**'s family migrated in 1870 to Canada. Both of his parents were active in the Underground Railroad. Roman spent his youthful years in Canada, graduating from Hamilton Collegiate Institute (Ontario). After returning to the United States, he enrolled at the HBCU, Meharry Medical College in Nashville, Tennessee. Graduating from Meharry in 1890, he also earned an MA in philosophy and history at (HBCU) Fisk University in Nashville. A pioneer in the field of Ophthalmology and Otolaryngology medicine, Roman did postgraduate medical studies at Medical School of Chicago (1899) and at the Royal Ophthalmic Hospital and Central London Nose, Throat, and Ear Hospital in England (1904).

4 **Joseph Charles Price** (1854–93) was born as a free person in 1854. He attended the HBCU Shaw University and completed his undergraduate work at Lincoln University (PA) in 1875. Valedictorian of his class, Price later founded the HBCU Livingstone College in Salisbury, North Carolina, in 1882. Price was only twenty-eight years old at that time and served as its president until his death.

5 Born in Guyana, **George G. M. James** (1893–1956) earned a Bachelor of Arts and Bachelor of Theology at Durham University (England) and worked toward his doctorate at Columbia University (New York). He was trained in classics. He was Professor of Logic and Greek at Livingstone College; Professor of Languages and Philosophy at Johnson C. Smith; Professor of Mathematics and Dean of Men at Georgia State College (which later became Savannah State); Professor of Social Science at Alabama A. & M. College and as Professor of Social Sciences at Arkansas A. M. & N. at Pine Bluff (which later became University of Arkansas at Pine Bluff). He was on faculty at this last institution when he wrote *The Stolen Legacy*.

6 **Winson R. Coleman** (1905–84) earned his BA from Penn College in 1928 and his MA from Haverford College in 1929. He won two fellowships funded by the General Education Board while working on his doctorate. He received his doctorate from the University of Chicago in 1950. He started teaching at Johnson C. Smith in the fall of 1929. He was chair of the philosophy department before becoming dean of the College of Liberal Arts and Sciences. While at Johnson C. Smith, he also started and coached the tennis team beginning in 1931, which won CIAA championships in 1934, 1935, 1940, 1941, 1942, 1943, 1944, and 1960. (The CIAA was formed in 1912 as the Colored Intercollegiate Athletic Association before changing to the Central Intercollegiate Athletic Association in 1950.) He retired after working at Johnson C. Smith for forty-five years.

7 **John Milton Smith** (1910–1983) was born in Fayetteville, North Carolina. He received the BA, S.T.B., and MA degrees from Lincoln University (Pennsylvania). He did further study at the Western Theological Seminary/University of Pittsburgh and received the S.T.M. degree. In 1941, he received the PhD from the University of Iowa. He taught at North Carolina A & T in addition to State Teachers College (Elizabeth City, North Carolina).

8 **Albert Millard Dunham Jr.** (1903–49) received his PhD from the University of Chicago in 1933. He was a student of the renowned philosopher Alfred North Whitehead. Dunham was married to a painter and social worker named Frances Taylor Dunham Catlett. After years of mental illness, Dunham died in Saint Elizabeth's Hospital, Washington, DC, in 1949. Among his published works is the coedited book *George Herbert Mead: The Philosophy of the Act*.

9 Born in Birmingham, Alabama, **Angela Yvonne Davis** (1944–) studied French at Brandeis University (BA) and philosophy in Frankfurt, West Germany. In 1965, she graduated magna cum laude, a member of Phi Beta Kappa. After returning to the United States, she studied with Herbert Marcuse at UC San Diego; she earned a master's degree from UC San Diego in 1968. While she completed all the requirements for the PhD, she never submitted a dissertation. She never actually received her PhD because her research and writings were stolen by the FBI in 1970. Her dissertation was never returned to her. She was reportedly working on a dissertation dealing with the theory of force in Kant's political philosophy and German idealism in general. She was a professor of Ethnic Studies at the San Francisco State University from at least 1980 to 1984. Davis was a professor in the History of Consciousness and the Feminist Studies Departments at the University of California, Santa Cruz and Rutgers University from 1991 to 2008. In the political arena, Davis ran unsuccessfully in 1980 and 1984 on the Communist Party ticket for vice president of the United States.

10 **Wayman Bernard McLaughlin** (1927–2003) was born in Danville, Virginia. In June 1948 he received his bachelor's degree from Virginia Union. In June 1952 he received a Bachelor of Divinity from Andover Newton Theological School. And then in 1958 he received the doctorate in philosophy from Boston University. While at Boston University, he was a classmate and good friend of Martin Luther King Jr. During their time at Boston University, King, McLaughlin in conjunction with other African American graduate students organized a philosophical club called the Dialectical Society. McLaughlin spent his academic career at four HBCUs: Virginia Union, Grambling, Winston-Salem State Teaching College (later Winston-Salem State University), and North Carolina A&T.

Chapter 2

1 Born in New Orleans, **John Wesley Edward Bowen** (1855–1933) graduated with the bachelor's degree at the (HBCU) University of New Orleans (1878). He also earned a Bachelor of Sacred Theology from Boston University (1885) and a PhD from the same institution in 1887, becoming the first African American earning such a degree from Boston. In addition to clerical duties, Bowen was Professor of Church History and Systematic Theology at (HBCU) Morgan College (now University); Professor of Hebrew at Howard University, and Chair of Historical Theology (Gammon Theological Seminary).

2 While **D. J. Jordan** had an extensive background in classics, his advanced training was in law. He was admitted to the bar in South Carolina in 1892, and then in Georgia in 1904. Jordan taught and was an administrator at numerous HBCU institutions under the administration of the African Methodist Episcopal Church.

3 Born in Eastville, Virginia, **Thomas Nelson Baker** (1860–1940) as a slave, he was thirty-three when he received the BA from Boston University. He continued his education, receiving a BD from Yale University. In 1903, at the age of forty-three, he was awarded a PhD in philosophy. He was the first African American to receive the PhD in philosophy from an educational institution in the United States.

4 Born in Marshall, Texas, **Roy Dennis Morrison II** (1926–95) graduated from Howard University in three years with a degree in philosophy, psychology, and classical Greek. He received a degree in divinity from Northern Baptist Theological Seminary in Chicago and a master's degree and a doctorate in the philosophy of religion from the University of Chicago. Morrison was the chair of the Master of Theological Studies degree program and Professor of Philosophical Theology, Religion, and Scientific Method, and Philosophy of Black Culture and Religion at Wesley Theological Seminary in Washington, DC. His book *Science, Theology and the Transcendental Horizon: Einstein, Kant and Tillich* was published in 1994. He was a former president of the North American Paul Tillich Society.

5 **Rufus L. M. H. Perry Jr.** (1868–1930) attended New York University for college and law school. He graduated from NYU Law at the top of his class in 1891. In 1912, he made news around the country when he converted to Judaism. He had his first name changed to "Raphael." He authored *A Sketch of the Philosophical Systems* in 1918.

6 **Rufus L. M. H. Perry Sr.** (1834–95) was born a slave. He later escaped from slavery and then became an ordained minister in 1861, attending Kalamazoo Seminary (Michigan). He was awarded the honorary PhD from the State University of Louisville, Kentucky (which was later known as Simmons College) in 1887. The Rev. Dr. Rufus Perry was one of the leading voices in Brooklyn's African American community. He authored *The Cushite or the Descendents of Ham* published in 1893.

7 **Joyce Mitchell Cook** (1933–2014) graduated from Bryn Mawr with a BA in philosophy in 1955. She then received a double MA in psychology and philosophy from Oxford University in 1957. She received her doctorate in philosophy from Yale University in 1965. Her dissertation was titled *A Critical Examination of Stephen C. Pepper's Theory of Value*. She taught at Howard University, Connecticut College, and Wellsley College. Cook also served on the Jimmy Carter administration as a speech writer and correspondence editor.

8 An alumnus of HBCU Talladega College, **Broadus N. Butler** (1920–96) earned his master's degree and a PhD in philosophy from the University of Michigan. He actually financed his graduate education via the GI Bill. Previously, Butler served in the Second World War as a member of the Tuskegee Airman. President of Dillard University in New Orleans from 1969 to 1973, Butler then served for three years as director of the Office of Leadership Development at the American Council on Education in Washington. Other administrative duties include assistant dean of the College of Liberal Arts at Wayne State University and vice president of the University of the District of Columbia. Also as the president of the Moton Memorial Institute, he assisted African American philosophers in gaining funding for postdoctoral research. A prolific scholar, in addition to writing articles in such outlets as *The Personalist*, *Liberal Education*, and *Current Issues in Higher Education*, Butler published in a number of Black journals including *The Negro History Bulletin*, *Crisis Magazine*, *Negro Digest*, and *Journal of the National Medical Association*, and *The Journal of Negro History*, among others.

Chapter 3

1 **Forrest Oran Wiggins** (1907–82) received his Bachelor of Divinity from Butler University (Indiana) in 1928. He went on to earn his MA and PhD in philosophy in 1938 from the University of Wisconsin. He taught at several Black institutions, including Morehouse College, Johnson C. Smith, and Howard Universities, before he joined the philosophy faculty at the University of Minnesota in 1946. Wiggins became the first African American to teach at the University of Minnesota. Wiggins was one of only four African American philosophers that by 1950 had regular faculty posts on predominantly white colleges. Wiggins taught from 1946 until 1952. However, in 1952, he was dismissed by the president of the University, despite the recommendation of the philosophy department that he be promoted. Wiggins was a victim of both McCarthyism and racism. Wiggins served as vice president of the Minnesota Progressive Party where he campaigned for Henry Wallace's presidential bid in 1948 and openly attacked capitalism, racism, and imperialist war.

Chapter 4

1 **Eugene Clay Holmes** (1905–80) received his bachelor and master's degrees from New York University and his PhD in philosophy from Columbia University. He joined the philosophy department at Howard University in 1930 and taught there for forty years. He followed Alain Locke as chair of the department. Holmes was an active member of the Communist Party USA. He retired from Howard in 1970 and died of cancer in 1980.

2 **Cornelius Lacy Golightly** (1917–76) received his doctorate in philosophy from the University of Michigan in 1941. He was a Rosenwald fellow in philosophy at Harvard during the academic year 1941–42. Alain Locke, chair of the philosophy department at Howard University, hired Golightly as an instructor of philosophy and social science for the academic year 1942–43. Thereafter, Golightly resumed his academic career as an academic philosopher when he was hired

at Olivet College in Michigan in 1945. This faculty appointment, as professor of philosophy and psychology at this small mid-state Michigan college, marked a historic moment when Golightly became the first Black philosopher permanently hired to teach at a white institution in the twentieth century.

Chapter 5

1 Born in South Carolina, **Gilbert Haven Jones** (1881–1966) was only the third African American to earn the PhD in philosophy. He finished his doctorate at the University of Jena in Germany. In doing so, he became the first African American to covet the doctorate from a German higher educational institution. After completing his doctorate, he began teaching at Wilberforce. During his time at Wilberforce he was a professor of philosophy and psychology as well as dean of the College of Liberal Arts (1914–24) and the University's fourth president (1924–32).

2 **Willis Jefferson King** (1886–1976) was president of both HBCU Samuel Huston College (1930–32) in Austin, Texas, and Gammon Theological Seminary (1932–44) in Atlanta, Georgia. He had previously taught as Professor of Old Testament Literature beginning in 1918. Served as a bishop in the United Methodist Church, King wrote several scholarly works, most notably, *The Negro in American Life: An Elective Course for Young People on Christian Race Relations* (New York: The Methodist Book Concern, 1926).

3 **William R. Jones** (1933–2012) received his undergraduate degree in philosophy at Howard University. He earned his Master of Divinity at Harvard University in 1958, and was ordained and fellowshipped as a Unitarian Universalist minister in that year. Jones went on to do doctoral work at Brown University, receiving his PhD in 1969. After receiving his PhD, Jones was an assistant professor at Yale Divinity School from 1969 to 1977 in addition to serving as coordinator of African American Studies. After leaving Yale in 1977, Jones became Professor of Religion and the Director of Afro-American Studies program in the College of Social Sciences at Florida State University (FSU) in Tallahassee. He was a regular participant in the Philosophy Born of Struggle conferences, and received the Philosophy Born of

Struggle Award in 2011. During the course of his long academic career, Jones held visiting professorships at Princeton Theological Seminary, Union Theological Seminary, and Iliff School of Theology. Jones received an honorary doctorate from Meadville/Lombard Theological School in 1990. Upon his retirement in 1999, Jones was honored by FSU with the title Professor Emeritus. Dr. Jones's magnum opus *Is God a White Racist?* (1973) and his article "The Legitimacy and Necessity of Black Philosophy: Some Preliminary Considerations" are foundational contributions to Black Liberation Theology and African American philosophy, respectively.

Introduction: Footnotes to History:

On the Recovery of African American Philosophers and Reconstruction of African American Philosophy

Chapter Summary

Here we establish the general case for the legitimacy and necessity for African American philosophy.

In the pages that follow, we unveil a complex and intricate story of persons, ideas, and sociohistorical events. During their own times, many African American philosophers shined brightly; now their light shines dark with anonymity. Today, these same philosophers have been relegated to footnotes in philosophical history. While there is the genteel mention of say W. E. B. Du Bois, Angela Davis, Alain Locke, Charles Mills, or Cornel West, the African American philosopher is not usually given more than a passing reference in most introductory philosophy courses, much less standard histories, encyclopedias of philosophy, anthologies, or textbooks. To be condemned to a footnote is to place the Black philosopher outside the pale of philosophical history. The classic illustration of this point is David Hume's infamous footnote in his essay on national character. Hume writes that he is "apt to suspect the negroes to be naturally inferior to the whites." The otherwise "skeptical Scotsman" was certain that any Black person who exhibits an inkling of intellectual ability is comparable to a parrot "who speaks a few words plainly."[1] Hume's racial law is an explanatory principle, an ultimate assumption that illustrates why Black people occupy a subordinate, if not marginal position in the philosophical canon. Philosophical history stands guilty of the sins of commission and omission from Hume to Immanuel Kant to G. W. F. Hegel. Its guilt rests in words said and also in words not said.[2]

Hume's racial law denied Black intellectual culture citizenship in world intellectual culture. It should not be lost on the reader that what was Negro History Week, which Dr. Carter G. Woodson popularized and is now known as Black or African American History Month, emerged as a solution to the sin of omission. The history of African American philosophy provides for future generations a resource of what would otherwise be a forgotten past.[3] Consequently, the *future* of the African American philosopher rests on a recovery of the *past* history of African American philosophy. As William R. Jones warned so many years ago, if we ignore the African American philosophical tradition, philosophy will continue to march under the banner of "FOR WHITES ONLY."

It is perhaps because of the philosopher's aversion to history that the reconstruction of the history of African American philosophers has lagged behind other disciplines. In the annals of history and the social sciences, groundbreaking revisionist efforts in various disciplines include in psychology Robert V. Guthrie, *Even the Rat Was White: A Historical View of Psychology* (1976); in history Earl Thorpe, *Black Historians* (1969) in addition to August Meier and Elliot Rudwick, *Black History and the Historical Profession, 1915–1980* (1986); and in sociology Stanford M. Lyman, *The Black American in Sociological Thought: A Failure in Perspective* (1972) and John Bracey et al., *Black Sociologists: The First Half Century* (1971).

This book was born in 1981. The Association for the Study of African American Life and History held its annual convention in October of that year. One of the panels focused on the philosophy of the Black experience, with Black philosophers John McClendon—my coauthor in this book—and Johnny Washington presenting papers. McClendon's presentation was a sampling of an eighty-five-page working paper he had written for the University of Illinois-Urbana's Afro-American Studies and Research Program titled "Afro-American Philosophers and Philosophy: A Selected Bibliography." The following year the National Council for Black Studies (NCBS) held its annual conference. One of the panels, organized and chaired by McClendon, was on "Black Philosophy" and consisted of presentations by Patrick Bellegarde-Smith, Leonard Harris, John Jackson, and Lucius Outlaw. By November 1982,

McClendon's trailblazing bibliographical essay "The Afro-American Philosopher and the Philosophy of the Black Experience: A Bibliographical Essay on a Neglected Topic in Both Philosophy and Black Studies" appeared in *Sage Race Relations Abstract*. Following the example of the great Black research librarian and leftist Ernest Kaiser, this often-ignored bibliographical essay provided a literature review of Black philosophers and the philosophy of the Black experience; he provided a critical summation of nearly 400 books, dissertations, essays, and speeches. McClendon's meticulous research, which was done before the advent of the Internet, provided the groundwork for the present work. Since its publication, no one has sought to reproduce McClendon's research. To say the least, even with the assistance of the Internet, it would take a team of philosophers to update his mammoth accomplishment.

For nearly twenty-five years, we have been on a journey to recover and reconstruct the history of the Black philosopher. This work is only a preliminary presentation of our collective research. It is in no way exhaustive and does not pretend to make a summation of all the work done by African American philosophers or all the philosophical trends within African American philosophy. Given the breadth of philosophical interests among African American philosophers, our purpose is to acquaint the reader with selective writings of African American philosophers and with some of the topical issues discussed in the philosophy of the Black experience. Our work is the first step in the recovery and reconstruction of an African American philosophical canon.

The history of the professionalization of philosophy, not unlike other disciplines in the academy, is firmly rooted in institutionalized forms of academic racism. The trunk of racism in philosophy has many branches. One of these branches is the professional organization of philosophy, the American Philosophical Association (APA). In light of academic racism in philosophy, in 1974, the renowned William R. Jones offered the following recommendations to the APA: (1) the establishment of a placement resource service to assist departments in meeting Affirmative Action goals, (2) compilation of an exhaustive roster of Black faculty and graduate and undergraduate students in philosophy, (3) a survey of the status of philosophy in Black colleges and universities, (4) graduate fellowships for Blacks in philosophy along the lines of the Rockefeller Doctoral Fellowship for Blacks in religion, (5) a colloquium on the topics: "Perspectives on Black Philosophy" and "Teaching Philosophy from a Black Perspective," (6) a curriculum writing conference to formulate basic materials for use in Black colleges, (7) the upgrading and enlargement of philosophy in Black schools, and (8) the establishment of frameworks for the discussion and teaching of topics in

Black philosophy on white campuses.[4] While the Committee on Blacks in Philosophy has assisted the APA in taking incremental steps toward fulfilling Jones's recommendation, in large part, the policies and practices of philosophy departments in addition to the APA have not gone beyond the horizon set by Jones nearly fifty years ago.

On the problem of universality and particularity

Through a dialectical tale of sorts, we demonstrate that African American philosophers have developed a formidable body of work about philosophy, particularly about how the Black experience is related to the "big questions" in the areas of metaphilosophy, ontology, epistemology, philosophy of science, philosophy of religion, and social philosophy. We contend that even when African American philosophers grappled with such questions without reference to the Black experience, this experience formed the social context of their work.

African American philosophy can be seen as a species of African American intellectual thought. Black philosophical traditions have tended historically to emerge from within the context of Black intellectual culture rather than from the confines of the white academy. The claim here is not that the history of African American philosophy is completely removed from European and/or Euro-American philosophy, only that it has a determinate identity and tradition.

Given its moorings outside the white academy, African American philosophical discourse has a considerable and extensive history. An investigation into that history requires linking the content of African American philosophical inquiry to the broader dimension of its intellectual and social history. This requires highlighting, on the one hand, how philosophical inquiry addresses distinct problems and themes that are deeply rooted in the normative practices and traditions of academic philosophy. But it also requires, on the other hand, understanding the particularities that emerge from concrete problems adjoined to Black intellectual and social history.

To advance African American philosophy as a legitimate area of philosophy requires us to defend the category of particularity as it relates to the content and methodology of philosophy. To accent the particularity of African American philosophy is not a dismissal of universalism tout court.

It is an attempt to link the Black experience in Africa, the United States, and the Africana diaspora to world philosophy. *The truth of particularity resides in its dialectical relationship to universality.* Though particularity and universality are distinct categories, they are, nevertheless, correlative categories. As correlative categories, they must of logical necessity be seen as a pair. The relationship of particularity to universality is not an either/or proposition. Hence, the call for particularity is not merely an act of transferring the citadel of philosophy from Mt. Olympus to Mt. Kenya, but a recognition that world philosophy is not located in Europe.

In some philosophical circles, even today, questions continue to be raised about the legitimacy and necessity of African American philosophy. And the continuing response of the philosophical guild to its presence confirms that its legitimacy is still not universally accepted. The universal character of philosophy, it is said, has no room for ethnic particularity. Though we speak of Greek philosophy, German philosophy, and even American philosophy, African American philosophy is seen as a semantic monstrosity bordering on self-contradiction, as William R. Jones has noted. Many Black philosophers have argued that such criticisms rest on questionable presuppositions concerning the nature of philosophy, its method, and its analysis.

The following chapters are provided to aid both students and teachers of philosophy as well as the general reader with interest in the field of African American philosophy. Chapter 1, "Through the Back Door: The Problem of History and the African American Philosopher/Philosophy," offers a history of African American philosophers. We argue that what constitutes African American philosophy is decidedly intertwined with how we account for the *historical formation* of African American philosophy. Therefore, Chapter 1 gives particular attention to the critical role of African American academic philosophers in the formation of African American philosophy, through both their philosophical work on general problems in the discipline and research directly related to the philosophy of the Black experience. Chapter 2 examines metaphilosophical questions concerning the nature of philosophy generally and African American philosophy specifically. Chapters 3 through 5 each cover a specific area in philosophy. Chapter 3 has as its focus issues in axiology, which include value theory, moral philosophy, and ethics as well as aesthetics. Here we examine what African American philosophers have had to say about the origin, nature, classification, and place of values in the world. In Chapter 4, we examine what African American philosophers have had to say about the relationship of philosophy to science, in both its natural and social forms. Chapter 5 is concerned with the philosophy of religion.

A note

We capitalize the word, "Black," when making reference to Black Africans and people of African descent. As a proper noun, we capitalize it like *Negro* or *African American*. Over a number of generations, there was a consistent fight to capitalize the word, "Negro," as a way of establishing racial respect and dignity. Since the word, "Black," has now come to replace "Negro" as the contemporary convention, we follow in that tradition with the capitalization of "Black." As Robert S. Wachal observes, "The failure to capitalize Black when it is synonymous with African American is a matter of unintended racism, to put the best possible face on it."[5]

Notes

1. David Hume, "Of National Characters," in *The Philosophical Works of David Hume*, ed. T. H. Green and T. H. Grose (London: Longmans, Green & Co., 1882). Hume's remarks on parroting were directed at Jamaican intellectual and educator Francis Williams. It is reported that Williams was a student at Cambridge University and studied mathematics and Latin. He attempted to introduce formal education for Jamaicans on the island in the eighteenth century. T. H. MacDermot, "From a Jamaica Portfolio-Francis Williams" *The Journal of Negro History* 2(2) (April 1917): 147–59 and Michele Valerie Ronnick, "Francis Williams: An Eighteenth-Century Tertium Quid" *Negro History Bulletin* 61(2) (April–June 1998): 19–29. Also consult, "Hume's Racism Reconsidered," in ed. Richard Henry Popkin, *The Third Force in Seventeenth-Century Thought* (Leiden: Brill, 1992).
2. Lerone Bennett, "The Negro in Textbooks: Reading, 'Riting and Racism," *Ebony* (March 1967), 130.
3. Lerone Bennett, "Black History/Black Power," in *The Challenge of Blackness* (Chicago, Illinois: Johnson Publishing Co., 1972), 195.
4. William R. Jones, "Crisis in Philosophy: The Black Presence," *Proceedings and Addresses of the American Philosophical Association* 47(1973–74), 118–25.
5. Robert S. Wachal, "The Capitalization of Black and Native American," *American Speech* 75(4) (2000), 365. For a further discussion of this issue, see John H. McClendon, "Black/Blackness: Philosophical Considerations," in *Encyclopedia of the African Diaspora: Origins, Experiences, and Culture*, ed. Carol Boyce Davies, vol. 3 (Santa Barbara, California: ABC-CLIO, 2008), 198–203.

1

Through the Back Door:

The Problem of History and the African American Philosopher/Philosophy

Chapter Summary

Initially we examine the historical formation of African American philosophy from 1865 to now. While there is a tendency to see philosophers and philosophical questions as outside the boundaries of history, we demonstrate that African American philosophy is a product of history. Moreover, we discuss the philosophical problems attached to defining African American philosophy. (54)

The French Marxist philosopher Louis Althusser provocatively says that philosophy has no history.[1] Althusser's somewhat cryptic statement brings to our attention that philosophy as a discipline often ignores the historical and social conditions for the emergence of philosophers and philosophical doctrines and trends. Accordingly, the popular image of philosophy reflects something so abstract that its subject matter stands apart from the social circumstances of working people and the dynamic events of everyday life.

On this point, African American philosopher Henry Theodore Johnson remarks the following:

> There is a general disposition on the part of the "common herd" (as Schopenhauer bluntly characterizes the unreflecting multitude) to regard all philosophy as so much moonshine in the abstract. To the conception of such, that is philosophy whatever they cannot comprehend, which is intelligible to no one and devoid of value as a human commodity to all men. Indeed, philosophy seems to have a bad name everywhere among the ordinary populace.[2]

Given the social division of labor where the separation of mental and manual labor persists, what often results is the viewpoint that philosophical reflection appears as the solitary dominion of those in the ranks above the toiling masses. Plato and Aristotle prominently held this view.

Concurrently, from the standpoint of certain philosophers, there persists the opinion that the love of wisdom (Philo—Sophia) exceeds the bounds of history as a timeless search for truth. It seems we are faced with a nagging dilemma. On the one hand, we have philosophical inquiry presented as a timeless search for truth, which transcends the historicized—material—world. On the other hand, we must confront the fact that philosophers are material (social) beings and thus are in—and of—the historically situated world of social reality. As Karl Marx insightfully notes,

> Philosophers do not spring up like mushrooms out of the ground; they are products of their time, of their nation, whose most subtle, valuable and invisible juices flow in the ideas of philosophy. The same spirit that constructs railways with the hands of workers, constructs philosophical systems in the brains of philosophers. Philosophy does not exist outside the world, any more than the brain exists outside man.[3]

If philosophy does not exist outside the world, then it cannot exist outside of history. Accordingly, the African American philosopher is very much the product of history. The history of African American philosophy is a complex and intricate story of persons, ideas, institutions, and sociohistorical events. The present work is only the beginning of the story; it is not the end. We contend that the future of African American philosophy is to be found in the judicious examination of its past.

Prior to Leonard Harris publishing his anthology *Philosophy Born of Struggle* in 1983, Percy E. Johnston's *Afro-American Philosophies: Selected Readings from Jupiter Hammon to Eugene C. Holmes*, published in 1970, was the only text devoted to the writings of African American philosophers and the philosophy of the Black experience. Presently, we are witnessing the production of an array of books attentive to African American philosophers. And we have seen a proliferation of anthologies devoted to African American philosophy and/or the philosophy of the Black experience. One of the most significant contributions is George Yancy's *African-American Philosophers: Seventeen Conversations* (1998), a collection of interviews from a wide range of African American philosophers.[4] Despite the array of available works, the professional field of philosophy—not to mention the general reading public—still knows very little about the history of Black philosophers, both professional and nonprofessional alike. Unquestionably, we need more solid—well researched—texts on this subject with a wide distribution inclusive of the scholarly and general reading audiences.

Solid texts in the history of African American philosophy can only emerge when certain core questions are meaningfully and adequately addressed as the focus of theory and method, particularly respecting the historical record. Now let us systematically interrogate the subject matter of the history of African American philosophy. In that regard, we submit the following questions as a brief sampling of possible interrogations. The first set of questions is empirical in nature and the second is more conceptual in tone.

Our first set of questions includes the following: Who are the African American thinkers that have grappled with philosophical questions and problems over the course of the history of African American philosophy? What type of training/education did they receive? What were the venues (institutional setting) available for their work? Were such outlets academic or nonacademic in makeup or did both come into play? What was the relationship between teaching and research for the earlier generations of African American philosophers? What audience did they seek to address? And what means were at their disposal for reaching an audience? What subfields in philosophy did they explore and what schools of thought captured their allegiance? It should be most apparent that the above questions require empirical research.

Our second set comprises the following: Does philosophical theory demand that the history of philosophy posed perennial questions—such as the mind/body problem—of which we witness changes only in form, while what remains as consistently true is an essential content that lasts over time?[5] Is the historical method a matter of knowing how to demarcate the past from the present via some method of periodization? How does one weigh the philosophical merit of ideas or issues in philosophy's history from more general notions concerning intellectual history in the broader nonphilosophical sense of the term—such as the history of ideas? In other words, what are accurately considered philosophical questions, issues, and problems? Finally, do we need the past as the primary yardstick for measuring current levels of philosophical attainment?

On the progress of African American philosophy

Can we see progress—as we discover with scientific inquiry—over the course of the history of philosophy? If there is some kind of progressive development with philosophical thought, then indisputably philosophy has its own substantive history. Of course, this proposition about philosophy's substantive history divorces us from the idea that philosophy has no history. Perhaps with this thesis—philosophy has no history—the most telling implication entails purging any progressive development from within philosophical thought. From early on, African American philosophers wrestle with the question, namely "what does it mean to talk about progress in Black life?" wherein life is experienced within the existential circumstances of hegemonic racial oppression and class exploitation. Such conditions are indicators for what philosopher Henry T. Johnson fittingly coined as *The Black Man's Burden*.[6]

In the nineteenth century, the philosophical problem of Black progress and its corresponding meaning shapes what transpires as a historic form of African American philosophical tradition. In part, this tradition offers up the view that a philosophy of progress is essential to the cause of racial development in the context of the Jim Crow segregationist regime and its institutional obstruction of sustained and progressive development by African American people. Black philosopher William D. Johnson in his 1895 essay, "Philosophy," states,

> When we come to consider the Negro, no race has probably been so oppressed with opposition and resistance. It has been like piling upon us the entire mountain system of the country. Yet, what are the facts? If the Negro had been a weak race, it must evidently have been crushed under this weight of slavery, ostracism, caste, and persecution. If he only survived he would by the law of action and reaction, be as strong as the combined weight of his opposition. But we find that as a race we have been more than equal to the surroundings, for our rapid advance since emancipation, in *the march of progress*, has become a wonder to the world.[7] (italics added)

What should be clear is that a *philosophy of progress* is grounded on the assumption that there is progressive development within the history of philosophy. Therefore, the notion of *philosophy of progress* is dialectically linked to the *progress of philosophy*.[8] Henry T. Johnson encapsulates this principle when he argues,

> With every curse of adversity peculiar to our career since emancipation there are associate blessings and clouds of despondence should not be allowed to curtain them from our view. *Faith and philosophy* are the glasses which, if well adjusted, will enable us to discern a silver lining to these ȯerhanging clouds, and gather apples of gold from the pictures of silver which crown the galleries of all people for whom heaven has reserved a larger destiny.[9] (italics added)

In the wake of slavery and Reconstruction, the segregated status of Black people (in the late nineteenth century) continually posed challenging questions about racial progress. The mass of Black people lived in the neo-slavery conditions of sharecropping and tenant farming—politically powerless, stripped of civil rights, and faced with forms of legal and extralegal terrorism. Consequently, the idea of social progress appeared elusive. If the arc of history marches toward progress, why does Black history seem to depart from this basic axiom? What kind of progress can there be under circumstances such as racist oppression and relentless class exploitation? How can the hurdle of racism, with all of its obstacles, allow for Black (racial) progress? What serves as the catalyst for historical progression? How can we measure progress? What truly is the meaning of progress in history?

As both W. D. Johnson and H. T. Johnson earlier avow, the affirmation of African American self-initiative remains the ever-present impulse within the idea of progressive racial development. This affirmation of self-initiative crucially serves as a counterargument to racist stereotypes of "lazy Negroes" fearful of hard work. With self-initiative comes creativity and originality, something clearly expressed in the Work Songs produced by the African American working masses as early as slavery. Work Songs are both constitutive and reflective of African American material culture.[10]

Subsequently, African American philosophy emerges from determinate material and cultural circumstances, thus assuming its precise *historic form*. What should not be overlooked is that African American philosophy in its *historic form* emerges from within the concrete conditions of Black life. While Work Songs also grow out of African American life, they are not an inquiry into these conditions. Thus, there emerges the vital need for philosophy as an intellectual instrument for comprehension of African American material conditions and cultural expression. Creative and critical thought—as sustained by the various *historic forms* of philosophy—demand requisite material and cultural circumstances. In other words, philosophy has its basis in the material conditions encountered in day-to-day life. Whereas Work Songs are reflections of African American life and culture, philosophy is a theoretical inquiry on African American life and culture. Moreover, the notion of historic forms amplifies the concrete particularity of African American philosophical traditions.

By African American philosophy, accordingly, we are not suggesting philosophical thought stands in principle exclusive of—or in opposition to—white philosophy; rather we are detailing its historic forms. The task of specification allows for both the universality and particularity of a general concept or problem to gain concrete relevance. In other words, the question "how relevant is the idea of progress—in the history of philosophy—to the African American experience?" necessitates we specify the meaning of "progress" in the context of the African American experience. Herein lies the philosophical import attached to the notion of *historic forms*.

The philosophical problem of Black progress and its corresponding meaning shapes what transpires as historic form. This idea particularizes what are universal principles and problems. Consequently, the general notion of "progress" in the history of philosophy assumes a distinct instance in the African American context. A review of African American philosophical reflections—over the course of history—is a necessary condition for grasping this determinate historic form. For illustration, in "Originality in Individual and in Race Development" (1891), A. B. Stidum remarks,

> However, it is of our own individual and race development I would speak, and, if to repeat, that this is essentially an age of originality. Do I aver too much when it is said that we, as a race class, are not too quick to discover that within ourselves are to be found unlimited resources for the development of this ever eagerly sought and world-wide demand? True, intelligent and worthy observers, un-biased by that false prejudice of caste and the stigma engendered by the past condition of the race, note with pride the rapid progress of its mental and material growth within the brief period of a quarter of a century.[11]

Comprehending the philosophical notion of "progress" (even in its particularized or historic form) is fundamentally a conceptual endeavor.

While empirical indicators are necessary tools, they are insufficient as theoretical instruments vis-à-vis the task of supplying us with philosophical definitions of progress. Subsequently, the philosophical conceptualization of progress exceeds any accessible quantitative measurement.

Obviously, our second set of interrogations involves conceptual examination in contrast to the empirical investigation for the former. The failure to pay attention to these theoretical and methodological problems (affixed to the history of African American philosophy) is prominently reflected in a considerable number of anthologies on African American philosophy. This is especially true of those designed to function as introductory texts. For teachers and students with little or no knowledge of the history of African American philosophy, these anthologies on many occasions take on a canonical veneer and they often shape basic conceptions about the very definition, character, and interpretation of African American philosophy.

Our fundamental notions about the nature of African American philosophy are grounded in the definitions and interpretations adjoined to the practice of philosophizing. They direct us toward the perennial question "what is philosophy?" And when we ask the question "what is philosophy?" we are actually approaching a largely conceived perspective on philosophical inquiry or what is technically expressed as *metaphilosophy*. Two key aspects of metaphilosophy are what we consider to be the tasks of philosophical definition and interpretation. These key aspects consecutively form both the substance and scope of philosophy as a discipline.

Early efforts in metaphilosophy by African American philosophers include Henry T. Johnson's "Philosophy Religiously Valued" (April 1891) and William D. Johnson's "Philosophy" (1895). William D. Johnson offers a definition and interpretation of philosophy via the method of etymological clarification:

> The word philosophy is derived from the Greek phileo, to love, and sophia, wisdom, and means the love of wisdom. But what is wisdom? You say, wisdom is the best application of knowledge. Still, going into the etymology of the word, we find it made up of the German wissen, to know, and the Latin domus, a house. Hence, wisdom means knowing what is in the house. The real man lives in several houses—first, in his own body; next, in the clothing he wears; then the house proper; next, the community; the state; after these in time and space; but, above all else, in God; for says the Apostle, "In him we live and move, and have our being." Philosophy, therefore, is an inquiry into the cause and nature of things.[12]

Johnson clearly argues that philosophy is situated in the world, which is nevertheless, a complicated and complex one of several dimensions in which humans live their lives. Johnson asserts that philosophy aims to take us beyond just living in the world to actually comprehending it. This search for understanding of the world ultimately leads to "an inquiry into the cause and nature of things." If philosophy consists of an inquiry, then it is more than merely reacting to one's place in the world. Critical reflection on the cause and nature of things grounds philosophical inquiry. This is why Work Songs—as expressive response—are the possible subject matter of philosophy, yet not philosophy itself. The defining characteristic and attribution of philosophy is that it constitutes a mode of inquiry.

With that said, most philosophers presume that philosophical inquiry—particularly with respect to definitions and interpretations—refers essentially to matters that are more conceptual rather than empirical in nature. For the most part, we think this presumption consistently holds true. For illustration, when philosophers ask the questions, "what counts as belonging in the world?" or "what constitutes the furniture of the universe?" it is conventionally understood that any detailed empirical description of all the items of the universe is not the intent.

Instead, philosophers are governed by the theoretical imperative to grapple with the ontological task of outlining what it means to exist in the world. An explanation of the nature of being and reality (i.e., *ontology*) becomes paramount. An empirical description of various forms of matter in their lawful motion, for example, can take a back seat to philosophical perspectives grounded in abstract reflection and theoretical considerations.

Similarly, answering the question, "how do we determine the ontological order of reality?" hence extends beyond phenomenal accounting and empirical descriptions. *Ontological ordering* establishes the primacy of some entities over others. In fact, some very significant phenomena from the standpoint of scientific inquiry may be consciously overlooked—or abstracted away—in the philosophical accounting about the nature of reality. The empirical reality of molecules, atoms, and quarks, while crucial in the physicist description of the world, subsequently may not be a matter of concern in philosophical discussion about the nature of being and reality, that is, the subject matter of the philosophical subfield known as ontology.

It follows that the concepts of *ontological reduction* and *ontological hierarchy* are necessarily attendant with this mode of philosophical inquiry. Black philosopher William D. Johnson provides us with a demonstration of ontological reduction. He states,

"Look out of the window and tell me what you see," were the words of Prof. J. P. Shorter to his class at Wilberforce University last year, during the summer school. One said: "I see a cow"; another, "I see a tree"; a third, "I see a house." "No," said the Professor, "the answer is I see one." Then he proceeded to show that there is no such thing as a concrete number. That same, "one" can be fitted to anything, and we can just as well say, "One man, one horse, one child," etc. Therefore, just what it is behind the appearance of things, and that makes them what they are, it has been the object of philosophy to find out.[13]

Obviously, while we can perceive a host of things that compose reality, Johnson brings to our attention that perception and conception respectively brings us qualitatively different results. The philosophical concept or idea of "One" is affixed to an ontological reduction, where the essence behind the appearance of reality issues forth the unity or oneness of reality. The reduction of reality to "oneness" is what philosophers call "monism." Johnson is a monist respecting his view on reality. The primary character of reality becomes the concept of one. What becomes key is that ontological reduction presumes there is a distinction between the appearance and essence of reality.

Similarly, philosophers holding to a *materialist* viewpoint argue that matter is primary, wherein reality is ultimately reducible to its material basis in nature and society. Consequently, nature is sui generis (self-generating) and does not require some kind of supernatural being(s) for its origins or continued existence, progression, and development.[14] On the scale of ontological ordering, subsequently, higher forms of matter such as living matter and hence human life have priority over other forms of material (nonliving) entities as well as vegetative and animal life.

This conceptualization regarding the hierarchy of being—with humans at the apex—is a philosophical presumption, which is affixed to ontology and specifically *ontological hierarchy*. We are required to note that the enslavement of African Americans had its corresponding white racist ontological hierarchy. The ontological placement of Black people as subhuman was an ideological justification for the political economic (bourgeois) reality that rendered Black slaves as chattel, that is, property that was exchanged on the capitalist market as commodities. The prior assumption about human life as the pinnacle of ontological hierarchy was distorted in the allowance for Black subhuman existence. While African American philosophers straightforwardly rejected such racist perversions, they in the meantime presupposed (as a matter of principle) the philosophical orientation that human beings are the summit of ontological ordering.

The salient point is that ontological ordering is not an empirical representation correspondingly attached to the specialized sciences. A pioneering force in the field of medical ethics, among other areas of philosophy, African American philosopher Charles V. Roman perceptively notes,

> Man is not only a member of the animal kingdom by consanguinity, but in many ways an inferior member. But nevertheless and notwithstanding, man is the undisputed lord of the world. Neither the keenness of the eagle's eye, nor the stretch of his mighty pinions has availed him to elude man's dominion. The lion is the king of the forest only so long as man is absent.[15]

If humans maintain higher ontological status over subhuman animals, then nonliving matter is even lower in ontological placement. Thus, it stands that a rock, for instance, does not have the same value as human life. Although rocks and human skulls are both hard objects, this description falls short of an ontological classification. The mineralogical description of rocks fails to convey how breaking rocks remains—in an ontological sense—qualitatively different from bashing in the skull of a human being. The value differentiation between rocks and skulls is quintessentially a conceptual distinction render by philosophy.

Dialectical idealism—which became the dominant thinking among African American philosophers in the nineteenth and early twentieth centuries—effectively served to bolster consciousness as the dynamic principle surrounding human life. By dialectical idealism, we mean that the catalyst for all motion, change, and development (laws of motion) reside in immaterial entities such as ideas, consciousness, or the human soul.

Dialectical idealism stands ontologically in stark contrast to *mechanistic materialism*, which espouses mechanical determinism that severely restricts—in fact nullifies—the notion of free will. Mechanistic materialism is the viewpoint on reality where the world becomes like an all-encompassing machine, devoid of any consciousness. African American philosophers clearly identified that the lack of human freedom is the defining feature of enslavement. It stands to reason that African Americans living in the shadow of the slave plantation would tend to find mechanistic materialism and its associated mechanical determinism as restrictive and encumbering in its social implications. The denial of free will is—in its social substance—no more than the negation of freedom. The African American turn to dialectical idealism was philosophically an affirmation of the principle of freedom.

Dialectical idealism—when regarded as a form of voluntarism—anchors a more favorable social philosophy that fosters freedom. "Voluntarism" is the philosophical notion captured in the popular saying "where there is a will, there is a way." If one's attitude determines one's altitude, then consciousness (idealism) sets the limits of human progression. This is the substance of H. T. Johnson and A. B. Stidum's viewpoints on racial progress. Thus, dialectical idealism comprised an African American philosophical tradition, which argued that such value differentiation—between rocks and human beings—resided in the immaterial essence of human existence. In concert, one must remain aware that all efforts at framing an ontological hierarchy consistently imply some measure of value differentiation. The subfield of philosophy that examines the problems surrounding value as a general notion is called "axiology"—which we will address in Chapter 3.

Herein we discover that Black philosopher J. C. Price focuses on "The Value of Soul" as the cardinal principle of distinction. Price asserts, "In the boundless and created universe there is nothing unnecessary or worthless. Everything from an angel to an atom has some value. But all things are not of the same value; for the nature and end of one thing causes its worth to differ very materially from that of another."[16] Price addresses the relationship of the soul to the body:

> How the soul is united to the body we can never tell in our present state, yet where is the man that believes there is no connection between soul and body? Men tell us these things, and we believe them. My dear friends, why do we not believe Christ when he tells us the soul is priceless in its worth?[17]

Noticeably, souls are not open to empirical observation; they are quite apparently absent when undertaking the dissection of the human body. It follows that biology, anatomy, and physiology are all silent on the existence of souls. Hence, the rule of thumb about the essentially conceptual nature of philosophical inquiry and interpretation congruently sets philosophy apart from the physical, natural, and even the social and behavioral sciences.

From Price's view, if all people have souls and souls are a defining feature of humanity then it follows that each and every person has *intrinsic value*. By intrinsic value, we mean human beings are ends in themselves and not means to some external purpose. Accordingly, slavery nullifies this cardinal principle of intrinsic value or worth. Likewise, racist notions about differences in cranial measurements—as indicators of racial superiority—are inadequate justifications in light of the value of soul. Clearly, dialectical idealism became a philosophical weapon in the fight against racism.[18]

In contrast to philosophy, empirical investigation is crucial to the very notion of scientific research and this continues regardless of the particular field of science. With that said, we cannot conclude that philosophy is completely bereft of an empirical dimension. Although definition and interpretation are paradigmatically conceptual, we observe that from the standpoint of cognitive progression, they are both grounded on the way we offer description(s), and we recognize that description of phenomena is categorically an empirical task.

An ontological ordering that is consistent with the findings of science must consider the restrictions attached to the results of experimental investigation. In addition, the predisposition to ground our philosophic definitions and historical interpretations within the realm of the possibility of empirical boundaries is a helpful safeguard against rampant idealist speculation and arid metaphysical contemplation. Undoubtedly, this is one of Immanuel Kant's most salient points in *The Critique of Pure Reason*.

We must not overlook the fact that even some subfields of philosophy are innately connected to experiential inquiry. The history of philosophy itself is both a matter of philosophy and history. Where beforehand we acknowledged that philosophy is quintessentially conceptual, we must also be cognizant that history as a discipline, in turn, is principally an empirical undertaking. The history of philosophy (more a subfield of philosophy than history per se) nonetheless must consider the facts of the case, that is, the empirical reality which our philosophical interpretation depends upon and derives from.

One immediate methodological outcome is that the historian of philosophy adopts primarily an expository mode of presentation. The historian of philosophy, however, is not involved in a word-for-word repetition of what a particular philosopher wrote. And yet the historian must provide accurate explanations of philosophical trends and the associated philosophical problems that philosophers historically encounter, which subsequently are grounded in the actual circumstances of given time periods.

This is why "periodization," in conceptualizing the history of philosophy, gives a needed coherence to historical interpretation. With the concept of historical periods, the continual motion of philosophical inquiry is structured to accent the decisive moments when the transformation of ideas becomes an indicator of not only quantitative but also qualitative change. Capturing how changes in philosophical thinking take place over the course of history is one of the crucial tasks of the historian of philosophy. We already discovered that dialectical idealism as system of thought emerged as hegemonic during the nineteenth and early twentieth centuries for African American philosophers. Only on careful historical review can it be asserted if the same is true or not of their white counterparts. African American philosopher Charles Leander Hill most appropriately conveys the following:

It is not the primary function of the historian of philosophy to give critiques of the philosophers whose system he delineates. It is his prime duty to give an exposition of the various system of thought surveyed by him. He should attempt to state, in clear and concise language, what a given philosopher taught on the sublime themes of philosophical science. It is not possible, however, for the historian of philosophy to hide his hand in any exposition of philosophy. He, like other men, has his own presuppositions and his own inclinations. . . . It is inevitable that the historian of philosophy will have greater sympathies for, and affinities with, certain philosophers than with others.[19]

The historical interpretation of African American philosophy must be grounded in a factual framework and its affixed descriptive accounts. We contend that the experiential side adjoined to philosophy's history has monumentally significant implications for conceptualizing African American philosophy. The set of empirical questions (outlined above) concerning the history of African American philosophy amplifies this point. Moreover, all talk about what constitutes an African American philosophy is decidedly intertwined with how we understand the history (the process of formation) of African American philosophy.

The interpretation of the history of African American philosophy has specific methodological problems attached to it that differ from how we often tackle philosophical issues per se via abstract conceptualization. Namely, in most contemporary philosophical circles, it is frowned upon if the philosopher gets her hands dirty with history. Philosophical questions are to be viewed in abstraction from the historical consideration of philosophical traditions.[20]

This method of ahistorical framing gains a measure of legitimacy precisely due to the epistemological task of the logical reproduction of the object in thought. Certain historical aspects of a given problem are deleted in view of accenting what is considered *the essence* of a given problem. The logical reproduction of the object stands as the opposite pole to chronological reproduction. Meanwhile, chronological reproduction—which is the substance behind the exercise of the historical method—is focused on the immediate process of development (or the detailed formation) of a given entity. Each step and every fact convert into building blocks in the chronological—historical—reproduction of an object.

Yet, in logical reproduction, the facts and events in history are subordinated to what is deemed as *essential* to grasping the meaning and importance of a given entity. The very *nature* or *essence* of the subject matter under review becomes paramount. Here we can return to William D. Johnson's caveat about the distinction between essence and appearance. Logical reproduction is the archetypal method of ontological reduction for it unearths what is deemed essential to definition and meaning.

This has particular meaning with respect to the philosophy of race. So, we observe that a philosophical interest in the essence of whiteness need not involve referencing or reflecting on previous traditions and other historical currents among African American philosophers. Of course, there are historical prototypes such as W. E. B. Du Bois's "The Souls of White Folk" that no doubt portends having contemporary relevance.[21] Yet, the previous encounters with this problem are not necessary for our own philosophical perspectives and judgments on whiteness today. Although we can take prior explorations into view, we are not faced with an imperative to do so. Put simply, contemporary inquiry into the issue of whiteness can legitimately take place and be removed from any concerns about the historical context for—and traditions within—African American philosophy.

Just as a mathematician need not know the history of mathematical thought to solve specific problems in the disciplines of geometry or calculus, the contemporary philosopher is not obligated to know the history of African American philosophical thought on the question of whiteness in order to obtain an adequate answer to this problem and other associated philosophical issues. In this sense, philosophical inquiry takes on the appearance of an "ahistorical" encounter. Here the use of the concept of "ahistorical" does not mean that there is no need for any reference to history as such, only that *the history of African American philosophy*—antecedent philosophical tradition—is not necessarily operative in our deliberations on race.

Although there are valid grounds for justifying the pursuit of philosophical investigation without historical context and traditions, the notion of a general conception of African American philosophy cannot be established without basic presumptions about the *history* of African American philosophy, that is, its specified process of development. Here, the empirical aspect of this history proves decisive. If one presupposes that a particular approach to a philosophical issue is novel, then that assumption must be established based on historical facts. For what may be thought of as "original" could be no more than the replication of an earlier idea, even a rehash of a rather long tradition of philosophic thinking. There is the real possibility that the putatively inventive idea is actually a preceding tradition that might have already proven to be misguided.

Hence, the replication and rehashing of old ideas could amount to falling into a trap, which had already been exposed and avoided by past philosophers. Also, knowledge about earlier philosophical traditions aids in informing our contemporary research and provides valuable insights into the complexities we are presently facing in society. Many of our current philosophical problems are ultimately no more than the products of history. How often does the concern about Black progress recur as the subject of debate and discussion? Why are the presence of racism and capitalism a repetitive issue in Black life? Thus, we have our penultimate question: Can the history of African American philosophy inform our approach to such queries and problems?

On the history of Greek philosophy: The problem of Afrocentric interpretations

For an exemplary case, wherein we can discern that the knowledge of Black philosophical history would have radically improved the examination of European thought, we should examine Marimba Ani's *Yurugu*.[22] Ani offers an Afrocentric critique of European philosophy, particularly the influence of Plato and the ancient Greek tradition. Her major thesis is that European and African philosophies are fundamentally opposed and, in fact, are basically antagonistic. This thesis quite evidently rests on a preconception about the history of both European and African philosophy.

Ani claims that the classical Greek tradition anchors the historic presence of European racism, chauvinism, and white supremacy. Ani holds that Plato is the chief progenitor of a monolithic Greek system of thought, which is based on mechanistic materialism. This argument (1) places Plato's philosophical system at the center of Western European thought, and (2) ignores the fact that Plato was an unrelenting idealist. In bold relief, African American philosopher Rufus Perry correctly notes that, for Plato

> life was only the conjunction of the soul with the body (mind with matter), and death was nothing but their separation. Matter was a mere *potentiality*, a *condition* for the appearance of *ideas* in a contingent form. Virtue was an imitation of God, or the effort of man to attain the image of his original.[23]

Perry's argument that matter is merely a contingent condition for ideas in effect gives ideas ontological primacy over matter; that is, matter as potentiality is dependent on the existence of ideas. It follows that Plato maintains the philosophical position of idealism.

Yet, we find that Ani's claim substantially rests on how Plato's alleged materialism harbors the seeds for white supremacy. Since Ani wrongly argues that Plato's materialism founds what constitutes Western metaphysics, then this factual error proves as decisive. If Western metaphysics ultimately relies on Plato's system of thought, it surely cannot be mechanistic materialism. Now we must ask, since materialism and idealism present us with starkly different philosophical implications, how does the fact of Plato's actual idealism impact the historical interpretation of Greek philosophy and its influence on Western civilization?

Ani presumes that Western/white civilization fosters an ontological ordering that is principally different than what we discover with African civilization. Correspondingly, Ani assumes the history of philosophy can be outlined by employing the broad stroke of civilizational frameworks. Thus, European/white presence (in the world) is founded on Western civilization. Concordantly, Black global existence issues from African civilization. The historic clash of civilizations—between Africa and Europe—is philosophically manifested as "metaphysical exclusivism." Ani's thesis about the antithetical nature of European and African thought and how it originates in the acute differences between ancient Greek and African philosophies has wide-ranging influence. As a foremost representative of Afrocentricity, Ani's text maintains canonical authority in this camp.[24]

However, Guyanese-born philosopher George G. M. James (Figure 1) offers a historical representation of Greek philosophy that contrasts with Ani.[25] James was an academic philosopher whose career emerges within the context of the historically Black college and university (HBCU) institutional network. Far from there being a determinate difference between Greek and African philosophy, James argues that Greek philosophy is nothing more than plagiarized African philosophy. James's controversial magnum opus *The Stolen Legacy*, published in 1954, has captured the attention of many Afrocentric advocates, including the historian of Africa and African peoples Dr. Yosef ben-Jochannan who replicates James's—stolen legacy—hypothesis.[26]

One can readily see that James's position is diametrically the opposite of Ani's. We must note that *The Stolen Legacy* stands as the second text written

Figure 1 George G. M. James (1893–1956).

by an African American philosopher dealing with the history of Greek philosophy. Rufus Perry's *Sketch of Philosophical Systems*, published in 1918, was the first book by an African American philosopher on Greek philosophy. It is noteworthy that Perry does not argue that Greek philosophy is reducible to Egyptian (Kemetic) philosophy. Nonetheless, he does not proclaim that philosophy originated in ancient Greece. Perry states,

> Greek philosophy and Ancient philosophy are so nearly one and the same thing, that a sketch of the systems of the one is but a little less than a sketch of the systems of the other. But, while this is true, it does not follow that philosophic thought had its origin in Greece, or first manifested itself in that age. As there were pre-historic nations of a certain degree of civilization, they must have had philosophers among them. But, in Greece, philosophic thought, which was subsequently transferred to Rome, reached a breadth, a depth and an acuteness, that led into the labyrinths of the most abstruse metaphysics.[27]

Prior to Perry's work, Black philosopher Richard T. Greener (Figure 2) actually anticipated James's thesis. We note that Greener's outstanding accomplishments are too numerous to cite in the body of this text. Nonetheless, this professor of philosophy at the University of South Carolina—and first Black graduate of Harvard—contends that the Greeks both borrowed and stole from Egyptian intellectual culture and thus its

Figure 2 Richard T. Greener (1844–1922).

philosophy. Furthermore, Greener posits that Egyptian philosophy springs from the Upper Nile region. In his 1880 essay, "The Intellectual Position of the Negro," Greener asserts,

> The Negro, moreover, has a share [of world intellectual] inheritance, for he remembers that Athens and Rome borrow what they did not steal from Egypt, where Pythagoras and Plato and Herodotus went for wisdom, and that Egypt, renowned still though dead, obtained the genius of her philosophy, her religion and art from Nubia and Abyssinia.[28]

Undeniably, Greener's position antedates a cardinal Afrocentric stance respecting the hypothesis that the very foundations of Egyptian civilization originate further along the Upper Nile. Yosef ben-Jochannan, Willis N. Huggins, and John G. Jackson are steadfast advocates of this thesis. This thesis ushers forth the real possibility that ancient African philosophy was more expansive than Egyptian philosophy.[29]

Other African American philosophers that specialized in Greek philosophy and specifically Plato include both Winson R. Coleman (Figure 3) and John Milton Smith. After receiving a doctorate from the University of Chicago (1950) Coleman taught at the HBCU Johnson C. Smith State University as professor of philosophy. Among Coleman's publications were "Knowledge and Freedom in the Political Philosophy of Plato."[30] Also, with his doctorate from the University of Iowa (1941) Smith published "A Critical Estimate of Plato's and Dewey's Educational Philosophies."[31]

Figure 3 Winson R. Coleman (1905–84).

What is most noteworthy here is that there are sources, by African American philosophers, which a serious present-day scholar can review regarding the history of Greek philosophy and Plato. Furthermore, given Ani's commitment to the African-centered approach, if she did not know about Perry's seminal book—along with Greener, Coleman, and Smith's research—she could have drawn on James, when formulating her own position. Besides, there are other works in the Afrocentric tradition such as Henry Olela, *From Ancient Africa to Ancient Greece: An Introduction to the History of Philosophy* (1981) and Innocent Onyewuenyi, *The African Origin of Greek Philosophy: An Exercise in Afrocentrism* (1993). The reader should note that the publication dates of both these works preceded Ani's *Yurugu*, which was published in 1994.

Nevertheless, Ani only briefly cites James and fails to address the basic point of contention between her work and James's study. An inspection of James's position is necessary to evaluate Ani's premise about the vast distinction between Greek and Egyptian philosophy. If we follow Ani's line of argumentation, one must assume no connection between Greece and Egypt (Kemet) and, hence, these two histories of philosophy are presumed as fundamentally different. This kind of fundamental difference or mutual antagonism we term "metaphysical exclusivism."

Metaphysical exclusivism embarks from the presupposition that contending systems of thought—when fundamentally differing on basic principles—cannot be reconciled in any manner. Hence, our prior example on the differences holding between dialectical idealism and mechanistic materialism is a prime illustration of metaphysical exclusivism. We confront what amounts to an either/or dilemma, with no room for the unity of the contending systems. Either one is a dialectical idealist or mechanistic materialist; adopting both positions is a contradiction in terms; at worst, it is a form of theoretical eclecticism.

Although it could very well be correct to say that ancient Greek and African philosophies are different in many ways; nonetheless, Ani's metaphysical exclusivism denies the possibility for any similar or shared aspects. Noteworthy for the student of philosophy is that a principle of difference need not entail mutual exclusion. Likewise, a measure of commonality does not imply identity. Contrastingly, James argues for an essential identity holding between the two ancient philosophies.

If James is correct, it follows that Ani's view concerning Greek philosophical autonomy from Africa—as working hypothesis—is patently false. But, also, Ani's thesis about metaphysical exclusivism becomes particularly duplicitous. Whatever the merits of James's history—and we think there are many demerits—Ani's chief arguments would have been seriously challenged, particularly if she had offered a detailed response to James's historical interpretation.

In addition, one of the chief demerits of James's methodology, we must point out, is that he conflates what are particular—commonly held—aspects sustained within both ancient Greek and African philosophy as an indication for identical systems. Moreover each are held as monolithic systems of thought. This identification—given the presumption of monolithic systems—neglects the historical facts that Greek philosophers such as Plato and Aristotle actually differed on basic philosophical issues and assumptions. If Plato and Aristotle are both plagiarizers of African philosophy, then it follows that African philosophy is far from monolithic.[32]

Case in point, Aristotle openly rejects the Platonic notion of Forms. This observation not only undermines James's historical interpretation but also has import for our analysis of Ani. Ani's claim of metaphysical exclusivism rests on a monolithic conception of Greek philosophy. However, Greek philosophy is not reducible to the solitary position of Plato's system. Aristotle not only rejects Plato's ontology of Forms but also sets out to erect an alternative system; wherein Forms—as general ideas—which ground reality become abstractions that result from experiencing the particular entities that make up our world.

Aristotle effectively transforms Plato's Forms from putatively "ontological" categories into "epistemological" ones. By epistemology, we mean confined to a theory of knowledge rather than principles founding the nature of reality. For Aristotle, Forms are no more than the product of abstract thinking—our way of knowing the world—and thus cannot exist in a distinct world/reality of their own making. Thus, we have radically different notions about ontology and epistemology within Greek thought. This is one of Aristotle's foremost contributions to the progressive advancement of philosophical thought. Unfortunately, the monolithic conception of Greek philosophy sorely misses this point.

Although Alfred North Whitehead once proclaimed that Western philosophy is a series of footnotes to Plato, the full measure of this dictum does not foster a monolithic viewpoint. Certainly, if Aristotle's response to Plato is said to be a footnote, it is one, which in its transmission comes with a critical annotation. In sum, Greek philosophy is neither reducible to Platonism nor monolithic in its substance. Ani's sweeping generalizations about Greek/Western philosophy—without the necessary factual support—undermines her interpretation of the history of racism. We cannot be remiss and neglect that Ani's convoluted excursion into Greek philosophy was aimed at providing an explanation for racism/white supremacy as system of thought, wherein this system has its peculiar origins in Western civilization.

Reading *modern* racism into the circumstances of *ancient* Greek philosophy effectively conflates whiteness with Western civilization. Nonetheless, we have demonstrated that the origins and continuance of white racism cannot find any justification by directing our attention toward Platonic thought and its legacy in Western philosophy. Transparently, we have an instance where the philosophy of race is founded on the history of philosophy. Ani's benign neglect—of the history of African American philosophy/philosophers—is detrimental in launching her Afrocentric treatise on firm grounds. The historical interpretation of classical Greek philosophy cannot escape these stubborn facts gathered from persistent inquiry. Ani's composite of errors therefore comprises the following ensemble:

First, rather than forming multiple schools of thought, ancient Greek philosophy is a singular/monolithic system of thought.
Second, this monolithic system is reducible to Platonic thought.
Third, Plato's system of thought is mechanistic materialism rather than idealism.

Fourth, Plato's mechanistic materialism grounds and fosters white supremacy.

Fifth, white supremacy is anchored in the very origins of Western civilization.

Ani's civilizational interpretation of Greek philosophy fails to consider some stubborn facts about the nature of Greek philosophy and its attendant history. Furthermore, it falls drastically short of providing a feasible explanation for the historic persistence of racism. Importantly, we discovered that both the ideas of "Western" and "whiteness" should not be conflated with racism. Such conflation amounts to an *anachronistic reading*.

Simply stated, an anachronistic reading entails incorrectly assuming that present-day categories—such as whiteness/white supremacy—are suitable for interpreting the entire past including antiquity. The truth of the matter is, however, that present-day racism is not reducible to the notion of Western civilization. Hence, the historic continuance of racism cannot be equated with the concept of Western civilization and its historical formation and legacy.

Empirical description, philosophical definition, and historical interpretation

Any and all basic presumptions about African American philosophy's history should be grounded on firmly supported knowledge, based on the careful review of acquired facts. When it comes to our assumptions about the history of African American philosophy, the use of imagination, creative thinking, and speculation may have a place in our examination; however, they all must be anchored in sound investigative (empirical) methods.

Therefore, empirical description becomes foundational in the cognitive process and hence anchors the definition and historical interpretation of philosophy. Empirical description is a composite rendering that is only possible given the factual groundings of observation. Hence, inadequate and incorrect descriptions, linked to historical account, can result only in weak philosophical definitions and misguided historical interpretations.

Unfortunately, some scholars of African American philosophy have a view of its history which is not founded on the rigorous empirical assessment of actual historical evidence. Their presumptive context for the very idea of what constitutes African American philosophy is often founded on implied and preconceived notions about its history, rather than drawing from the results of explicit research projects directed specifically at its history.

One prevailing and dominant preconception is that the history of African American philosophy is essentially one that derives from nonacademic (rather than with academic) intellectuals. In fact, nonacademic philosophers are often given priority over those trained as philosophers. This preconception is especially evident in a host of books that are designed to function as introductory text in African American philosophy.

By nonacademic sources, we do not mean non-scholarly or even nonphilosophical work; rather we are pointing to philosophical works and philosophers who are not in—or connected to—the academy. Nonacademic philosophers are intellectuals who were not formally trained in philosophy or who do not teach or do philosophical research at academic institutions. Some very important philosophical works by nonacademic thinkers—from Maria Stewart and Martin Delaney to Claudia Jones to more contemporary thinkers such as Malcolm X (Figure 4)—form a crucial part of the history of African American philosophy. Yet, we should not ignore the fact that African American academic philosophers have also played a vital role in the history of African American philosophy.

Figure 4 Malcolm X (1925–65).

But on reading certain works on African American philosophy, African American academic philosophers—especially before the year 1965—are conspicuously absent. The year 1965 is employed as a periodization marker for two reasons. First, most philosophers who earned their doctorates in philosophy or who taught philosophy before or beginning in that year are more than likely no longer formally in the academy; we have the example of Joyce Mitchell Cook—the first African American woman to obtain a doctorate in philosophy, from Yale in 1965. Second, Malcolm X remains a prominent nonacademic philosopher and his death in 1965 marks a significant turning point in the emergence of the distinctive subfield—the Philosophy of the Black Experience.[33] Consequently, we have a scenario where African American philosophers in the academy (pre-1965), apart from Alain Locke, have virtually disappeared from view in general treatments on African American philosophy.

James Montmarquet and William Hardy's *Reflections: An Anthology of African-American Philosophy* (2000) and Tommy Lott's *African-American Philosophy: Selected Readings* (2001) highlight how the historical character of African American philosophy is primarily nonacademic. This is indicated by including nonacademic African American philosophers in the historical (noncontemporary) parts of their respective books and simultaneously they exclude academic African American philosophers. Alain Locke is the single African American philosopher who was an academic philosopher (before 1965) presented in both texts. The academic African American philosophers who are included are all contemporary philosophers, that is, post-1965 Black intellectuals.

As a result, we are left with the impression that the advent of academic-oriented African American philosophers is more of a recent matter tied to present concerns, not something emerging from the concrete historical development of African American philosophy. Since these works are not texts specifically designated as the history of African American philosophy, then all the assumptions concerning the history of African American philosophy are implicit, thus resting primarily as presuppositions that are embedded in the very organization of the texts. Hence, this reflects the authors' underlying conception of African American philosophy. Each book is conceived as a comprehensive introductory text on African American philosophy that includes both past and contemporary dimensions of the subject.

Noteworthy, the racist character of academic philosophy, over the last two centuries, certainly provides some degree of justification for calling attention to the nonacademic sources of African American philosophy. Undoubtedly, the full measure of the historical sweep of African American philosophical work cannot be confined to just academic philosophers and philosophy. After all, due to slavery and then to racial segregation in institutions of higher education, there were few opportunities for African Americans to enter the academy.

Moreover, the very exclusion of Black people from the academy—for the most part—does not in any way point to the lack of philosophical traditions among African Americans. Clearly, philosophical reflection is not exclusively restricted to the academy and thus nonacademic sources can and do provide a meaningful reservoir. Given the racist nature of the white academy, the alternatives that African Americans pursued in their quest for carrying out philosophical work involved academic as well as nonacademic avenues.[34]

So, therefore, when we see that the Montmarquet and Hardy text includes Martin R. Delaney, Frederick Douglass, and Sojourner Truth, and the Lott book has Maria Stewart, Mary Ann Shadd Carey, Edward Blyden, and Booker T. Washington, among others, there are reasonable and considerable grounds for their inclusion in their respective works. But what happened to the academic philosophers of the nineteenth century and even the twentieth century before 1965?

In our estimation, there is real danger with the historical interpretation of African American philosophers and philosophy, where the prevailing assumption is that nonacademic philosophy remained the limits of African American philosophical contributions and works are nonacademic sources. The presupposition that somehow only during our contemporary time do we find that African American philosophers made real (first) strides in academic philosophy is patently ahistorical and grossly inaccurate. In this sense, the aforementioned texts are considerably lacking in the historical depth congruent with the African American tradition in academic philosophy as was positively demonstrated in (and especially with the 1983 first edition of) Leonard Harris's *Philosophy Born of Struggle*.

It is noticeable that the historical interpretation of philosophy is not removed from the philosopher's given political orientation. As Hill suggests, the historian of philosophy "will have greater sympathies for, and affinities with, certain philosophers than with others." The matter of how political orientation is linked with historical interpretation is specifically prominent—in modern-day African American texts—with the virtual silence concerning any Marxist tradition. For instance, the Montmarquet and Hardy's work says nothing about how Marxism fits into the historical scheme of African American philosophical traditions.

However, unlike Montmarquet and Hardy, we find that Lott refreshingly has a section on Marxism. While he gives a nod to Cornel West—who is openly anti-Marxist-Leninist—Lott, nevertheless, leaves out Eugene C. Holmes. You may wonder, "who was Eugene C. Holmes?" We discover that before—then Communist—Angela Davis came onto the academic scene, Holmes, for many years, was the only African American Marxist philosopher *in the academy*. Lott's section entitled, "Marxism and Social Progress" could have drawn from the numerous articles Holmes published in this area. Of particular note is the fact that Holmes presented a provocative and inspiring paper before the APA titled, "A General Theory of the Freedom Cause of Negro People."[35]

Holmes's various essays on African American social/political philosophy, the aesthetics of Black art, Black education, biographical sketches on Locke, Langston Hughes, and Du Bois, as well as his works[36] on the materialist conception in the philosophy of science could have offered Lott's text invaluable insights into the philosophy of Marxism via the Black experience. Moreover, not only are there at least two published bibliographies of Holmes's publications but as recently as 1998 Albert Mosley talks explicitly about Holmes as the Marxist philosopher at Howard University in an interview with George Yancy.[37]

As for the issue of African American academic philosophers, rather than presume there is no academic philosophical traditions of value, let us dig long and deep into the empirical treasure chest and build on that. For when we integrate the academic with the nonacademic philosophers of the past, we will come closer to recovering and reconstructing the history that can aid us in our contemporary needs. The measure of our progress will be our comprehension of the past, especially from the standpoint of our present realities and future ambitions.

As we transition forward, the latter part of this chapter addresses the empirical description of various academic African American philosophers and their historical context. This can make real sense only in considering the host of empirical and conceptual questions posed at the onset. Herein is the raw material, that is, the factual foundation of the descriptive stage. It is from here that we can move to definition and interpretation, knowing full well that the parameters of our inquiry into the history of African American philosophy are dictated by empirical research.

The lacuna in the historical research on African American philosophy has invariably shaped the viewpoints we have on present-day evaluations of African American philosophers. For instance, contemporary discourse—on

African American philosophy—commonly views Cornel West as a canonical figure. West's various positions at Ivy League institutions, the range of his philosophical writings, and his extraordinary success as public intellectual, for some, position him as one of the most creative and insightful of present-day African American philosophers.

Whatever merit there is to West's importance, we should not presuppose that African American philosophers made "Giant Steps" in academic philosophy only in recent times. Such a mistake would explicitly indicate a gross ignorance of the history of African American philosophy and thus, we become saddled with the ill-fated yoke of presentism as the surrogate for a historical perspective.

In this regard, we deem West's own treatment of the history of African American philosophers as problematic. In *The American Evasion of Philosophy: A Genealogy of Pragmatism*, West acknowledges only one African American philosopher, Dr. W. E. B. Du Bois, as belonging to the pragmatic tradition and therein casting him as "The Jamesian Organic Intellectual." Transparently, with the exception of Du Bois, West concludes that African American philosophers were not inclined to join the pragmatist movement. As to why this virtual Black absence from pragmatism, West fails to give us any explanation.

This silence, nonetheless, engenders a host of questions: Why were African American philosophers not attracted to such an important school of thought? What were the justifications for not joining the bandwagon? Did pragmatism address the issue of Black (racial) progress? Earlier, we established why mechanistic materialism was generally rejected and why dialectical idealism had certain appeal. How was/is pragmatism situated as a definitive philosophical stance vis-à-vis dialectical idealism? Yet, on more than one occasion, we discover that West suggests that his own "Prophetic Pragmatism" offers a viable—philosophical—alternative for African Americans. Notwithstanding Du Bois's supposedly Jamesian pragmatism, could it be that West is the only African American philosopher to envision the (pragmatist) light?

Anyhow, West is certain that Du Bois belongs in the ranks of pragmatism. However, we should bring to the reader's attention that David Levering Lewis and Shamoon Zamir present different interpretations of Du Bois's relationship to pragmatism, particularly William James. In 1890 Du Bois wrote an essay, "The Renaissance in Ethics: A Critical Comparison of Scholastic and Modern Ethics," for a seminar conducted by James. Du Bois presents, in opposition to James, the perspective that values can be grounded on the basis of scientific ontology. Later, during his social scientific stage of development, and when Du Bois consciously departs from formally doing philosophy, James's pragmatic separation of ontology and axiology remains problematic within the context of Du Bois's dialectical conceptual framework. Lewis maintains that Du Bois exhibits a dialectical materialist approach closely approximating the philosophical viewpoint of Karl Marx and Frederick Engels. Here Lewis offers us a strikingly different picture of Du Bois than the one presented by West.[38] Whereas, Zamir highlights how Du Bois sought a science of ethics through the reconciliation of science and philosophy, manifested in a synthetic "Spenserian-Hegelian" form. While Zamir differs from Lewis's quasi-Marxist interpretation, nevertheless, the thrust of Zamir's reading is against the grain of West's Jamesian perspective of Du Bois and in that respect more akin to Lewis's reading.[39]

Paradoxically, West conveys that although Du Bois belongs within the camp of pragmatism, nonetheless, his philosophical worldview differed radically from the perspectives of key figures in this movement. Could it be that this radical difference was due to the fact that Du Bois was not a pragmatist? If we have anything closely amounting to radical difference, then we cannot overlook the possibility of Du Bois standing outside of the pragmatist tradition. This historical fact of the case must serve as the measuring rod for our interpretation. Anything less is merely vacuous speculation masquerading as rigorous historical interpretation. Let's now review West's comments on this issue:

> The career of W. E. B. Du Bois serves as a unique response to the crisis of American pragmatism in the twentieth century. . . . As an American intellectual of African descent . . . Du Bois looks at the United States through a different lens from those of Emerson, Peirce, James, Dewey, Hook, and Mills. As one grounded in and nourished by American pragmatism-both by personal choice and by social treatment-allies himself in word and deed with the wretched of the earth.[40]

Pragmatism is a particular form of empiricism that emerged in the United States. Empiricism is a theory of knowledge (epistemology) that not only asserts that experience is the source of knowledge but also experience constitutes the very limits of knowledge. Pragmatism is overwhelmingly the historic form of empiricism in the United States. Thereby, its content and focus explicitly signify a philosophical viewpoint from—and importantly on—the realities of US life. The glue cementing the link between pragmatism's various internal strands and trends remains an allegiance to empiricism, wherein it shapes not only matters of epistemology but also matters relating to ontology and value theory.

Of course, while empiricism is not unique to the United States, its pragmatist formulation chiefly derives from this country. As with other philosophical schools of thought in the United States, pragmatism cannot be removed from issues concerning race and racism. Concurrently, what should not be overlooked is that race and racism were pivotal in Du Bois's philosophical outlook.[41]

If Du Bois had a qualitatively different philosophical lens than that found with key members of the school of pragmatism, it stands to reason that his take on the United States was not due to "nourishment" from pragmatism. Clearly, pragmatism was not on Du Bois's philosophical plate. It makes little sense to say, "unlike his fellow vegetarians, Du Bois enjoyed a good steak from time to time." While it is true that Du Bois was an undergraduate student of William James at Harvard, nevertheless, we submit that the early course of Du Bois's philosophical development is more adequately grasped as dialectical idealism—which is preeminently articulated in the philosophy of Hegel. Du Bois was quite aware of how dialectical idealism was associated with Hegel's philosophy. We discern that Du Bois's allegiance to philosophical idealism is vividly captured in this statement from Shamoon Zamir:

> It is in *Souls* that the crisis of confidence and the struggle to gather up the self out of chaos are most imaginatively and complexly dramatized. Here Du Bois is able to describe a history in which, to use Sartre's terms, the instruments are broken and unusable and "plans blasted." In this defeat Du Bois the theorist of action and *Du Bois the idealist philosopher of history* begins to give way to Du Bois the poet who tries to contest and appropriate the new universe.[42] (italics added)

While Zamir finds in Du Bois's *Souls of Black Folk* the basis for a transition from philosophy of history to poetry, African American philosopher Robert Gooding-Williams offers a penetrating and compelling criticism on West's proposal that Du Bois was pragmatist. Gooding-Williams argues, "Du Bois's discussion of the American Negro revises Hegel's philosophy of history, first, by transporting the Hegelian dialectic into North America and second, by bringing the 'message' of Africa, which Hegel relegates to the non-narratable 'threshold' (Schwelle) of historical time and development into the drama of world history."[43]

Du Bois was quite aware of the fact that James's founding role in pragmatism—as a school of thought—was an important departure from

Hegel and Hegelianism. Du Bois continued his studies of Hegelianism, at the University of Berlin, precisely after his Harvard undergraduate (philosophical) work with James. This fact is of no small matter in our discussion on the locus of Du Bois.[44] The vast philosophical distance separating Du Bois and James precisely centers on Hegelianism. From the very standpoint of pragmatism, James steadfastly opposes Hegel and Hegelianism to its core. In turn, Du Bois embraces Hegel in such a pivotal and fundamental manner that the claim about "The Jamesian Organic Intellectual" proves forced and superficial. In this connection, the historian David Levering Lewis asserts,

> Du Bois felt … [an] affinity for Hegel, from whose monumental *Phenomenology of Mind* he borrowed more or less intact notions of distinct, hierarchical racial attributes. And for all James's supposed pragmatic and empirical influences upon him, Du Bois found in the Hegelian World-Spirit, dialectically actualizing itself through history, a profoundly appealing concept.[45]

In concert with this statement, pragmatism and dialectical idealism are fundamentally at odds respecting whether knowledge of reality is rooted in the immediate appearances of perception. Pragmatism remains a form of empiricism and openly rejects the *dialectical distinction* of appearance/essence as foundational to knowing reality. We previously observed that William D. Johnson differentiated between perception (experience/empiricism) and the conceptual notion of observing the "One." Notably, both Johnson and Du Bois belong to the African American philosophical tradition of dialectical idealism, which has a close kinship with Hegel. Contrary to Johnson's looking out the window example, William James argues that experience (perceptual observation) is not defective, since we *actually see the many things of reality* and not some mystical "One."

James argues that experience grounds our knowledge of reality, rather than merely arriving at deceptive appearances. *The Will to Believe*—James's first book in philosophy—includes the essay "On Some Hegelians." This essay contains James's key arguments in his attack on Hegelianism. From the empiricist standpoint, James critically remarks about Hegel's philosophy:

> But the trouble that keeps us and Hegel from ever joining hands over this apparent formula of brotherhood is that we distinguish, or try to distinguish, the respects *in which the world is one from those in which it is many*, while all such stable distinctions are what he most abominates. The reader may decide which procedure helps his reason most. For my own part, the time-honored

formula of *empiricist pluralism*, that the world cannot be set down in any single proposition, grows less instead of more intelligible when I add, "And yet the different propositions that express it are one!" The unity of the propositions is that of the mind that harbors them. Anyone who insists that their diversity is in any way itself their unity, can only do so because he loves obscurity and mystification for their own pure sakes.[46] (italics added)

Consequently, we contend that interpreting Du Bois as a pragmatist significantly misses the boat. Here, we must return to our prior question, "what schools of thought captured the allegiance of African American philosophers?" We submit that for African American philosophers—specifically Du Bois—dialectical idealism remained paramount. The failure to concretely grasp the history of African American philosophy pointedly comes to the forefront, with West's misplacement of Du Bois. Such failure signals why historical interpretation and philosophical definition cannot be jettisoned from empirical inquiry, that is, if the history of philosophy stands as a viable means for recovering the true meaning of the past.

While West inspects such figures as Ralph Waldo Emerson, Charles Peirce, William James, John Dewey, Sidney Hook, C. Wright Mills, Reinhold Niebuhr, and Richard Rorty, among others, he is silent about any African American philosopher—besides Du Bois—within the ranks of pragmatism. Given the prominence of pragmatism in the United States, we ask, how did African American thinkers respond to its philosophical influence? Now that we have demonstrated that Du Bois was not a pragmatist, is it the case that there were no African American pragmatists? It should go without saying, the ascendency of dialectical idealism does not imply that all African American philosophers held allegiance to it. Consequently, our task continues in uncovering the facts surrounding this issue.

Contrary to West, we find there is considerable scholarly justification for placing Alain Locke as pragmatist. Among a host of philosophers, Leonard Harris contends that Locke assumes a prominent space in the ranks of pragmatism as a "Critical Pragmatist." Furthermore, Booker T. Washington is no less significant than Emerson respecting a nonphilosopher of pragmatist leanings. Black philosopher Bill Lawson effectively articulates that Washington should be situated within the tradition of Deweyan pragmatism.[47]

Unfortunately, West completely ignores African American philosophical research on pragmatism. We have, for example, the case where Holmes offers a critical study of pragmatism with his dissertation *Social Philosophy and Social Mind: A Study of the Genetic Methods of J. M. Baldwin, George Herbert*

Mead and J. E. Boodin. We additionally have John Milton Smith's dissertation *A Comparison and Criticism of the Educational Policies of Plato and John Dewey*, and Broadus Butler's *A Pragmatic Study of Value and Evaluation.* Accordingly, West—like so many others—ignores the "lost voices" of African American philosophers who labored under the "Color Line," as W. E. B. Du Bois so fittingly called Jim and Jane Crow.

Professional philosophy and academic racism

Professional academic philosophy, like other disciplines in the bourgeois academy, is firmly rooted in institutionalized racism. Therefore, we must answer the question, "what is racism?" Racism is not just the attitude or belief that there exist superior and inferior races, but more importantly, it is behavior and institutions that give material support to such attitudes and beliefs by the suppression of the supposed inferior groups. Thus, academic racism is the practice associated with the complex of institutions such as colleges and universities, including the posture of the APA, which function together and assert institutional power by erecting standards that, under the guise of professionalization, were and are racist.[48]

Resistance to Black philosophers (and Black scholars more generally) as teachers of white students has a rather long history. Albert Millard Dunham Jr., the elder brother of the African American dancer and choreographer Katherine M. Dunham, illustrates the racism faced by African American philosophers. After having studied at Harvard with Alfred North Whitehead and at Chicago with John Dewey and George Herbert Mead, Dunham received his doctorate from the University of Chicago in 1933. Dunham was considered by many, at that time, to be one of the most promising among African American philosophers to rise in the profession.[49]

In due course he was assigned to teach a summer class in the philosophy department of his alma mater. The appointment was to be a gateway to becoming a full-fledged member of the philosophy faculty at Chicago. However, over half of the students dropped the class when they discovered that their professor was a Black person. Although the administration managed to gather enough students to continue the class, the idea of Dunham joining the Chicago faculty, in light of the student response, was quickly abandoned. Later Alain Locke recruited Dunham to teach at Howard University. Those that knew him, including his sister Katherine, believed that the racial restrictions, which were imposed on him as a Black philosopher, especially with regard to the possibility of teaching at white institutions, caused Dunham's long-term affliction with depression. Sadly, we discover that by 1949 (after many years of mental illness) Dunham died in a psychiatric institution.

Institutionalized academic racism is the context in which African American philosophers operated and the setting in which their work must be interpreted. Therefore, African American philosophers consistently responded to how academic racism maintained a virulent attack on the intellectual capacity of Black people. Three specific occasions are Richard T. Greener's insightful essay, "The White Problem" (1894); Alexander Crummell, "Civilization—The Primal Need of the Race: The Attitude of the American Mind Toward the Negro Intellect" (1897); and George Washington Henderson, "In Defence [sic] of Higher as Well as Industrial Education" (1901).[50]

Harvard's first Black graduate and former professor of philosophy at the University of South Carolina Richard T. Greener acutely notes,

> If one wishes to observe the eccentricity, vagary, platitude, and idiosyncrasy all combined, let him read the literary effusions of the so-called "Caucasian" intellect from Thomas Jefferson's "Notes on Virginia." . . . Jefferson, fresh from Hume, uttered some platitudes about the two races living together in freedom, treading very cautiously, as is his custom, when not too sure of his premises. . . . A phase of the white problem is seen in the determination, not only to treat the Negro as a member of a child-like race, but the grim determination to keep him a child or ward. In every advance, since emancipation it has, with true Caucasian gall, that everything must be done for him, and under no circumstances must he be allowed to do for himself.[51]

Segregation determined that African Americans in the late nineteenth and on through most of the twentieth century were afforded little opportunity to pursue either undergraduate or graduate study in philosophy at white colleges. Therefore, prior to 1840, approximately no more than fifteen Black students attended white colleges.[52] For the vast majority of African American philosophers who had in fact completed graduate work at white institutions, the "Color Line" of segregation also meant that they were either excluded from or had limited participation in the white academy, along with its subsidiary professional organizations. In fact, by 1936, there were only three Black scholars with PhDs serving on the faculties of white colleges. The sad truth is that nearly 80 percent of Black PhDs in 1936 taught at three HBCUs: Atlanta (founded in 1865), Fisk (founded in 1866), and Howard (founded in 1867) universities.[53]

Given the racist obstacles to acquiring an education, in some instances, African Americans were forced to leave the United States to study and teach abroad. Before Black institutions were viable alternatives for pursuing academic philosophy, a few African Americans boldly departed from this country to engage in academic philosophy. We discover, for example, that antebellum philosophers such as Alexander Crummell and Patrick Francis Healy (Figure 5) left the United States to gain a higher education in philosophy. Healy, who was the first African American to earn a PhD, earned his degree in 1865 from the University of Louvain.[54]

A graduate of Cambridge University (class of 1853), Alexander Crummell studied with the Cambridge Platonist, William Whewell. Furthermore, Crummell's teaching career in philosophy was also outside of the United States. Crummell taught philosophy in Liberia where he was a professor of mental and moral science. Crummell made a particular mark on the history of African American philosophers and their connection to Africa. After his return to this country, he advanced the institutional development of African American academic life. Crummell's crowning intellectual achievement was perhaps his founding of the American Negro Academy in March 1897. This

Figure 5 Patrick Francis Healy (1834–1910).

first attempt at founding a national Black think tank included scholars of the caliber of W. E. B. Du Bois.[55]

With respect to Patrick Francis Healy, he was the only African American with a doctorate to teach philosophy at a white institution prior to the turn of the twentieth century. The son of a slaveholder and slave mistress, Healy taught philosophy at Holy Cross, St. Joseph (Philadelphia), and Georgetown. He later became the president of Georgetown in 1874 making him the first African American to head a white higher educational institution. An ordained Catholic priest, as with most of his siblings, Healy was a leading member of the Catholic Church. One of his brothers actually achieved the rank of bishop, the first African American to do so.[56]

The "Color Line" restricted most African American philosophers to teaching at HBCUs prior to the 1970s. When Cornelius Golightly joined the philosophy faculty at Olivet College in 1945, he became the first Black philosopher, in the twentieth century, hired in a permanent position within a philosophy department at a predominantly white institution.[57] Subsequently, the segregation of African American philosophers in often underfunded Black institutions limited their ability to pursue research and publication. Faced with enormous teaching loads, low salaries, professional isolation, limited resources, and enormous administrative responsibilities, many African American philosophers were unable to publish their work. For example, Wayman B. McLaughlin (Figure 6) taught at North Carolina

Figure 6 Wayman B. McLaughlin (1927–2003).

A&T for over thirty years. Yet, he never published his book with the proposed title *The Psychic Gifts of the Spirit: A Study in Philosophy and Parapsychology*. In some instances, the doctoral dissertation is the only available source for a clue into the philosophical views of Black philosophers.

Because HBCUs were teaching institutions, many administrators like Ferdinand D. Bluford (North Carolina A&T) and Mordecai Johnson (Howard) did not reward or value scholarship. They made it impossible for Black scholars to engage in sustained research and writing. The historian Earl Thorpe recalled how Bluford despised scholarship so much that he "would fire a few Ph.D.s once in a while just to be sure that it was clear that he was president."[58]

A classic example is the case of Francis A. Thomas (Figure 7) at HBCU Central State University in Wilberforce, Ohio. Although Thomas desired to write a book (with the proposed title *A Philosophy for the Small Planet Earth*), this project unfortunately never came to fruition. Nonetheless, his intellectual contributions as philosopher are more significantly and relevantly measured by his teaching, mentoring, and dialoging with students and colleagues. Furthermore, his administrative role both as chair of the philosophy department at Central State University and as director of the Audio-Visual Center, then later as dean of Payne Theological Seminary did not afford him the public exposure adjoined with being employed at more prestigious white institutions.[59]

How odd it seems that a philosopher and theologian would be saddled with the duty of running the Audio-Visual Center. After receiving his BA from Wesleyan and BD from Yale University, Thomas elected to pursue post-baccalaureate degrees in education with an emphasis on audiovisual communications. Thomas's Indiana University doctoral dissertation,

Figure 7 Francis A. Thomas (1913–2001).

"Philosophies of Audio-Visual Education as Conceived in a University Center and by Selected Leaders," graphically captures how he conceptualized his combined responsibilities in philosophy and communication technology. The anchoring and overriding principle, for such organizational diversity, is rooted in the complex needs of the HBCU context. Practical demands were ubiquitously adjoined to academic work. Thomas succinctly proffers how this ubiquitous link finds its philosophical expression in the unity of theory and practice, which is allied with the content of philosophy itself:

> Theory, unless ultimately grounded in empirical data tends to fancy; practice not founded on theory, leans too heavily upon chance and usually results in chaos. In the history of mankind, communication through language and conceptualization constitutes both the mark and method whereby man distinguished himself from subhuman animals. This ability to think on a high level of abstraction, and the desire to prove both the implications and consequences of thought have resulted in the development of the special field of philosophy which concerns itself with the formulation of theoretical assumptions.[60]

The demands on a professor in the HBCU setting are not without philosophical imperatives. This fact harbors a tremendous narrative and testament, for it conveys that Thomas was part and parcel of the HBCU struggle to survive and flourish amid the challenges of white power and domination. Therefore, Thomas's intellectual contributions could not and did not revolve around the conventional academic ethos of publish or perish. Rather, his motivating intellectual and political principles were "push and persist" and "survive yet resist" white supremacy, even when the financial resources were meager and more than often the acquisition of funds repeatedly mandated going to white sources.[61]

Also, the particular status of African American women in academic philosophy is an integral chapter in the history of African American philosophy. The additional burden of sexism plays no small part in this history. Recently, the incipient Black feminism of Anna Julia Cooper has been embraced by some Black women philosophers and credited as making a pioneering "feminist" contribution to African American philosophy. Unfortunately, as historian Kevin Gaines observes,

> Much of what contemporary readers recognize as "feminist" in Cooper's writing cannot easily be disentangled from her Western ethnocentrism, her staunch religious piety, and a late-Victorian bourgeois sensibility distrustful of social democracy. Of course, these were views she shared with the predominantly male black intelligentsia, complicated, however, by her gender

consciousness in such a way as to produce multiple and at times conflicting identities. Out of the multiplicity of her voices emerged that of a southern, nativist apologist for antilabor views.[62]

So, to the extent to which Cooper was a feminist, her social philosophy was grounded on a petit-bourgeois ideology of racial uplift, which measured racial progress and the "Woman's Question" from the standpoint of a "late-Victorian bourgeois sensibility distrustful of social democracy." At the age of sixty-six, Cooper remarkably earned a doctorate (in 1925) from the University of Paris-Sorbonne in French literature.[63]

As previously noted, Joyce Mitchell Cook was the first African American woman to be granted a doctorate in philosophy, which she received in 1965 from Yale University. From a historical viewpoint, this is crucial since African American males earned doctorates in philosophy from Yale as early as 1903 with Thomas Nelson Baker—the first African American to earn the doctorate in philosophy from an institution in the United States—leading the way.[64] She was also the first woman appointed to teach at Yale and in the Howard University philosophy departments (1959–61 and 1970–76, respectively). Between 1959 and 1961, she was the managing editor of the prestigious *The Review of Metaphysics*.[65] Cook opened the door for future generations of Black women philosophers such as Adrian M. S. Piper, Anita Allen, Angela Yvonne Davis (Figure 8), Michele M. Moody-Adams, Blanche Radford-Curry, Joy James, Claudette Jones, Barbara McKenny, La Verne M. Shelton, Jacqueline Scott, Janine Jones, Sybol Cook Anderson, Vanessa Wells, Anika Mann, and Kathyrn Gines, among others.

Many of the first generation of Black women in philosophy faced unbelievable material and ideological barriers (such as gender discrimination and sexist

Figure 8 Angela Yvonne Davis (1944–).

ideology) which greatly impacted their advancement in the discipline of philosophy. Joyce Mitchell Cook (by Howard University), Laverne Shelton (by Rutgers), and Adrian Piper (by Michigan) were all denied tenure despite excellent backgrounds and training at Yale, Minnesota, and Harvard, respectively. And, in 1969, philosopher Angela Davis was fired (from her professorship in the Philosophy Department at the University of California, Los Angeles [UCLA]) by the Board of Regents of the University of California, urged by then-California Governor Ronald Reagan, because of her membership in the Communist Party. It is reported that her dissertation was stolen by the federal government. From our research, she never actually completed her dissertation nor received the doctorate.[66]

In 1970, there were at least two Black women with full time faculty positions in philosophy. In the last forty years, we have seen a remarkable growth in the number of Black women with a doctorate in philosophy nor teaching in philosophy departments; today, there are more than thirty Black women philosophers in the field (see Table 1).

Table 1 Selected listing of African American women philosophers

	Year	Name	Doctoral Institution
1.	1965	Joyce Mitchell Cook	Yale University
2.		Angela Davis	
3.	1975	La Verne Maria Shelton (Leeb)	University of Minnesota
4.	1979	Anita L. Allen	University of Michigan
5.	1979	Blanche Radford-Curry	Brown University
6.	1981	Adrian M. S. Piper	Harvard University
7.	1981	Ramona Hoage Edelin	Boston University
8.	1985	Georgette Sinkler	Cornell University
9.	1986	Michele M. Moody-Adams	Harvard University
10.	1987	Joy James	Fordham University
11.	1993	Janine Jones	University of California-Los Angeles
12.	1994	Barbara Massey McKenney	The American University
13.	1995	Renee A. Hill	University of Virginia
14.	1995	Jacqueline Renee Scott	Stanford University
15.	1997	Daseia Y. Cavers-Huff	University of California-Riverside
16.	1997	Delia Graff Fara	Massachusetts Institute of Technology
17.	1997	Barbara Hall	University of Arizona

(Continued)

Table 1 Continued

	Year	Name	Doctoral Institution
18.	2000	Al-Yasha Ilhaam Williams	Stanford University
19.	2000	Gertrude Gonzales de Allen	Binghamton University
20.	2000	Tracy Annette Edwards	University of Wisconsin-Madison
21.	2002	Devonya N. Harris	Boston College
22.	2003	Kathryn T. Gines	University of Memphis
23.	2003	Pamela Hood	Claremont Graduate University
24.	2004	Anika Maaza (Simpson) Mann	University of Memphis
25.	2004	Donna-Dale Marcano	University of Memphis
26.	2005	Jeanine Weekes Schroer	University of Illinois-Chicago
27.	2006	Desiree Helen Melton	State University of New York at Binghamton
28.	2006	Sybol Cook Anderson	John Hopkins University
29.	2006	Lina Buffington	Emory University
30.	2007	Kris Sealey	University of Memphis
31.	2008	Kristie Dotson	University of Memphis
32.	2008	Vera Denise James	Emory University
33.	2008	Yolonda Yvette Wilson	The University of North Carolina at Chapel Hill
34.	2011	Tina Fernandes Botts	University of Memphis
35.	2011	Vanessa Wills	University of Pittsburgh
36.	2012	Nena Davis	UNC-Chapel Hill
37.	2013	Keisha Shantel Ray	University of Utah
38.	2013	Camisha Russell	Pennsylvania State University
39.	2014	Qrescent Mason	Temple University
40.	2015	Brittany O'Neal	Michigan State University
41.	2015	Ronke A. Oke	Pennsylvania State University
42.	2015	Jameliah Shorter-Bourhanou	Pennsylvania State University
43.	2015	Natalia Washington	Purdue University
44.	2015	Monique Wonderly	University of California-Riverside
45.	2016	Catherine Clune-Taylor	University of Alberta (Canada)
46.	2016	Céline Leboeuf	Harvard University
47.	2016	Lindsey Latraille Stewart	Pennsylvania State University
48.	2017	Lisa R. Cassell	University of Massachusetts-Amherst
49.	2018	Alisa Bierria	Stanford University
50.	2018	Kimberly Ann Harris	Pennsylvania State University
51.	2018	Briana Toole	University of Texas-Austin
52.	2018	Desiree Valentine	Pennsylvania State University

In 2007, the Collegium of Black Women Philosophers (CBWP) was formed to increase the number and visibility of Black women in the field of philosophy. Despite the progress of Black women in professional philosophy, Anita Allen observes, "We all have horror stories and bruises. We have all been demeaned, disrespected, harassed, regarded as problems or burdens of affirmative action, and denied our due. But what I would like to emphasize is that we are here."[67]

Excluded from the opportunity to participate in the white academy, African American philosophers were faced with a dual professional imperative: on the one hand, they undertook work that would gain the scholarly approval of their white counterparts. On the other hand, these segregated philosophers had a commitment to address the philosophical issues confronting the African American community. This dual imperative, which Du Bois had framed as double consciousness, remained a salient feature of the history of African American philosophers, up through the final decades of the twentieth century.[68]

When addressing the problems raised by the African American experience (such as the nature and impact of racism as well as philosophical problems and topics of interest to mainstream white philosophers) African American philosophers utilized resources available to them within the framework of Black institutions and often were forced to publish in Black publications. White control of major university and commercial presses limited the opportunities to publish books. And, moreover, few white publishers were interested in publishing the works of Black scholars. Michael Winston mordantly observes how the "shortsightedness" of administrators at HBCUs, for example at Howard, led to the failure of HBCUs to support a university press of any kind.[69]

In fact, for the Black philosopher, the available academic journals were generally focused on disciplines outside of philosophy. Nevertheless, Black philosophers actively continued to present their philosophical viewpoints in these journals. Thus, we must address and answer our earlier questions, namely, what were the venues (institutional settings) available for their work? Were such outlets academic or nonacademic in makeup or did both come into play? What audience did they seek to address? And what means were at their disposal for reaching an audience?

Founded by W. E. B. Du Bois, the scholarly journal *Phylon* served as an outlet for several African American philosophers.[70] For instance, Boston University doctorate holder and classmate of Martin Luther King Jr., African American philosopher Wayman Bernard McLaughlin published his "Symbolism and Mysticism in the Spirituals" within the pages of *Phylon*. Our content analysis reveals how McLaughlin examines the double meaning of the spirituals, that is, the symbolic language used in and mystical meaning behind the spirituals. These songs, as McLaughlin notes, were "born out of the aches, pains, and joys of existence." However, within the tradition of philosophical personalism, McLaughlin emphasizes that the spirituals express an intuitive personal experience that African American slaves had with God. When we unveil the mystical meaning of the spirituals, McLaughlin argues, we can see the spirituals as expressing the "direct communion of the soul with God."[71]

Similar to McLaughlin's experience, several African American religious journals provided outlets for Black philosophers. For example, *The Journal of Religious Thought* (hereafter JRT) in its autumn/winter issue of 1949 alone had three philosophers publish essays in that particular issue: William A. Banner's "Fundamentals of Christian Social Order," Carleton L. Lee's "Toward a Christian Critique of British Socialism," and Samuel W. Williams's "Communism: A Christian Critique." Banner was a 1947 graduate of Harvard and later served as chair of the Howard University Philosophy Department. And Carleton L. Lee's doctoral dissertation (University of Chicago 1951), *Patterns of Leadership in Race Relations: A Study of Leadership among American Negroes*, was one of the first African American dissertations explicitly focused on the Black experience. A graduate of HBCU Talladega College, Lee taught at several HBCUs before starting the Black Americana Studies program at Western Michigan State University[72] (see Tables 2 and 3).

Table 2 African American philosophers who served as presidents of HBCUs

Name	Institution	Years
J. W. E. Bowen	Gammon Theological Seminary	1906–10
John Burrus	Alcorn A & M	1882–93
Broadus Butler	Dillard University	1969–73
Marquis L. Harris	Philander Smith	1936–61
Charles Leander Hill	Wilberforce	1947–56
Glibert Haven Jones	Wilberforce	1924–32
Willis J. King	Samuel Huston College	1930–32
Willis J. King	Gammon Theological Seminary	1932–44
Benjamin Mays	Morehouse College	1940–67
Richard I. McKinney	Storer College	1944–55
William Stuart Nelson	Shaw University	1931–36
William Stuart Nelson	Dillard University	1936–40
Joseph C. Price	Livingston College	1882–93

Table 3 African American philosophers as chairs of philosophy departments

Name	Institution	Years
Lewis Baxter Moore	Howard University	1899–1919
Alain Locke	Howard University	1928–53
Eugene C. Holmes	Howard University	1953–66
Winston K. McAllister	Howard University	1966–76
William A. Banner	Howard University	1976–81
Max William Wilson	Howard University	1981–88
Jacqueline Anderson	Olive-Harvey College (Chicago)	?
Winson R. Coleman	Johnson C. Smith	?
Everett F. S. Davies	Virginia State College	1954–71
James L. Farmer Sr.	Wiley College	?
William T. Fontaine	Morgan State University	1946–47
Thomas F. Freeman	Texas Southern University	?
Francis M. Hammond	Seton Hall	1946–51
Gilbert Haven Jones	St. Augustine	?
Richard I. McKinney	Morgan State University	1951–78
Darryl Scrivens	Florida A & M	2014–18
Jesse Taylor	Appalachian State University	1997–2004
Francis A. Thomas	Central State	1947–78
Rudolph Vanterpool	California State University, Dominguez Hills	?
Samuel W. Williams	Morehouse College	1946–70

Samuel Woodrow Williams (Figure 9) was a student of Alain Locke and Eugene C. Holmes at Howard University and would eventually serve as chair of the Philosophy Department at Morehouse College. Williams was philosophy professor and mentor to Martin Luther King Jr. Of particular note, Williams gave an address, "The Legacy of Martin Luther King Jr., Violence and Nonviolence in the Struggle for Equality," at Hebrew University in 1970. Unlike King, Williams does not completely dismiss the use of violence in the struggle to obtain civil rights. For Williams, in contrast with King, violence is not an absolute principle of immoral fiber. Thus, we discern the philosophy of nonviolence—among African American philosophers—is a rather complex conception with rich variance.[73]

Also, Richard I. McKinney—with a BA in philosophy and religion— received his doctorate from Yale in 1942. After serving as the president of Storer College (a West Virginia HBCU) McKinney became chair of the philosophy department at Morgan State University. Concerned with how

Figure 9 Samuel Woodrow Williams (1912–70).

philosophy and specifically existentialism could be linked to the civil rights movement, McKinney published his "Existential Ethics and the Protest Movement" in *The Journal of Religious Thought* (1965–66).[74]

For McKinney, if existentialism was relevant to protest movements, then we have another important exemplar respecting the unity of theory and practice. As with Francis A. Thomas, McKinney is particularly concerned on how philosophy can inform social activism:

> The question of the relation of theory to practice has often been of concern to philosophers. Sometimes it is claimed that all action proceeds from some recognized philosophical presuppositions. On the other hand, there are those who maintain that we develop habits of action and then seek philosophical justification for them. In any case, we recognize that every philosophy represents some foundation for conduct, whether or not it is developed in advance of that conduct. It is probable that among the participants in the protest movement, examples of both claims may be discovered.[75]

Along the same lines of Black activism, Black philosopher Everett F. S. Davies (Figure 10) published "Negro Protest Movement: The Religious Way," in the *JRT* of 1967–68. Born in Sierra Leone, Davies earned his MA from Yale and doctorate from Columbia University. Davies began membership with the APA in 1956. Administratively, Davies was chair of the Philosophy

Figure 10 Everett F. S. Davies (1900–77).

Department at the HBCU Virginia State College in Petersburg, Virginia.[76] Additionally, three pioneering philosophers of African American religion, William R. Jones, Robert C. Williams, and Roy D. Morrison II, found their way to the pages of *JRT*.

Jones wrote "Theodicy: The Controlling Category for Black Theology" (1973), while Robert C. Williams submitted his "Moral Suasion and Militant Aggression in the Theological Perspectives of Black Religion" (1973–74). Jones was both a student of Eugene C. Holmes at Howard University and later a faculty member in the philosophy department there. Jones would later chair African American Studies at FSU. As for Williams, he taught at Fisk University and Central State University (both HBCU) before moving on to Vanderbilt and then finally Muhlenberg College as vice president, academic dean, and professor of philosophy.[77]

In 1976, *The Journal of Religious Thought* entered the ever-growing discussion on the nature and substance of Black philosophy. While some philosophers such as William A. Banner of Howard University stood in opposition to this notion, others, for instance, such as Roy D. Morrison II declared in no uncertain terms, "Black Philosophy: An Instrument for Cultural and Religious Liberation" (1976). After undergraduate work at Howard University, Morrison gained his University of Chicago PhD in 1972, and he uniquely stands as one of the few philosophers of African American religion holding the status of atheist.[78]

Long before *The Journal of Religious Thought*, *The AME Church Review* was a rich source for philosophical works by African American thinkers. Given the religious basis of the journal, it is no surprise that idealism formatively emerged as the dominant tradition among African American philosophers writing in the late nineteenth and early twentieth centuries. Indeed, many of the early Black philosophers were also theologians, if not ordained ministers. This tendency toward religion did not mean that the philosophy of science was absent from the agenda.

In his 1893 article "Philosophy of Progress," D. J. Jordan argues, "Philosophers tell us of the inertia of matter. According to the definition of inertia their teaching is correct; but no matter in all creation is inert; every particle and atom is acting upon every other."[79] Jordan's conceptual distinction between "inert" and "inertia" is of no minor philosophical importance. Newton's laws of motion rest on the premise that matter remains in the state of inertia or rest, unless an external force is applied.[80]

Philosophically, some thinkers identified inertia with inertness and hence the idea of "dead" matter. Newton's own mechanistic conception of the world—coupled with the notion of dead matter—gave rise to two philosophical problems. One, what is the source of motion itself and the other related to the very origins of life. With Newtonian mechanics the source of motion is a circular problem of action and reaction, where reaction is a corresponding action ad infinitum. The theory of "vitalism" originated as a response to this notion of dead matter with its ancillary mechanical determinism. Vitalism is the view that the sources of life are outside the parameters of matter. The substance of life therefore is immaterial as well as dynamic.

In contrast, Jordan recaptures a dynamic principle for matter. Since inertia is distinguishable from inertness then matter is far from lifeless and thus lacking a principle of internal motion. Consequently, Jordan eschews any form of mechanical determinism adjoined to matter. From this insight, Jordan establishes the dialectical (dynamic) premise for an ontological principle of internal motion. Forces within matter rather than outside it become primary. Subsequently, he develops his social philosophical perspective, which conceptualizes how Black progress attains realization in the very process inherently situated within the progression of history.

Additionally, we find in the pages of this religious journal an intriguing debate over the validity of Darwin's theory of evolution. A. J. Kershaw rejects the theory of evolution as speculative philosophy that is inconsistent with science as a system of thought. Edward A. Clarke seeks to reconcile evolution with biblical Scripture. Hence, in the pages of *The AME Church Review*, the philosophy of science had a tremendous bearing on African American social-political philosophy.[81]

Later in the pages of *The AME Church Review* (1955) philosopher Charles Leander Hill published the first English translation of Anton Wilhelm Amo's "Dissertation on Apathy." A native of modern-day Ghana, Anton Wilhelm Amo arrived in Amsterdam and then migrated to Germany during the early eighteenth century. It is likely that Amo arrived in Amsterdam as a slave. Amo was given the opportunity to gain a formal education at the highest level. Consequently, Amo became the first person of African descent to earn a PhD in philosophy. He submitted his inaugural dissertation to the Wittenberg University faculty in 1734. It was this doctoral dissertation—written in Latin—that Hill translated into English.[82]

Comparably, Hill was the second African American to earn a doctorate in philosophy from the Ohio State University (1938) and authored *A Short History of Modern Philosophy from the Renaissance to Hegel* (1951)—the first history of modern philosophy written by an African American philosopher. A scholar on co-reformer Philip Melanchthon of the Protestant Reformation, Hill substantially advanced Melanchthon studies with his translation of *The Loci Communes*. Furthermore, Hill served as president of Wilberforce University (1947–56) and was also an ordained minister in the A.M.E Church.[83]

In addition to *The AME Church Review* and *The Journal of Religious Thought*, the following African American journals often served as the publishing outlets for African American philosophers: *A.M.E. Zion Quarterly, Quarterly Review of Higher Education Among Negroes, The Negro Journal of Religion, Journal of Negro History, Journal of Negro Education,*

Phylon, Freedomways, Negro History Bulletin, and *Western Journal of Black Studies,* among others. Hence, we have Joseph C. Price, "The Race Question in the South," *A.M.E. Zion Quarterly* (1893); Forrest O. Wiggins's "Reflections on Education," in the *Quarterly Review of Higher Education Among Negroes* (1936); Charles Leander Hill penned his critical discussion on "American Democracy," in *The Negro Journal of Religion* (1940); William T. Fontaine elected to submit his article "An Interpretation of Contemporary Negro Thought from the Standpoint of the Sociology of Knowledge," to the *Journal of Negro History* (1940); Cornelius Golightly's "Negro Higher Education and Democratic Negro Morale," in the *Journal of Negro Education* (1942); Alain Locke's "Self-Criticism: The Third Dimension in Culture," appeared in *Phylon* (1950); Broadus Butler wrote "In Defense of Negro Intellectuals," as a rebuttal to E. Franklin Frazier's essay "The Failure of the Negro Intellectual," in *Negro Digest* (1962); Eugene C. Holmes's article "W.E.B. Du Bois: Philosopher," was in *Freedomways* (1965); Carleton L. Lee presented his article "Black Americana Studies," in the *Negro History Bulletin* (1971); and *Western Journal of Black Studies* published Charles Frye's "Black Studies: Definition and Administrative Model" (1977).

The post-1965 period increasingly became the take-off point for the advancement of the Philosophy of the Black Experience or Black philosophy. In 1976, Joyce Mitchell Cook, William R. Jones, and Robert C. Williams participated in a groundbreaking panel, convened by the APA, which explored the meaning of Black philosophy and more broadly its relationship to metaphilosophy.[84]

While research opportunities for Black philosophers were restricted, a considerable number of these figures were pivotal mentors to social activists. In addition to Samuel Williams, George D. Kelsey was another faculty member in the Philosophy and Religion Department of Morehouse College whose ideas contributed to King's development as an advocate of the philosophy of nonviolence. Kelsey's role as a philosopher of nonviolence is a vital yet neglected chapter in the history of African American philosophy. Kelsey received his PhD in philosophy from Yale in 1946 and would go on to write an important book representative of the Christian conception of nonviolence. Kelsey's *Racism and the Christian Understanding of Man* is a significant text for understanding African American contributions to the philosophy of nonviolence.

William Stuart Nelson—who at Howard University developed the first academic course on the philosophy of nonviolence at an institution of higher education—advised King on the principles of nonviolence during the

Montgomery bus boycott.[85] Nelson was also founding editor of *The Journal of Religious Thought*, which remains a major source for intellectual discussion in the philosophy of religion. The import of Black journals such as *The Journal of Religious Thought* for understanding the history of African American philosophical inquiry cannot be overstated. The reading audience of these journals not only included members of the academy but also those outside of its doors, specifically those in search of a deeper understanding of how philosophy was pertinent to Black life.

Concomitantly, African American philosophers found in these scholarly journals an outlet for teaching philosophy, with the aim of sharpening philosophical insights about the formidable challenges of institutionalized racism and Black liberation. What Dr. Francis A. Thomas articulated about the unity of theory and practice serving as the substance of philosophy was far from an aberration. Certainly, he gave expression to a very important tradition, which is foundational to the notion of the public intellectual.

Notes

1. Louis Althusser, *Lenin and Philosophy and Other Essays* (New York: Monthly Review Press, 1971), 55.
2. Henry T. Johnson, "Philosophy Religiously Valued," *The A.M.E. Church Review* 7(4) (April 1891), 423. See also Read "H. T. Johnson, D. D.," *The Christian Recorder* (June 4, 1896), 1.
3. Karl Marx, "The Leading Article in No. 179 of the Kölnische Zeitung," in *Collected Works of Karl Marx and Frederick Engels*, Vol. 2 (Moscow: Progress Publishers, 1975), 195.
4. Percy E. Johnston, ed., *Afro American Philosophies: Selected Readings from Jupiter Hammon to Eugene C. Holmes* (Upper Montclair, New Jersey: Montclair State College Press, 1970). Johnston also founded the first scholarly journal in the field, *Afro American Journal of Philosophy* (1982–83). This journal was a publication of the Afro American Philosophy Association, started by Johnston and not linked with any university. Johnston majored in philosophy at Howard University and was a student of Eugene C. Holmes.
5. Since minds are immaterial and bodies are material their relationship of interaction persists as a continuous philosophical puzzle called "dualism." In the history of Western philosophy Rene Descartes (1596–1650) is the most noted name associated with the mind/body problem and its

corresponding dualism. Read Rene Descartes, *Meditations on First Philosophy*, trans. John Cottingham (Cambridge: Cambridge University Press, 1996). For treatments of the mind/body question by philosophers of African descent consult, Anton Wilhelm Amo, Inaugural Philosophical Dissertation, *On the Apathy of the Human Mind or the Absence of Sense and of the Faculty of Sensing in the Human Mind And the Presence of these in our Organic and Living Body* (Doctoral Dissertation, University of Wittenberg, 1734) and Thomas Nelson Baker, *The Ethical Significance of the Connection Between Mind and Body* (Doctoral Dissertation, Yale University, 1903).

6. Henry T. Johnson, *The Black Man's Burden* (Philadelphia, PA: Privately Printed, 1899).

7. William D. Johnson, "Philosophy," in *Afro-American Encyclopedia*, ed. James T. Haley (Nashville, TN: Haley and Florida, 1895), 288.

8. D. J. Jordan, "The Philosophy of Progress," *The A.M.E. Church Review* 10(1) (July 1893), 118–28.

9. Henry T. Johnson, *The Negro Tried and Triumphant, or, Thoughts Stirred by Race Conflict* (Philadelphia, PA: A.M.E. Publishing House, 1895), 5. Also see, D. J. Jordan, "The Philosophy of Progress," *The A.M.E. Church Review* 10(1) (July 1893), 118–28.

10. "Slave Work Song: Shuck That Corn Before You Eat," The Colonial Williamsburg Foundation, http://www.history.org/history/teaching/enewsletter/volume2/september03/primsource.cfm. For a treatment of Black music by an African American philosopher, consult Alain Leroy Locke, *The Negro and His Music* (Washington, DC: Associates in Negro Folk Education, 1936). See also Ted Gioia, *Work Songs* (Durham, North Carolina: Duke University Press, 2006).

11. A. B. Stidum, "Originality in Individual and in Race Development," *The A.M.E. Church Review* 7(4) (April 1891), 409.

12. William D. Johnson, "Philosophy," 284; and Henry T. Johnson, "Philosophy Religiously Valued," *The A.M.E. Church Review* 7(4) (April 1891), 421–24.

13. Johnson, "Philosophy." See William D. Johnson, *Lincoln University: Or the Nation's First Pledge of Emancipation* (Philadelphia: Privately Printed, 1867). See, Richard R. Wright, *Centennial Encyclopaedia of the African Methodist Episcopal Church* (Philadelphia: Book Concern of the A. M. E. Church, 1916), 137. And consult, "The Rev. William Decker Johnson," in *Afro-American Encyclopedia*, 590–92. The reference to Prof. J. P. Shorter is to Joseph Proctor Shorter (1845–1912); Shorter graduated from Wilberforce University in 1872, with a major in Classics. He later assumed the chair of the mathematics department at Wilberforce, serving for

twenty-three years. Consult, Richard R. Wright, *Centennial Encyclopaedia of the African Methodist Episcopal Church* (Philadelphia: Book Concern of the A. M. E. Church, 1916), 201–02.

14. See C. V. Roman, "Philosophical Musings in the By-Paths of Ethnology," *The A. M. E. Church Review* 28(1) (July 1911), 446–47.

15. C. V. Roman, *A Knowledge of History is Conducive for Racial Solidarity and Other Writings* (Nashville: Sunday School Union Print, 1911), 14. Consult, Nerene Virgin, "Charles Victor Roman," *The Canadian Encyclopedia* (Toronto: Historica Canada, 2014). Casey Nichols, "Charles Victor Roman (1864–1934)," in *BlackPast.org Remembered & Reclaimed*, http://www. blackpast.org/aah/roman-charles-victor-1864-1934.

16. J. C. Price, "The Value of Soul," in *Afro-American Encyclopedia*, 518. Read Lucy Burnett, "Joseph C. Price 1854–1893," in *BlackPast.org Remembered & Reclaimed*, http://www.blackpast.org/aah/price-joseph-charles-1854-1893. The definitive biography on Price is William Walls, *Joseph Charles Price: Educator and Race Leader* (Boston: Christopher Publishing House, 1943).

17. Price, "The Value of Soul," 520.

18. See Joseph C. Price, "The Race Question in the South," *A.M.E. Zion Quarterly* 3 (April 1893).

19. Charles Leander Hill, *A Short History of Modern Philosophy: From the Renaissance to Hegel* (Boston, MA: Meador Publishing Company, 1951), 9–10.

20. For a contemporary discussion of the history of philosophy, see Richard Rorty, J. B. Schneewind and Quentin Skinner, *Philosophy in History: Essays on the Historiography of Philosophy* (Cambridge: Cambridge University Press, 2004). For a Marxist discussion of the history of philosophy, see Theodor Oizerman, *Problems of the History of Philosophy*, trans. Robert Daglish (Moscow: Progress, 1973).

21. W. E. B. Du Bois, "The Souls of White Folk," in *W. E. B. Du Bois: A Reader*, ed. David Levering Lewis (New York: Henry Holt and Company, 1995), 453–65.

22. Marimba Ani, *Yurugu* (Trenton: Africa World Press, 1994).

23. Rufus L. M. H. Perry, *Sketch of Philosophical Systems* (Privately Printed, 1918?), 16. Emphasis in the original.

24. Indeed, Ani's publisher once indicated—to one of the author's—*Yurugu* was his top seller. For a critique of Ani's book, see Stephen C. Ferguson, *Philosophy of African American Studies: Nothing Left of Blackness* (New York: Palgrave, 2015), particularly chapter 3.

25. Handel Andrews, "Guyana's Shining Star George G. M. James," *Rasta Livewire* (May 29, 2009), http://www.africaresource.com/rasta/sesostris-

the-great-the-egyptian-hercules/george-gm-james-guyanas-shining-star-a-tribute/. Charles D. Johnson, "An Investigation into the Death of Professor George G. M. James" *Medium* (December 29, 2015), https://medium.com/@afrdiaspora/an-investigation-in-the-death-of-professor-george-g-m-james-cfe4401be83e

26. See George G. M. James, *The Stolen Legacy* (New York: Philosophical Library, 1954). See also William Leo Hansberry, "Stolen Legacy," *Journal of Negro Education* 24(2) (Spring 1955), 127–29. Yosef ben-Jochannan, "In Pursuit of George G. M. James' Study of African Origins of Western Civilization," Yosef ben-Jochannan Virtual Museum, http://www.nbufront.org/html/MastersMuseums/DocBen/GGJames/OnGGJamesContent.html. For a fuller discussion of the "Stolen Legacy" thesis, see Stephen C. Ferguson, *Philosophy of African American Studies: Nothing Left of Blackness* (New York: Palgrave, 2015), particularly chapter 3.

27. Rufus L. Perry, *Sketch of Philosophical Systems* (Privately Printed, 1918?), 4. Perry gave the graduation oration, "Liberty as Embraced in the Constitution of the United States." Perry had a strong background in classics and was fluent in Greek, Hebrew, and French. It is reported when he took the New York State Bar Examination, he wrote the entire exam in Latin. Along with engaging in private practice, Perry served as assistant district attorney of Kings County in 1895. Consult, Suzanne Spellen, "The Tale of a Pioneering African-American Father and Son: Rufus L. Perry Sr. and Jr.," *Brownstoner* (February 1, 2017), https://www.brownstoner.com/history/brooklyn-black-history-rufus-l-perry-crown-heights/.

28. Richard T. Greener, "The Intellectual Position of the Negro," *The National Quarterly Review* (July 1880), 186. A contemporary of Frederick Douglass, Greener's accomplishments include first Black faculty member at the University of South Carolina, dean of Law School (Howard University) and US diplomat to Vladivostok, Russia. Consult, Katherine Reynolds Chaddock, *Uncompromising Activist: Richard Greener, First Black Graduate of Harvard College* (Baltimore: Johns Hopkins University Press, 2017). Allison Blakely, "Richard T. Greener and the 'Talented Tenth's Dilemma,'" *The Journal of Negro History* 59(4) (October 1974), 305–21.

29. Willis N. Huggins and John G. Jackson, *An Introduction to African Civilizations: With Main Currents in Ethiopian History* (New York: Negro Universities Press, 1969); John G. Jackson, *Ethiopia and the Origin of Civilization* (Eastford, CT: Martino Fine Books, 2017); and Yosef ben-Jochannan and John Henrik Clarke, *New Dimensions in African History: The London Lectures of Dr. Yosef ben-Jochannan and Dr. John Henrik Clarke* (Middletown, DE: Brawtley Press, 2017).

30. Winson Coleman, "Knowledge and Freedom in the Political Philosophy of Plato," *Ethics* 71(1) (October 1960), 41–45.

31. See John Milton Smith, "A Critical Estimate of Plato's and Dewey's Educational Philosophy," *Educational Theory* 9(2) (April 1959), 109–15.

32. John H. McClendon, "A Critical Examination of George G. M. James 'Legacy' in the Presentation of the 'History of Philosophy,'" a paper presented at 77th Annual Conference of the Association for the Study of Afro-American Life and History, Kansas City, Missouri (October 10, 1981).

33. For comprehensive biographical material on Cook, read Chapter 13 of George Yancy, ed., *African-American Philosophers: 17 Conversations* (New York: Routledge, 1998). For philosophical treatments of Malcolm X, see John H. McClendon III and Stephen C. Ferguson II, "On the Dialectical Evolution of Malcolm X's Anti-Capitalist Critique: Interrogating His Political Philosophy of Black Nationalism," in *Malcolm X: From Political Eschatology to Religious Revolutionary*, ed. Dustin J. Byrd and Seyed Javad Miri (Leiden: Brill, 2016), 37–90; William R. Jones, "Liberation Strategies in Black Theology: Mao, Martin, or Malcolm?," in *Philosophy Born of Struggle*, ed. Leonard Harris (Dubuque: Kendall Hunt, 1983), 229–41.

34. For a case study on the African American academic philosopher read, Bruce Kuklick, *Black Philosopher, White Academy: The Career of William Fontaine* (Philadelphia: University of Pennsylvania Press, 2008).

35. Eugene C. Holmes, "A General Theory of the Freedom Cause of Negro People," in *Afro American Philosophies*, 18–36.

36. For Holmes's writings, see John H. McClendon, "The Afro-American Philosopher and the Philosophy of the Black Experience," *Sage Race Relations Abstracts* 7(4) (November 1982), 41. Also see John H. McClendon, "Eugene C. Holmes: A Commentary on a Black Marxist Philosophy," in Leonard Harris, ed., *Philosophy Born of Struggle* (Dubuque: Kendall Hunt, 1983), 37–50.

37. See John H. McClendon, "Eugene C. Holmes: A Commentary on a Black Marxist Philosophy," in Leonard Harris, ed., *Philosophy Born of Struggle* (Dubuque: Kendall Hunt, 1983), 37–50. "Interview with Albert Mosley," in *African-American Philosophers: 17 Conversations*, 148. Ironically, Lott was one the seventeen philosophers that Yancy interviewed.

38. See David L. Lewis, *W. E. B. Du Bois, 1868–1919: Biography of a Race* (New York: H. Holt, 1993), 94–96.

39. See Shamoon Zamir, *Dark Voices: W. E. B. Du Bois and American Thought, 1883–1903* (Chicago, Illinois: University of Chicago Press, 1995), 57–60.

40. Cornel West, *The American Evasion of Philosophy: A Genealogy of Pragmatism* (Madison: University of Wisconsin Press, 1989), 138.

41. Bill E. Lawson and Donald F. Koch, eds., *Pragmatism and the Problem of Race* (Bloomington: Indiana University Press, 2004).

42. Shamoon Zamir, *Dark Voices: W. E. B. Du Bois and American Thought, 1888-1903* (Chicago: University of Chicago, 1995), 6.

43. See Robert Gooding-Williams, "Evading Narrative Myth, Evading Prophetic Pragmatism," which is chapter 5 in Robert Gooding-Williams, *Look, a Negro!: Philosophical Essays on Race, Culture, and Politics* (New York: Routledge, 2006), 76.

44. For the German influence on Du Bois, see Joel Williamson, *The Crucible of Race* (New York: Oxford University Press, 1984), 407–08.

45. David Levering Lewis, *W. E. B. Du Bois, 1868-1919: Biography of a Race* (New York: Henry Holt and Company, 1993), 139–40.

46. William James, *The Will to Believe: And Other Essays in Popular Philosophy, and Human Immortality* (New York: Dover Publication, 1956).

47. On Locke, read Leonard Harris, ed. *The Critical Pragmatism of Alain Locke* (Lanham: Routledge, 1999). For Washington as situated within the tradition of Deweyan pragmatism consult, Bill Lawson, "Booker T. Washington: A Pragmatist at Work," in *Pragmatism and the Problem of Race*, ed. Bill E. Lawson and Donald F. Koch (Bloomington: Indiana University Press, 2004), 125–41.

48. See John H. McClendon III, "On the Politics of Professional Philosophy: The Plight of the African-American Philosopher," in George Yancy, ed., *Reframing the Practice of Philosophy Bodies of Color, Bodies of Knowledge* (Albany: SUNY Press, 2012), 121–45; and William R. Jones, "Crisis in Philosophy: The Black Presence (Report of the Subcommittee on the Participation of Blacks in Philosophy)," *Proceedings and Addresses of the American Philosophical Association* 47 (1973–74), 118–25. See also, Michael R. Winston, "Through the Back Door: Academic Racism and the Negro Scholar in Historical Perspective," *Daedalus* 100(3) (1971), 678–719.

49. W. Morris with John M. Brewster, Albert M. Dunham and David Miller, eds., *The Philosophy of the Act* (Chicago: University of Chicago, 1938).

50. Richard T. Greener, "The White Problem," in *Blacks at Harvard: A Documentary History of African-American Experience at Harvard and Radcliffe*, ed. Werner Sollors, Caldwell Titcomb, and Thomas A. Underwood (New York: New York University Press, 1993), 42–56; Alexander Crummell, "Civilization – The Primal Need of the Race: The Attitude of the American Mind Toward the Negro Intellect," in *Occasional Paper of the American Negro Academy*, No. 3 (New York: Amo Press, 1969), 3–19; George Washington Henderson, "In Defence [sic] of Higher as Well as Industrial Education," *The A. M. E. Church Review* (April 1901), 311–13.

51. Richard T. Greener, "The White Problem," in Werner Sollors, Caldwell Titcomb, and Thomas A. Underwood, eds. *Blacks at Harvard: A Documentary History of African-American Experience at Harvard and Radcliffe* (New York: New York University Press, 1993), 42.

52. See John E. Fleming, *The Lengthening Shadow of Slavery* (Washington, DC: Howard University Press, 1974), 217–46.

53. See Roger L. Geiger, *The History of American Higher Education: Learning and Culture from the Founding to World War II* (Princeton, New Jersey: Princeton University Press, 2015), 476.

54. For information on Patrick Healy read James O'Toole, *Passing for White: Race, Religion, and the Healy Family, 1820–1920* (Amherst, MA: University of Massachusetts Press, 2002); and Cyprian Davis, *The History of Black Catholics in the United States* (New York: Crossroad, 1990).

55. Wilson J. Moses, *Alexander Crummell: A Study of Civilization and Discontent* (New York: Oxford University Press, 1989). Alfred Moss, *The American Negro Academy* (Baton Rouge: Louisiana Press University, 1981); C. R. Stockton, "The Integration of Cambridge: Alexander Crummell as Undergraduate, 1849–1853," *Integrated Education* (Winter 1979); and Alexander Grisby, *Crummell: Pioneer in Nineteenth-Century Pan-African Thought* (New York: Greenwood, 1987). In many respects, James McCune Smith (1813–65) was the progenitor of the study abroad tradition. As far as the historical record indicates, Smith was the first African American to earn a medical degree. He obtained his degree from the University of Glasgow, Scotland, in 1837. Smith had previously obtained both a bachelor's and master's degree from the same institution and completed his physician's residency in Paris. John Stauffer, ed., *The Works of James McCune Smith: Black Intellectual and Abolitionist* (New York: Oxford University Press, 2007). David W. Blight, "In Search of Learning, Liberty, and Self Definition: James McCune Smith and the Ordeal of the Antebellum Black Intellectual," *Afro-Americans in New York Life and History* 9(2) (July 1985), 7–25.

56. Albert S. Foley, *Dream of an Outcaste: Patrick F. Healy* (Tuscaloosa: Portals Press, 1989). Cyprian Davis, *The History of Black Catholics in the United States* (New York: Crossroad, 1990). "Patrick Francis Healy Inaugurated," American Memory Project, Library of Congress, http://memory.loc.gov/ammem/today/jul31.html (accessed January 5, 2019).

57. The Rosenwald Fund offered to pay Cornelius Golightly's salary if the College would hire him. Gilbert A. Belles, "The College Faculty, the Negro Scholar, and Rosenwald Fund," *The Journal of Negro History* 54(4) (October 1969). Reginald Wilson, "Why the Shortage of Black Professors? Slack Enforcement," *The Journal of Blacks in Higher Education* 1 (Autumn, 1993), 25. Shawn Woodhouse, "The Historical Development of Affirmative Action: An Aggregated Analysis," *The Western Journal Black Studies* 26(3) (2002), 155–58. In 1949, only four Black philosophers taught as regular faculty at white institutions; see R. B. Atwood, H. S. Smith, and Catherine O. Vaughan, "Negro Teachers in Northern Colleges and

Universities in the United States," *The Journal of Negro Education* 18(4) (Autumn 1949), 451–62; and William R. Jones, "Crisis in Philosophy: The Black Presence," Report of the Subcommittee on the Participation of Blacks in Philosophy *Proceedings and Addresses of the American Philosophical Association* (1973), 118–25. See also chapter 4, note 89.

58. Quoted in Jerry Gershenhorn, "Earl Thorpe and the Struggle for Black History, 1949–1989," *Souls* 12(4) (2010), 386.

59. John H. McClendon III, "My Tribute to a Teacher, Mentor, Philosopher and Friend: Dr. Francis A. Thomas (March 16, 1913–September 17, 2001)," *APA Newsletter on Philosophy and the Black Experience* 3(1) (Fall 2003), 36–37.

60. Francis A. Thomas, *Philosophies of Audio-Visual Education as Conceived in a University Center and by Selected Leaders* (Doctoral Dissertation, Indiana University, 1960), 1.

61. John H. McClendon III, "My Tribute to a Teacher, Mentor, Philosopher and Friend: Dr. Francis A. Thomas (March 16, 1913–September 17, 2001)," 36–37.

62. Kevin K. Gaines, *Uplifting the Race: Black Leadership, Politics, and Culture in the Twentieth Century* (Chapel Hill, NC: University of North Carolina Press, 1996), 129.

63. Vivian M. May, *Anna Julia Cooper, Visionary Black Feminist: A Critical Introduction* (New York: Routledge, 2007). Beverly Guy-Sheftall, "Black Feminist Studies: The Case of Anna Julia Cooper," *African American Review* Special Section on Anna Julia Cooper 43(1) (Spring 2009), 11–15. Anna Julia Cooper, "The Ethics of the Negro Question," in Charles Lemert and Esme Bhan, eds., *The Voice of Anna Julia Cooper* (Lanham, MD: Rowman & Littlefield Publishers, Inc., 1998), 206–15; Karen Johnson, "Gender and Race: Exploring Anna Julia Cooper's Thoughts for Socially Just Educational Opportunities," *Philosophia Africana* 12(1) (March 2009), 67–82.

64. The list of African American males in academic philosophy with a PhD from Yale includes Thomas Nelson Baker (1903), Richard I. McKinney (1942), and George D. Kelsey (1946).

65. For comprehensive biographical material on Cook, read Chapter 13 of Yancy, *African-American Philosophers: 17 Conversations*, 263–85.

66. For comprehensive biographical material on Davis, read Chapter 1 of Yancy, *African-American Philosophers: 17 Conversations*, 13–30. See also Angela Davis, *An Autobiography* (New York: Random House, 1974); and Angela Y. Davis, *The Angela Y. Davis Reader*, ed. Joy James (Malden: Blackwell, 2008).

67. Anita L. Allen, "Novel Thought: An African American Woman Philosopher at Mid-Career," *Newsletter On Feminism and Philosophy*

9(2) (Spring 2010), 3. See also Naomi Zack, ed., *Women of Color and Philosophy: A Critical Reader* (Malden: Blackwell, 2000); and George Yancy, "Situated Black Women's Voices in/on the Profession of Philosophy," *Hypatia* 23(2) (Spring 2008), 155–89.

68. For a discussion of the petit-bourgeois nature of Du Bois's notion of double consciousness, see Adolph Reed, *W. E. B. Du Bois and American Political Thought: Fabianism and the Color Line* (New York: Oxford University Press, 1999).

69. Michael R. Winston, "Through the Back Door: Academic Racism and the Negro Scholar in Historical Perspective," 707.

70. See, for example, Marc Moreland, "Roger Williams: Discipline for Today," *Phylon* 6(2) (1945), 136–40; Forrest O. Wiggins, "Ethics and Economics," *Phylon* 6(2) (1945), 154–62; John A. Davis and Cornelius L. Golightly, "Negro Employment in the Federal Government," *Phylon* 6(4) (1945), 337–46; Alain Locke, "Reason and Race: A Review of the Literature of the Negro for 1946." *Phylon* 8(1) (1947), 17–27; George D. Kelsey, "Protestantism and Democratic Intergroup Living," *Phylon* 8(1) (1947), 77–82; Samuel W. Williams, "The People's Progressive Party of Georgia," *Phylon* 10(3) (1949), 226–30; and Eugene C. Holmes, "Alain Leroy Locke: A Sketch," *Phylon* 20(1) (1959), 82–89.

71. Wayman B. McLaughlin, "Symbolism and Mysticism in the Spirituals," *Phylon* 24(1) (1963), 69. Stephen C. Ferguson II, "Understanding the Legacy of Dr. Wayman Bernard McLaughlin: On the Problem of Interpretation in the History of African American Philosophy," *The APA Newsletter on Philosophy and the Black Experience* 13(2) (2014), 2–11. Ann Anderson, "Local Man's Legacy Began as Classmate of King," *Danville Register Bee* (January 18, 2005). The Spirituals as an area of African American cultural philosophy are also explored by Drs. Miles Mark Fisher, Howard Thurman, and Robert C. Williams, among others. Miles Mark Fisher, *Negro Slave Songs in the United States* (Ithaca: Cornell University Press, 1953). Also read, Lenwood G. Davis, "Miles Mark Fisher: Minister, Historian and Cultural Philosopher" *Negro History Bulletin* 46(1) (1983); Howard Thurman, *Deep River: Reflections on the Religious Insight of Certain of the Negro Spirituals* (New York: 1955); Robert C. Williams, *A Study of Religious Language: Analysis/Interpretation of Selected Afroamerican Spiritual, With Reference to Black Religious Philosophy* (Doctoral Dissertation, Columbia University, 1975).

72. See the Resume of Carleton L. Lee (August 16, 1970) in Box 2, Folder 23 of the Department of African and African American Studies Records, Duke University Archives, David M. Rubenstein Rare Book & Manuscript Library, Duke University. We thank the David M. Rubenstein Rare Book

& Manuscript Library of Duke University Archives for access to this document.

73. Eugene Holmes sent a copy of the previously mentioned, "A General Theory of the Freedom Cause of the Negro People," to Williams with the signature, "To my esteemed and most favorite student, Sam Williams . . ." Box 14, Folder 5, the Samuel W. Williams Collection, Robert W. Woodruff Library, Atlanta University Center, Archives/Special Collections. All other references to Box and Folder pertain to the Samuel W. Williams Collection. See Correspondence from Alain Locke on December 2, 1947, in Box 8, Folder 1, Williams was not only King's professor in philosophy but they also collaborated on civil rights demonstrations as well as team taught a course in philosophy at Morehouse. See "Special Meeting with Doctors M. L. King, Jr. and Samuel W. Williams." Box 11, Folder 1. Samuel W. Williams, "The Legacy of Martin Luther King Jr., Violence and Nonviolence in the Struggle for Equality" Speech Delivered March 9, 1970 at Hebrew University, Jerusalem, Israel. Box 12, Folder 72. We would like to thank the Archivist of the Robert W. Woodruff Library for assistance with the Samuel W. Williams Collection. Julian Bond indicates that while King was a very capable teacher of philosophy, Williams was more polished. On King as philosophy teacher, see John W Whitehead, "A Powerful Figure: An Interview with Civil Rights Activist Julian Bond" *Old Speak: An Online Journal Devoted to Intellectual Freedom*, http://www.rutherford.org/oldspeak/Articles/Interviews/bond.html and David J Garrow, *Bearing the Cross* (New York: HarperCollins Publishers, 1986) p. 164.

74. See John H. McClendon III, "Dr. Richard Ishmael McKinney: Historical Summation on the Life of a Pioneering African American Philosopher," *American Philosophical Association Newsletter on Philosophy and the Black Experience* 5(2) (Spring 2006), 1–4.

75. Richard I. McKinney, "Existential Ethics and the Protest Movement," *Journal of Religious Thought* 22(2) (1965–66), 108–9.

76. On Davies see, Archie J. Bahm, *Directory of American Philosophers*, Volume 5 (Philosophy Documentation Center, Bowling Green State University, 1971). Previously Davies was honored with his picture in Du Bois's *The Crisis*. Consult, Davies to Du Bois (June 16, 1932). For another work linking religion to activism, see Carleton L. Lee, "Religious Roots of the Negro Protest," in Arnold M. Rose, ed., *In Assuring Freedom to the Free: A Century of Emancipation in the U.S.A.* (Detroit: Wayne State University Press, 1964), 45–71.

77. Read, John H. McClendon III, "Dr. William Ronald Jones (July 17, 1933–July 13, 2012): On the Legacy of the Late 'Dean' of Contemporary African American Philosophers," *American Philosophical Association Newsletter on Philosophy and the Black Experience* 12(2) (Spring 2013), 21–29.

Stephen C. Ferguson II, "On the Occasion of William R. Jones's Death: Remembering the Feuerbachian Tradition in African-American Social Thought," *American Philosophical Association Newsletter on Philosophy and the Black Experience* 12(2) (Spring 2013), 14–19. Also consult, "Memorial Minutes: Robert C. Williams 1935–1987," *Proceedings and Addresses of the American Philosophical Association* 61(2) (November 1987), 385.

78. See Janae Moore, *What Is That Thing? Poetry for Spiritual Introspection & Dialogue That Leads to Action* (Xlibris Corporation, 2017). Moore was a former student of Morrison. She claims that Morrison declared himself an atheist.

79. D. J. Jordan, "The Philosophy of Progress," 119.

80. Read Richard R. Wright, *Centennial Encyclopaedia of the African Methodist Episcopal Church* (Philadelphia: Book Concern of the A. M. E. Church, 1916), 143.

81. Edward A. Clarke, "Evolution: God's Method of Work in His World," *The A. M. E. Church Review* 15(3) (January 1899), 729–34. Also consult A. J. Kershaw, "Evolution: Its Darwinian and Jordanic Theories Compared," *The A. M. E. Church Review* 14(4) (April 1898), 429–35. For a treatment of Kershaw on Evolutionary theory see John H. McClendon III, *Philosophy of Religion and the African American Experience: Conversations with My Christian Friends* (Leiden: Brill/Rodopi, 2017), 221–26.

82. Charles Leander Hill, "William Ladd, the Black Philosopher from Guinea: A Critical Analysis of His Dissertation on Apathy," *The A.M.E. Church Review* 72(186) (October–December 1955), 20–36.

83. Charles Leander Hill, *The Loci Communes of Philip Melanchthon* (Boston: Meador Publishing Co., 1944). John H. McClendon III, "Charles Leander Hill: Philosopher and Theologian," *The A.M.E. Church Review* 119(390) (April–June 2003), 81–105; and John H. McClendon III, "Introduction to Drs. Anton Wilhelm Amo and Charles Leander Hill," *APA Newsletter on Philosophy and the Black Experience* 2(2) (Spring 2003), 42–44.

84. Ed Hinshaw, Joyce M. Cook, William R. Jones, and Robert C. Williams, *The Black Philosopher* (Racine, Wisconsin: The Johnson Foundation, 1976). This is an audio recording.

85. Dennis Dickerson, "Teaching Nonviolence: William Stuart Nelson and His Role in the Civil Rights Movement," *The A. M. E. Church Review* (July–September 2009), 16–27. On Nelson's role in founding *The Journal of Religious Thought* and his leadership in the philosophy of nonviolent movement, see the special issue of *The Journal of Religious Thought* 35(2) (Fall–Winter 1978–79).

2

The Problem of Philosophy: Metaphilosophical Considerations

Chapter Summary

In this chapter, we examine metaphilosophical questions concerning the nature of philosophy generally and African American philosophy specifically. We are particularly concerned with offering a broader conception of what African American philosophy is. (37)

In Chapter 1, we extensively reviewed the problem of history's relation to philosophy. History was our salient focal point for bringing serious consideration to philosophy as distinctive—disciplinary—inquiry. The question "what is philosophy?" is one of the most basic questions of philosophy. We may experience no particular difficulty in answering such questions as "what is Karl Marx's philosophy?," "what is Eugene C. Holmes' philosophy?," "what is Roy D. Morrison's philosophy?," or "what is Anita Allen's philosophy?" Not because these are simple questions but because their content may be strictly defined. But in order to answer the question "what is philosophy?" we must break away from that which distinguishes Marx, Holmes, Morrison, and Allen, and many others from one another.

Metaphilosophy (sometimes called the "philosophy of philosophy") is the investigation into the nature of philosophy. Its subject matter includes the aims of philosophy, the boundaries of philosophy, and its methods. Several metaphilosophical questions arise for us. How is philosophical inquiry unique in character? What is the constitutive theory/methodology that stamps its analysis as distinctive? How do we differentiate philosophical inquiry from other disciplinary endeavors? How is metaphilosophy relevant to the process of defining African American philosophy? Are there specific metaphilosophical parameters adjoined to African American philosophy? How do the concrete (historic) forms of African American philosophy relate to defining African American philosophy?

The meaning of the question "what is philosophy?"

Previously, we unearthed that philosophy belongs to history and how historical features essentially form its meaning, along with its corresponding tasks and mission. For the attentive reader, it is most transparent that we have already made considerable strides in comprehending the measure and import of *metaphilosophy*. The meaning, tasks, and mission of philosophical inquiry is at the crux of metaphilosophy. By examining how philosophy was the subject of history, we were able to outline the material and intellectual basis for the advent of African American philosophy and its respective schools of thought. We uncovered that dialectical idealism was the foremost school in the late nineteenth and early twentieth centuries. The reader should not forget that a form of mechanistic materialism—adjoined with pseudoscientific declarations of white superiority—was one of the key catalysts for the African American embracement of dialectical idealism. The defense of Black intellectual capacity was a crucial aspect in the ensuing polemics.

As we previously noted, both philosophy and Work Songs are components of cultural life. Yet, philosophy stands out as a mode of inquiry, which delineates it from all other forms of cultural expression. This defining feature as *mode of inquiry* establishes philosophy as more than just a form of cultural response to material circumstances. Guided by critical theory and erudite methods, self-conscious discernment on matters of human value is the engine behind philosophy as mode of inquiry. *Mode of inquiry* explicitly details that philosophical analysis is a conscious intervention into intellectual culture and, consequently, demands vigorous methodological skills with cogent insights. Concurrently, it is apparent that metaphilosophical reflections are allied with the tasks, scope, and substance of philosophy.

Undeniably, the relationship of history to philosophy sheds important insights on the mission of philosophy. Our former thesis decisively posited that philosophy has a substantive history. We also found that history itself was an acute philosophical problem and was significantly associated to the issue of progress in philosophic thought. If we grant there is historical progression with philosophical thinking, then this implies that philosophy is subject to change. Now we observe that there are immediate metaphilosophical questions for our consideration: How does this historical dimension of philosophy relate to its tasks, scope, and substance? In other words, how is it interrelated to metaphilosophy? Does the very definition of philosophy undergo alteration? Can philosophy have multiple meanings over time?

Philosophy takes shape historically and for a number of centuries develops as the first and, in fact, the only form of theoretical knowledge. It follows that philosophy's scope and substance is dynamic rather than fixed. Simply put, the subject matter of philosophy has in the course of history been prone to dialectical change. For illustration, ancient philosophy had within its scope the natural and physical sciences, along with mathematics. We detect that respecting geometry—which originated in ancient Egypt—that Egyptian philosophers considered it as an integral part of philosophy and philosophizing. As well, Plato had the same perspective on geometry and philosophy. And the Ionian thinker Thales is recognized today as a pioneering contributor in both geometry and philosophy.[1]

However, we find that a contemporary expert in geometry would not of necessity have any substantial comprehension of philosophy. In the same order, our presently competent philosophers are most likely ignorant of geometry, that is, with respect to its intricate subject matter and procedures in problem solving. This historical difference regarding contemporary and past philosophy is also why Newton's physics, during his time, was often referred to as natural philosophy.

We observe that currently these areas of inquiry are sharply detached from the core subject matter of philosophy. The historical process of growth in knowledge was the objective basis for this transformation in the scope and substance of philosophy. As knowledge advances forward, there is an equivalent process of specialization. Specialized disciplines conclusively reflect the fact that knowledge becomes identified as more complex in its content.

This anterior alteration of knowledge's content parallels the historical variations in philosophy's scope. In one manner, we observe the historic deflation of its scope, with the advent of new (autonomously positioned) disciplines, for example, geometry and physics. In another way, we have the expanded transformation of its substance. This emerges by means of philosophy's theoretical association with specialized sciences, specifically by highlighting the philosophical implications attendant with scientific work. Although biology and physics are no longer designated as natural philosophy, modern-day philosophy concurrently allows for their incorporation. This integration falls under the disciplinary specification *philosophy of science* which we will explore in Chapter 5. The philosophical investigation of the sciences, of course, is not the same as pursuing the study of biology or physics; it is the employment of a philosophical lens onto scientific subject matter.

Often philosophy extends normative insights on scientific theory and methodology as it relates to the specialized sciences. While physics studies the motion and structure of matter, philosophy expands on how this research has ancillary ontological implications and epistemological dimensions. Notably, African American philosophers have entered this arena, for instance, Robert T. Browne's research in philosophy of geometry, William T. Fontaine's work in philosophy of biology, and Eugene C. Holmes, Charles Frye, and Roy D. Morrison II's investigations into the philosophy of physics.[2]

Modern-day philosophy of science is an ever-growing field of study. Even so, contemporary philosophy would appear quite strange to philosophers of the ancient world. Clearly, the contemporary scope and substance of philosophy has drastically transformed since ancient times.[3] These momentous changes in philosophy present a formidable metaphilosophical challenge. Given that the scope and substance of philosophy is ever-changing then its duties are subject to transformative influences rooted in tangible material circumstances and the adjoining cultural/intellectual context. This, in sequence, shapes its determinate historic forms. However, there remain certain underlying and persistent obligations associated with metaphilosophy.

We previously outlined two key and very significant tasks of philosophy: the matters of *philosophical definition* and *interpretation*. Carrying out such tasks principally involve—by way of method—crafting a highly developed theoretical framework. This notion of theoretical framework or conceptual orientation brings to light the qualitative dimension of philosophy, that is, the inspection of that phenomena which cannot be captured by quantitative measurement or analysis.

Here the distinction between appearance and essence importantly continues with our metaphilosophical endeavors. Consecutively, the process of grasping what is the essence of the matter is a decidedly theoretical undertaking. Theoretical abstraction become apparent as pivotal for this equivalent mode of inquiry. Herein, the value of ontological reduction presents itself as an expected procedure. As William D. Johnson would likely point out, counting the number of leaves on a branch surely will not result in comprehending the "One." Johnson highlights the delimitation of perceptual and conceptual methods of knowing. He also explicitly informs us about his metaphilosophical stance that philosophy aims at the penetration of formal appearances to the essence of reality. This remains, in Johnson's estimation, the fundamental task of philosophical interpretation. Compatibly, from an epistemological standpoint, he rejects empiricism and its dependence on perceptual reporting.

Johnson is not alone in thinking along such metaphilosophical lines. African American theologian and philosopher of personalism J. W. E. Bowen argues that there are earlier stages of cognition before one develops the necessary maturation for philosophical investigation. Bowen claims the transition from immediate perception to philosophical conception is a function of intellectual growth. His metaphilosophical concern addresses the aspect of *philosophic interpretation* rather than definition.[4] Hence, metaphilosophy not only seeks to define philosophy but also prescribes what it should do. In other words, *philosophic interpretation* also broadly implies all *normative references* concerning prescriptions about philosophical theory and method. *Normative reference* involves outlining what should be *the general tasks* of philosophy and the requisite means to accomplish them.

Consequently, philosophic interpretation has its own interior dimension, which serves as the obligatory condition for the exterior process of interpreting the world. Without this interior examination, then the actual activity respecting the interpretation of reality lacks the needed procedural guidelines. Bowen's exploration into metaphilosophy highlights this interior aspect, that is, by spelling out the requisite cognitive setting. He asserts,

> It is a characteristic of youth that it is untaught and formative; philosophic interpretations are never entered into during this period. *Perception* rather than *conception*, and the acceptance of the symbolic teaching of nature, rather than an actual reading of its meaning characterize the thought of incipient investigation.[5]

For Bowen, the work of *philosophic interpretation* is not a natural disposition. Put simply, human beings do not innately have (or inherently acquire) the capability of philosophical interpretation. Instead, this decrees a measure of academic guidance and a certain level of intellectual maturation. This maturation is a necessary mental function for advancing to philosophical interpretation. At the core of Bowen's metaphilosophy is the idea that philosophy—in its essential composition—persists at high levels of conceptual deliberation, which is attendant with rigorous theoretical reflection. Therefore, immature minds, for Bowen, cannot effectively engage in philosophical interpretation.

The problem of philosophical definition

When we further probe the question "what is philosophy?," the cardinal issue of *philosophical definition* appears on the radar screen. However, the reader should be cognizant that the concept of "philosophical definition" pertinently has two connotations. The *first* relates to how philosophy, from its disciplinary perspective, offers up technical terminology that may have a substantially different meaning than in common parlance.

Here we find the notion of "philosophical definition" connotes how philosophy defines concepts by means of specialized vocabulary. For the student of philosophy, grasping this lexicon is an essential imperative for comprehending philosophy. Bowen's caveat about the mature understanding requisite for philosophical interpretation crucially amplifies this cognitive issue. Without sufficient knowledge of philosophical terminology, the novice in philosophy can make little headway in interpreting philosophy.

The *second* connotation encompasses undertaking the definition of philosophy itself. This juncture is precisely where we enter the realm of metaphilosophy proper. The pedestrian idea surrounding the concept of "theory" is a good illustration of the former. Everyday vernacular often confuses the notion of guess-work with the nomenclature for theory as applied in science. For example, the scientific "Theory of Evolution" associated with Darwin or Einstein's "Theory of Relativity" are not the same as the everyday viewpoint on theory as guess-work or conjecture. Philosophers know that "theory" explicitly represents—in these cases—the proven hypothesis maintained in the respective fields of biology and physics. In these instances—the terminology regarding—"theory" is far removed from having a personal hunch or mere speculation.

Another case of terminological confusion, we observe, pertains to the idea of materialism as philosophic category. *Materialism* has a precise meaning within the framework of philosophical lexicon. The popular view on this notion is often expressed as the propensity toward avarice or greed. In contrast, the philosophical conception focuses on the ontological question of how material circumstances (with its lawful motion) founds reality. This popular confusion is certainly why knowledge of philosophical terminology can be a valuable source for clarification.

African American philosopher Samuel W. Williams addresses this question—about philosophical materialism—specifically regarding the Marxist-Leninist viewpoint on *dialectical materialism*. Before we move to Williams's explication, a preliminary overview on dialectical materialism becomes most apropos. Earlier, in Chapter 1, we saw how D. J. Jordan brought to our attention that while matter remains lawfully subject to *inertia*, nonetheless, it does not emerge as *inert*. He argued, "No matter in all creation is inert; every particle and atom are acting upon every other."[6] Jordan shows that inertia encompasses the scientifically accurate concept regarding, what the physicist terms, matter at rest. In contrast, the philosophical notion of *inert matter*, erroneously signifies the absence of internal motion.

Moreover, we have the contiguous philosophic belief, which stipulates— in a parallel way—the condition of "dead" matter. This "dead" matter appraisal is no more than a philosophic abstraction on inert matter. Indeed, this misconception about inertia leading to "dead" matter, under the influence of idealism, masquerades as a legitimate philosophical category. Nonetheless, Jordan's explication uncovers the ontological pitfalls with this "dead" matter conceptualization.

Jordan correctly argues that matter is internally dynamic. Today, we know that subatomic processes are vital to the composition of matter. With the contemporary advancement of quantum theory, the subatomic structure and active (inner) processes of matter is a well-established scientific notion. Indeed, quantum physics later confirms Jordan's philosophical hypothesis, which remarkably he pronounced in 1893. The exploration into subatomic physics did not advance until Max Planck's treatment of the black-body radium problem (1900), Albert Einstein's published research on photoelectric effect (1905), and Niels Bohr's atomic model (1913).

Obviously, the conflation of inert with inertia is inconsistent with the findings of modern physics. It follows that the adjacent philosophical notion of "dead matter" is a misconceived impression. Now, we must explore how scientific observations on matter are linked to the philosophical viewpoint of dialectical materialism.

Dialectical materialism as an ontological position stands in full agreement with this proposition about the interior dynamics of matter. This aspect of internal forces at work is summarized by the philosophical term—"dialectics." In part, dialectics is a philosophical generalization on the laws governing the very motion of matter. While there can be no matter without motion; likewise, there can be no motion without matter. Since motion cannot be detached from any given material entity, then we have the more concise terminology—*dialectical materialism.*

African American philosopher Eugene C. Holmes affirms how dialectical materialism—as expounded by Marx and Engels—concurrently supports the results of modern science. Holmes's subject matter is the philosophical issues attendant with the physics and mathematics of space and time. Holmes critically analyzes how idealist philosophers approached this topic, with attention to their ancillary denial on the primary reality of matter. From his Marxist philosophical standpoint, Holmes explains,

> These attempts to deny the primacy of matter and the objective nature of mathematical science were opposed by Marx and Engels and their followers, dialectical materialists who believed that the universe was matter in motion and that matter in motion could not be separated from each other. Since, in this conception, moving matter existed in space and time, it was declared that space and time were objectively real forms of existence.[7]

Holmes continues,

> Such a conception, Marx and Engels declared, were founded on the observations of physical science which had been attested to throughout the historical development of science and human knowledge. Science and human knowledge have established as empirical facts this objective existence, which have been concurred in by the achievements of physics, geometry, and mathematics. Thus, the existence of space and time have been established by the physical sciences, but this existence was not depended on man's thought of them or his methods of measuring them. Their properties depended solely on objectively existing matter.[8]

In accord, this scientific conceptualization issues forth—by way of theoretical reflection—an ontological viewpoint. This viewpoint renders the associated laws of motion, change, and development as inherent within the very composition of matter. Dialectical idealism, the reader may recall, suggests that the source of motion derives from immaterial forces. Unlike dialectical idealism, this alternative materialist perspective posits that the immaterial entities of mind, consciousness, or ideas are products of matter in motion and not ontologically primary in themselves.

Furthermore, the idealist response to mechanistic materialism presumes that matter is inert, hence, the adjoining premise of "dead matter" leads directly to idealism. It becomes transparent that the grounds on which dialectical idealism seeks to rectify the snares of mechanistic materialism— from the dialectical materialist standpoint—proves as misdirected. Successively, dialectical materialism stands in ontological opposition to both dialectical idealism and mechanistic materialism. The fundamental difference between dialectical and mechanistic materialism is that the latter denies consciousness as an ontological category, while the former situates consciousness as an attribute or property of matter.

For example, according to dialectical materialism, the distinction between mind/consciousness and brain transpires as one of ontological dependence of the former on the latter. There can be no consciousness without a fully functioning brain and nervous system; consciousness can only be embodied in matter. In accord, the concepts of mind and consciousness are synonymous terms. All discussions about mind are simultaneously references to consciousness. Sequentially, minds are not discoverable as an organic constituent within the human body; that is, the dissection of the body would not result in the mind resting next to the brain.

Yet, while consciousness/mind is immaterial, its source is indeed material in makeup. Although consciousness is more than intentional behavior, it nevertheless gains expression by such means. African American philosopher Thomas Nelson Baker clearly brings this fact to our attention. Baker is ontologically an idealist and believes that God is the creator of the universe. Yet, regarding his stance on the mind/body problem, he plainly demonstrates his philosophical allegiance to materialism. Baker has penetrating acumen on the topic at hand. In his momentous Yale doctoral dissertation (1903), "The Ethical Significance of the Connection between Mind and Body," Baker states the following:

> Now we know only the "natural body" and it is through this body that the mind manifests itself. For us, the body is the condition of the mind. We do not say that the mind cannot exist without the body, but we do say that apart from the body mind has no existence for experience, i.e. it can be known only

through the body. The condition of a thing is that without which the thing could not exist. The body is that, so far as we are concerned, without which the mind could not exist.[9]

Although there is a hint of ambiguity in Baker's statement, nevertheless, he concludes, "the mind could not exist" without the condition of the body. It follows that the mind has a different ontological locus in the scheme of reality than would the brain, which is obviously a key component of the body. Consciousness or ideas have dependent ontological existence. A concussive blow to the head or experiencing a stroke—drastic changes in the physiology of the brain—have immediate results respecting consciousness. In fact, a strong enough blow or severe stroke can lead to unconsciousness. Clearly, the state of consciousness depends on the status of the brain.

The thesis that consciousness or ideas depend on material entities (bodies) for its existence in the world is even acknowledged by idealists such as Baker and James B. Carter. In his essay, "Wanted-An Idea," Carter discusses the relationship of religion and science along dialectical idealist lines. The upshot is that he does not reject science to affirm religion. Isomorphic to Plato's notion of *methexis*—where sensible entities of the world participate in the Forms—Carter theorizes that human ideas "faintly" correspond to God's notions. Transparently, he is an idealist concerning this ontological issue, for God's thought grounds reality.

More importantly—from an epistemological perspective—Carter argues that correct ideas result from knowledge reflective on material reality. Congruently, the ontological relationship of consciousness to bodies has an epistemological outcome; which is reflected in the objective truth of our ideas. Ideas in relationship to matter, as Carter reveals, have significant epistemological implications. He pronounces,

> Man's correct ideas, even his most original ones, are deductions and inferences from environment even when higher inspiration helps to define, elucidate and fix them. But let this be ever remembered, that new ideas when useful and progressive, come more readily to him who has the more correct knowledge of the relationships, influences and effects upon each other of the different forms, shapes and conditions of matter.[10]

Carter's claim is that innovative ideas are the product of "the more correct knowledge of the relationships, influences and effects upon each other of the different forms, shapes and conditions of matter." The correct idealization on material circumstances is the necessary condition for novel thinking.

Consequently, innovative thought is not whimsical considerations devoid of an anchor in "the different forms, shapes and conditions of matter." This epistemological thesis is decidedly materialist in its substance. The reader should not let Carter's superseding ontological idealism obscure this important epistemological fact.

Baker and Carter's conclusion about ideas/consciousness and body/matter are also a cardinal premise of dialectical materialism. With that said, now let us return to Samuel W. Williams's exposition on philosophical materialism. As Eugene C. Holmes formerly noted, dialectical materialism is preeminently associated with the philosophy of Karl Marx, Frederick Engels, and V. I. Lenin. All of whom are advocates of Communism. While far from committed to Marxism-Leninism, however, Williams was a student of philosophy with the previously mentioned Marxist philosopher Eugene C. Holmes at Howard University. Therefore, Williams is quite cognizant of the full measure on the meaning associated with dialectical materialism. As philosopher, Williams has a scholarly appreciation for what is at stake regarding how philosophical idealism and materialism are contrasting ontological standpoints:

> One of our speakers suggested that we and the Communist were materialistic. This is only superficially true. Ours is not a philosophic materialism—it is at best economic materialism—a desire to have things, conveniences in abundance and we are developing an ethic around this. For example: "Business is business" is a cardinal ethical principle of economic materialism. *Communism is not materialistic in that sense at all. Theirs is an ontological materialism.* Ontologically we are idealists. Let me try to explain the difference: (1) matter not spirit is the ground of all existence for Communism and while (2) Spirit is the ground for all being. This is a most significant difference. Marx called his philosophy Dialectical and historical materialism and never economic determinism as so many economic textbooks delight in labeling it.[11] (Italics added)

Williams's explanation of economic materialism and the adjoining philosophical demarcation of idealism and materialism—conflicting ontological positions— clearly renders the transparent difference between the popular and philosophical notions. The popular treatment of materialism insufficiently conveys the complexities surrounding the philosophical conceptualization.

The serious student of philosophy can ill afford to conflate these very different approaches concerning the ontological idea of materialism. Comprehending the philosophical conception of matter is crucially linked to a whole host of problems and questions within several subfields of the discipline. With Williams effectively clarifying these notions, we can now return to the question of the metaphilosophical intricacies adjacent with the second connotation of "philosophical definition," namely, the definition of philosophy. With this definition, we are back on the road to the irrepressible metaphilosophical question "what is philosophy?"

The definition of philosophy and metaphilosophical discourse

When the conception of "philosophical definition" becomes relevant to metaphilosophical discourse, then we approach the task of providing the very definition of philosophy itself. In fact, Wilfred Sellars goes so far to state, "It is this reflection on the place of philosophy itself, in the scheme of things which is the distinctive trait of the philosopher . . . [such that] in the absence of this critical reflection on the philosophical enterprise, one is at best but a potential philosopher."[12] Black philosopher Roy D. Morrison II attempts to capture the core meaning and primary implications about what philosophy is. He offers the following:

> What is philosophy? We conceive of this discipline *as an on-going critical activity of the mind*. To philosophize means to think well, to think as critically and carefully as is possible for the human mind. More precisely, philosophy is an inquiry into the basic value judgments and the basic postulates of all of the special sciences—including those of theology and philosophy itself. By a "postulate," we generally mean a basic principle which is taken as absolute, universal, and necessary, and then employed decisively for all consequent thinking and behavior. . . . Postulates, in general, are not verifiable and are often partially based upon value judgments.[13]

In conjunction with Morrison's declaration that "philosophy is an inquiry into the basic value judgments and the basic postulates of all of the special sciences—including . . . philosophy itself," we discern that metaphilosophy— is sometimes called the "philosophy of philosophy." This rather curious and queer formulation—philosophy of philosophy—signifies that the very definition of philosophy emerges as philosophical problem.

In many ways, this is unique to the character of philosophy and philosophizing. When in pursuit of their research and problem solving—we witness—biologists, physicists, and mathematicians are not encumbered with defining the very nature of their equivalent disciplines. While the meaning of life may perhaps be a covering principle for the discipline of biology, nonetheless, the meaning of biology is not on the research agenda of present-day biologists. With that said, let's return to Morrison and the notion of postulate.

Notice that Morrison begins by declaring that a postulate is taken as absolute, universal, and necessary. First, what are the implications for a basic principle—that grounds thought/practice—which combines such characteristics as absoluteness, universality, and necessity? An *absolute* principle stands without qualification or equivocation; it is self-subsistent and depends on nothing else. If postulates serve as absolute principles, then with embracing them comes the demand for unwavering allegiance. For the beholder, absolute principles remain beyond question. They require no interrogation concerning veracity. The committed believer is convinced that her/his postulates give expression to absolute truths.

The addition of universality conveys that such basic principles are sovereign for each and all. The universal character of absolute principles suggests that if one is not in alignment, then we have a deviation from universal conformity. The presupposition encompasses that postulates as universal foundation are not, in any manner, subjective in character. Concurrently, universal principles are self-evident to all rational thinking persons.

In concert with the universality of postulates comes necessity. Whatever is universally established must also stand as compulsory, that is, remain (of necessity) binding for all. For instance, the notion of cause and effect is both universal and necessary. The concept of cause/effect involves believing that what takes place actually *happens everywhere* (universally) and this is accompanied with the deductive mandate—necessarily—*at all times*. Universally and necessarily, it is established that water at 32 degrees Fahrenheit becomes ice. There is no particular place or time—we can discern—that this instance of cause and effect is not true.

Any phenomena that is necessarily true arises as a matter of *deductive reasoning*. It is necessarily true that bachelors are single men; deductive reasoning allows for no deviations. Bachelors never cease to be single men without a contradiction in terms. Successively, the deductive—necessary—makeup of postulates provides the putative logical foundation for the persistence of universality over time.

This case sustains cause and effect as its overall binding principle. With this binding principle—as general postulate—then every cause (out of necessity) must have its corresponding effect. Undoubtedly, the cause/effect relationship functions as elementary postulate. Successively, this principle of cause/effect assumes an *a priori* status; that is, we need not experience each case of cause/effect to assert its truth.

As a matter of deduction, it stands as self-evidently true. *Deductive reasoning* starts from basic principles and by inference reaches conclusions concerning the method of general application to particular instances. This extrapolation from the cause/effect principle signals why the formation of ice from liquid water persists as universally and necessarily true.

Yet, when we empirically regard this postulate of cause and effect, our experience compels restricting cause/effect to the region of high probability, rather than necessity. When we operate from experience, the logic we employ is *inductive reasoning*. With inductive reasoning, we cannot establish absolute certainty. In other words, with each cause, a *prospectively* corresponding effect *might* follow. We cannot muster experimental results, which would provide certain truth about this postulate.

Clearly, when we moved from particular experiences to generalizations on them—the defining feature of inductive reasoning—then probability restricts how far we can take our conclusion respecting its truth condition. As a theory of knowledge, empiricism is anchored in inductive reasoning. A philosopher committed to empiricism would not agree that cause/effect is universal and necessary, in any objective sense. The rationale behind this conclusion—about the subjective character of cause/effect—is that empiricism demands that the limits of knowledge are constricted by experience.

Experience confines our prospects in achieving certainty; that is, we can only have probable results as the measure of truth. Empirical verification restricts what grounds truth conditions with regard to certainty. For illustration, the meteorologist in predicting the weather can never give certain results. We can only receive a forecast based on probability, hence the chance for rain or snow is always presented as a matter of percentages. Thus, the idea that a cause must have its correlative effect cannot be inductively determined. The principle of cause/effect is not empirically verifiable; in the same manner, basic postulates remain unverified.

This brings us to the heart of Morrison's notion about basic postulates. Since we have no way of verifying such principles, therefore, when questioning our basic postulates, they are beyond all experimental considerations. Absolute principles are merely positioned as axiomatic. This axiomatic or dogmatic manner of thinking, Morrison contends, prevails as the counter-position to philosophical inquiry. Philosophy cannot rest on the weight of basic postulates. Philosophy questions its own existence—hence, we have the philosophy of philosophy or metaphilosophy.

Morrison's last point returns to why philosophy is primarily theoretical in substance. Given "postulates, in general, are not verifiable and are often partially based upon value judgments," the empirical methods of verification are virtually useless, while value theory (axiology) can perhaps emerge as helpful. Often, we find, clashes over basic postulates are manifestations of fundamental value conflicts.

Our prior illustrations on white racism and African American progressive development reveal how value judgments are reliant on basic postulates. Explicitly, racist postulates deny in principle African American progressive development. The claim supporting this progressive development, on the other hand, finds its anchor in the foundational belief of Black self-initiative. The values expressed—with each respective position—center on more than just an empirical assessment of the issues under contention. The fundamental contradiction associated with theoretical or conceptual meaning— correspondingly affixed to rudimentary values—is the impulse for the conflict over foundational assumptions.[14]

In Chapter 1 we found that African American philosophers were quite vocal in their condemnation of racist postulates. White racism operates on the assumption—basic postulate—that Black people are inherently inferior. Furthermore, this notion about inferiority is an explanatory principle—ultimate assumption—that illustrates why Black people occupy a subordinate position in society.

In synopsis, Black inferiority develops into the key social problem. If Morrison is correct in his metaphilosophical viewpoint, then philosophical inquiry must provide a critical assessment. It is worth repeating Richard T. Greener's prior remarks on the white problem:

> A phase of the white problem is seen in the determination, not only to treat the Negro as a member of a child-like race, but the grim determination to keep him a child or ward. In every advance, since emancipation it has, with true Caucasian gall, that everything must be done for him, and under no circumstances must he be allowed to do for himself.[15]

Greener subjects the white racist denial of African American self-determination to intense philosophical interrogation. The clash of values is visibly offered for public scrutiny. Furthermore, Greener initiates what is a *categorical inversion*. By categorical, we mean (in this instance) how the specification of racial categories is successively employed to describe and analyze what is considered as problematic. *Categorical inversion* encompasses a major shift in the employment of such categories, resulting in the qualitative transformation on the conceptualization, which establishes the given problem.

Greener's intervention in the battlefield of philosophy directly confronts the ontology of white racism via dismantling its foundational premise, that is, the operative ultimate postulates. The *real problem* no longer persists as the Negro or Black problem. Rather it becomes apparent that the problem is a *white problem* which derives from institutional racism. In this regard, Greener anticipates W.E.B. Du Bois's *The Souls of Black Folk*, where he raises the question, what does it mean to be a problem?

The so-called Negro Problem remains as a rudimentary presumption of white racism. Consequently, the postulation of this alleged "Negro Problem" masks the actual problem of institutional racism and its consequences. Greener's rendering effectually and radically converts our philosophical perspective on what is problematic and successively our value judgments— on African American circumstances—must take a qualitatively different turn.

This turn can be summarized with the following questions: How are racist postulates operative as the "white problem"? What does it mean to face white racism in its institutional form? Considering the white problem as material reality, how can Black progress emerge as a real possibility? Why is the realization of Black self-determination essential for overcoming the white problem? Obviously, this cluster of questions provisionally serves as mode of inquiry, one relevant for establishing a philosophical critique of racist (decisive) presumptions. The principle of Black self-determination finds its needed intellectual support with philosophical criticism of such postulates. Appropriately, it follows that the philosophical definition of Black progress is a theoretical issue adjoined to value judgments on the white problem.

Fittingly, what Morrison demonstrates is that ultimate postulates fall under the purview of philosophical scrutiny. The cluster of unquestioned beliefs is what we term "presumptive context." In short, presumptive context is the systemic cluster of founding presuppositions. It follows, as such, that philosophical inquiry in its main thrust is an investigation of our most rudimentary assumptions and presumptions. Morrison suggests that philosophy—as mode of inquiry—mandates a critical mind or thinking, especially when encountering founding presumptions.

By questioning our basic value judgments and postulates, philosophical critique, therefore, requires us to face up to the false security render by our presumptive context. Philosophical inquiry often comes into conflict with our rudimentary—if not unjustified—beliefs. In summation, while Morrison provides the general outline for philosophical inquiry into basic postulates, Greener supplies the concrete example for the examination of African American philosophy, as the explicit mode of inquiry for the critique of such claims that surround white racism.

Clearly, the metaphilosophical question "what is philosophy?" is not an exercise in ruminations that have no relevance to African American philosophy as mode of inquiry. The challenges that metaphilosophy presents are impending tasks we cannot ignore. How we confront problem solving is very much a question about the anterior issue of correctly formulating what constitutes the problem. Absolute postulates employed in framing the problem cannot operate without subject to critical scrutiny. Often, we hear in day-to-day discourse the statement, "we know the problem, however, what about offering the solution?" Critical thinking—as philosophical analysis—does not allow for the blanket consensus that we actually know the problem. Indeed, the very formulation of the problem demands our critical reflection. Such critical reflection also includes considerations on the very foundation and scope of philosophy as mode of inquiry.

Metaphilosophy: The foundation and scope of philosophy

The first Black Rhodes scholar Alain Locke is particularly concerned with the dangers of viewing philosophy in terms of absolute categories which exist outside of real life circumstances.[16] The propensity for system building, among some philosophers, often leads to the notion that philosophy can be established on absolute grounds. Perhaps the classic representation of absolute system building emerged with the nineteenth-century German philosopher Georg W. F. Hegel. He interpreted the history of philosophy— indeed world history—according to his absolute system. Sequentially, the history of philosophy and world history were manifestations of what Hegel called *Absolute Consciousness*.

Reason was the compelling force for the progressive advancement of philosophic thought and the primary impulse for world material development. The substance of Absolute Consciousness, Hegel argued, was the dialectical unfolding of Reason. He famously declared, "The Real is

Rational and the Rational is Real." Absolute Consciousness was embodied in Hegel's system, which he considered as the apex of Western philosophy and civilization. Consecutively, the zenith of Reason was indeed Hegel's own system of philosophy. Western civilization, he asserted, was paradigmatic of rational thinking. We should not forget that Hegel claimed that the capacity for rational thought eluded African people. Hegel additionally argued that people of African descent stood outside of the history of philosophy and on the margins of world history.[17]

In sharp contrast to Hegel, Alain Locke metaphilosophically returns to "historicized worldliness" for grounding philosophy:

> All philosophies, it seems to me, are in ultimate derivation philosophies of life and not of abstract, disembodied "objective" reality; products of time, place and situation, and thus systems of timed history rather than timeless eternity. They need not even be so universal as to become the epitomized *rationale* of an age, but may merely be the lineaments of a personality, its temperament and dispositional attitudes projected into their systematic rationalizations. But no conception of philosophy, however relativistic, however opposed to absolutism, can afford to ignore the question of ultimates or abandon what has been so aptly though skeptically termed "the quest for certainty."[18]

Locke's metaphilosophical response—that all philosophies are "systems of timed history rather than timeless eternity"—is an open declaration for philosophy's substantive history. Plainly, there is no capitulation to Althusser's thesis on philosophy's ahistorical existence. Indeed, for Locke, philosophy is alive, dynamic, and socially situated. Additionally, this sociohistorical (contextual) reality has direct bearing on our judgments about the scope of philosophy. The conventional viewpoint that philosophy must occur as an absolute system of universal proportion, Locke warns, is not mandatory.

Locke's perceptive declaration that philosophies "need not even be so universal as to become the epitomized *rationale* of an age," effectively—yet implicitly—permits for historic forms of philosophy such as African American philosophy. Since the affirmation of an African American philosophy does not (of necessity) denote a claim for universal philosophy— as with the case of Hegel's proclamations about his system of (German?) philosophy—therefore, it can very well capture philosophy in its particularity.

Metaphilosophically, Locke's insights are important for our inspection. If we can conceive of philosophy *qua* philosophy as an inquiry consisting of "the lineaments of a personality, its temperament and dispositional attitudes projected into their systematic rationalizations," subsequently, African American philosophy can embody the concrete content of Black material and intellectual culture. In other words, African American philosophy—in its particularity—*can achieve* metaphilosophical justification. Concurrently, this philosophy *should be* established on firm metaphilosophical grounds; what Locke categorically specifies as "ultimates" and "the quest for certainty."

Locke's latter reflection on "ultimates" and "the quest for certainty" incorporates the important caveat that a philosophy of particularity— although in opposition to philosophies that claim universality and even absolute character—should not neglect the grounding principles contain within metaphilosophical endeavors. Locke's affirmation of "ultimates" and "the quest for certainty" places him in the ranks of what philosophers conventionally term as "foundationalism." Given "foundationalism" is an epistemological position that centers on what grounds our beliefs, Locke is primarily concerned with such founding and at the same time affirming the historical nature of philosophy.

For some philosophers, the historical character of philosophy implies "anti-foundationalism." The anti-foundationalist counterargument presumes that the affirmation of philosophical "foundations" encompasses neglecting philosophy's ever-changing place in history. History is congruent with the existential basis of philosophy, that is, philosophy is always in process. Therefore, philosophy cannot serve as the lasting foundation for our beliefs. In sequence, history nullifies "permanent" philosophical foundations respecting our beliefs and the possible achievement of certainty. Among present-day African American philosophers, this stance is most representative with Cornel West's conception of neo-pragmatism.

However, Locke maintains that matters of philosophical definition and interpretation, along with philosophy's meaning, tasks, and mission are no less important as metaphilosophical considerations, especially in the instance of historicized philosophies of particularities. For Locke, "ultimates" and "the quest for certainty" need not imply that philosophy is ahistorical; indeed, they are the essential fundamentals of not only epistemology but also metaphilosophy. From Locke's standpoint, this is vitally something which we cannot afford to overlook.

Although certainly within the parameters of a long tradition of philosophical pondering, Locke's treatise on philosophical foundations does not, however, exhaust other possibilities. For example, H. T. Johnson approaches this concern in a qualitatively different manner. Rather than argue for (or against) the import of philosophical foundations, Johnson reveals how philosophy functions as the theoretical grounds for religion. His metaphilosophical perspective summons how the scope of philosophy includes serving as the identical buttress for religion. In summary, the very crux of philosophy is foundational.

In his essay, "Philosophy Religiously Valued," Johnson details the historical interdependence of religion and philosophy, with the precise view on the value of philosophy. We must point out that all considerations on *the value of philosophy*—contra the philosophy of value—are essentially metaphilosophical concerns. The *philosophy of value or axiology* remains a subfield of philosophy, that is, the interior subject matter of philosophy. In distinction, uncovering the value of philosophy involves *an external judgment* on philosophy's very worth—as an intellectual undertaking. In asking the question "what is the value of philosophy?," we venture into the realm of "the philosophy of philosophy." It transparently follows that Johnson's essay is a work in metaphilosophy.

Johnson observes that when venturing back into ancient history, one would discover that religion and religious beliefs were hegemonic over the fledging beginnings of philosophy. He notes that the Scholastics relegated philosophy's status to the handmaid of theology. Visibly, the value of philosophy was effectively subordinated to religion. The metaphilosophical outcome is most transparent. With philosophy as the subordinate partner to religion, the foundations for religious beliefs are not a matter of rational concern. Faith—rather than reason—founds religious beliefs. The value of philosophy for religion is of minor importance.

Yet, over time an alternative viewpoint finally appeared, which considerably elevated the status of philosophy. This elevation encompasses serving as the theoretical foundation for religion. While religion primarily depends on faith, philosophy as theoretical knowledge becomes the grounds anchoring faith claims. In metaphilosophical terms, this transformation is momentous. At this interval, philosophy becomes crucially significant in sustaining religious belief. Faith ceases to be an adequate theoretical anchor for religion. This radical change in the relationship between philosophy and religion constitutes a drastic metaphilosophical shift. Johnson explains,

> Indeed so vital seems the relation inhering between the two [religion and philosophy] in the light of these earlier systems that but for philosophy there would have been no constructed religion. . . . By this claim in behalf of philosophy it is not contended that religion owes so much or aught to the

former in its practical bearings and outcome, but that throughout its theoretical form, articulations of the philosophical genius are to be plainly traced.[19]

Johnson continues,

As the pyramid must have a basis so the religious structure of humanity ever towering upward must have a groundwork on which to rest. That resting-point is not the passive faith that marks the religious votary as he leans upon the crutch of mental imbecility in his dungeon of ignorance. He rests only upon a sure foundation when his creed maintains its strength and loveliness in the light of intelligence.[20]

Johnson concludes that the value of philosophy rest in its function as the theoretical form grounding religion. Philosophy is essentially the groundwork of religious belief. This conclusion is quite daring because—unlike such thinkers as Augustine (the African philosopher and theologian of Christianity) and Thomas Aquinas—Johnson is compelled to place philosophy as the foundation for religion over "passive faith."[21] Johnson's claim is unequivocal. Without philosophical intelligence, the religious devotee declines into "the crutch of mental imbecility," and hence, residing in the "dungeon of ignorance."

Johnson effectively expands the scope of philosophy into the very realm of the theoretical foundation for religion. In Johnson's estimate, faith remains passive phenomena without the active role of philosophical theory. He does not allow for relegating philosophy into a subsidiary position vis-à-vis faith. In dissimilarity, both Augustine and Aquinas place faith above reason and thus philosophical thinking. Johnson declares that philosophy itself is foundational for religion, concomitantly possessing the characteristics of intelligence and genius, which sustains an otherwise passive religious faith. Clearly, his treatment of foundationalism provides a new twist on this discussion on what grounds philosophy via the claim about the philosophical foundations for religious beliefs. Philosophy becomes—in itself— *foundational.*

In many respects, this nineteenth-century African American philosopher is also light years ahead of many contemporary Black philosophers of religion. The key that philosophy holds for us, Johnson contends, lies specifically with its attribute of reason. Reason offers intelligent light, which we previously discovered is relevant since faith remains in perennial need of illumination. At root, philosophy is systematic reason and the foundation for religious belief. Johnson's metaphilosophical commitment derives from this very important principle.

Though Johnson is firmly convinced that the value of philosophy is founded on the attribution of reason, Rufus L. Perry has a fundamentally different perspective on this matter. Perry's opposing metaphilosophical viewpoint orbits around the limitation of reason, which is directly correlated to the scope of philosophy. Perry addresses metaphilosophy by claiming that reason—via philosophical speculation—cannot provide us with an understanding of the world. Human reason is an insufficient means for knowing about the universe. The complexity of reality defies all human efforts; hence Perry becomes a staunch advocate of "agnosticism" in his theory of knowledge. In effect, for Perry, the universe is unknowable. He argues,

> The Universe and the Supreme Power that controls it, is a problem that has provoked more discussion and wild speculation, than any other subject that has attracted the attention of man from the beginning. *It commenced with philosophy*; and the primary principles advanced in the systems of its votaries are as much a matter of dispute to-day, as they were, when Thales announced that water was the simple substance of all things visible,—the prima materia. (Italics added)

Perry continues,

> This dispute must always be, for the problem of the Universe cannot be solved on principles of philosophy. The aim of philosophy will never be achieved. Science sought the solution, but found the problem beyond its reach, and reason surrendered the task, as beyond its power. Man cannot fathom the fathomless; the mind of man cannot penetrate the impenetrable. There is a limit to mental capacity; there is a bound to reason.[22]

With respect to Perry's declarations, there are several important points of deliberation. First, what are the ideas that inform his notion of metaphilosophy? Prima facie, Perry does not offer an alternative metaphilosophical perspective, which in any manner contradicts the notion that philosophy chiefly aims to understand the world around us. However, it is of no small measure that Perry's conception of the history of philosophy, as interrelated to metaphilosophy, clearly demonstrates that he does not embrace the idea about historical progression in philosophic thought.

This becomes manifest when he says that humanity's search to understand the universe, "commenced with philosophy; and the primary principles advanced in the systems of its votaries are as much a matter of dispute to-day, as they were, when Thales announced that water was the simple substance of all things visible." Along the same trajectory as Althusser, Perry believes that the history of philosophy does not in any manner reflect a progression in thought.

Consequently, we are no more philosophically advanced today, than when Thales—in antiquity—claimed that water was the basis of reality. For Perry, philosophical inquiry is a recurring attempt at explaining the universe with no tangible results. What we know today is just about the same respecting the universe, which Thales obtained in antiquity. Some readers may wonder, who was Thales? And what was his contribution to the history of philosophy?

Conventional opinion regards Thales as the first philosopher in Western philosophy. This Ionian philosopher played a crucial role in advancing Greek philosophy outside of the clutches of mythological thinking. African philosopher Kwame Nkrumah offers a compelling examination of Thales's import in the history of philosophy. Thales rejected the supernaturalism attendant with Greek mythology and religion. Rather than the gods, Thales posited that water was the fundamental ontological principle anchoring the universe. Nkrumah warns that "by this, he [Thales] did not of course mean that everything was drinkable. That everything was directly water or constructible from water alone as raw material is in fact the heart of his epigram. Thales recognized just one basic type of substance."[23]

Nkrumah's keen observation that water, for Thales, consisted of one type of substance is of no small matter. In philosophical terms, *substance* is that which depends on nothing else. All other entities are either the properties or derivatives of substance. Obviously, Thales is a monist. Thus, water singularly functions as the building block of nature. Arguably, there is a short theoretical leap from the philosophical idea that water serves as the fundamental building block of nature to claims about atoms at the basis of nature, which we know is the very modern conception associated with physics.

Accordingly, Thales's ontology points to philosophical materialism. Keep in mind, all species of supernaturalism are ultimately reducible to philosophical idealism. Therefore, the philosophy of Thales, Nkrumah argues, considerably advanced philosophical materialism and thus anticipates scientific thinking. In this manner, Thales was the progenitor of an intellectual revolution.[24]

Without question, an intellectual revolution encompasses a qualitative change in thinking. Perry's viewpoint considerably deviates from Nkrumah because of the dismissal of progressive development within philosophical discourse. Moreover, the scope of philosophy—a cardinal aspect of metaphilosophy—is constrained by the limits of reason. This limitation transpires as the upshot of Perry's epistemology and how it subsequently intersects with metaphilosophy. The epistemological conception put forth is that the universe in principle cannot be known.

The unknowability of the universe or reality is the fulcrum which delineates why philosophy can never meet its aims. Perry's epistemology is best described as "agnosticism." "Agnosticism" declares that not only is the universe (in many essential respects) unknown but also in principle it is unknowable. Therefore, Perry's agnosticism corresponds with his metaphilosophical perspective on the scope of philosophy.

Let's return to Perry's precise words: "The aim of philosophy will never be achieved. Science sought the solution, but found the problem beyond its reach, and reason surrendered the task, as beyond its power." From this statement we can discern that Perry does not offer up science as an alternative to philosophy by way of an epistemological option. Yet, some philosophers point out that philosophy has certain limitations, which are rectified with scientific knowledge. They argue that the boundaries of knowledge are expanded by scientific advancement and hence this knowledge supplements what philosophy cannot provide. From Eugene C. Holmes's treatment of dialectical materialism, we can discern the value of scientific advancement for human knowledge. Marx's dialectical materialism, Holmes argued, was based on drawing from scientific research in founding its ontological and epistemological commitments.

However, Perry's epistemological position not only limits philosophy but also science vis-à-vis the restricted capacity of the human mind. Perry's agnosticism obviously encompasses all fields of knowledge regarding the comprehension of the universe. The limits regarding the scope of philosophy—metaphilosophy at base—emerges from the human condition associated with the myopia of reason. The boundaries of reason set the limits of knowledge and thus the unknowability of the universe. Consequently, we have Perry's concluding remark, "The aim of philosophy will never be achieved. . . . Man cannot fathom the fathomless; the mind of man cannot penetrate the impenetrable. There is a limit to mental capacity; there is a bound to reason."

For Perry, the prospects of constructing a better philosophy—than found with previous efforts—is not the answer. Furthermore, scientific investigation faces the same fate. As a matter of principle, philosophy falls short of the mark. In outline, philosophy's failure is not due to its distinctive mode of inquiry. Better yet, the pitfalls of philosophy rest in its mooring as an inherent human endeavor; one that remains imprisoned within the circumstances of a very limited human reason.

It follows that Perry, unlike H. T. Johnson, would not trust philosophy to serve as the groundwork of religion. Indeed, Perry's agnosticism directly points to religion as the answer to the drawbacks of philosophy. After all, for Perry, it is the "Supreme Power" that controls the universe. While this "Supreme Power" could very well be all-knowing (omniscient), Perry also implies humans can only reach this Power by faith, and surely not by way of reason. In conclusion, the ontological basis for Perry's agnosticism ultimately rest in his conception of this "Supreme Power" and the limitations of human knowledge. He declares,

> In the systems of the philosophers from Thales to Schopenhauer . . . the problem "of the Universe is found still unsolved, and it must remain unsolved." In Job we read. "Canst thou by searching find out God? Canst thou Find out the Almighty unto perfection? It is as high as heaven; what canst thou do? Deeper than hell; what canst thou know?"[25]

There are other African American philosophers that hold to a firm belief in God, yet, find agnosticism as disconcerting and woefully inadequate as a theory of knowledge. In a nutshell, belief in God does not automatically point to agnosticism. At this juncture, C. V. Roman's critique of agnosticism is most fitting for our review.

What Roman brings to the table of discussion is a high level of appreciation for the capacity of human thought. Human reason is not in conflict with the concurrent belief in the existence of God. In fact, he is quite critical of agnosticism as an epistemological position. This critique of agnosticism is both relevant to epistemology and metaphilosophy. At base, the point of contention is that the scope of philosophy centers on the expanse of human reason. The glaring contrast between Perry and Roman is immediately apparent. Roman states,

> Mankind cannot be satisfied with mere negation. "I don't know" is not answer enough to the cry of the cradle, nor explanation enough to the silence of the coffin. The devotees of the so-called practical sciences may continue to asseverate that first causes and final effects are beyond human comprehension, yet the majority of mankind will reject Agnosticism and regard Eschatology, Ontology and Teleology as sciences worthy of study.[26]

Roman offers a diametrically opposed metaphilosophical viewpoint from what we witnessed with Perry. In dissimilarity to Perry, Roman maintains that reason is the treasure house for knowledge and human progress. Although Roman affirms religious belief—his stance is concertedly idealist—yet, he does not render human ideas to the scrapheap. Roman outright rejects the notion that belief in God mandates an epistemology of agnosticism. Thought is crucially important to human existence and knowledge. Hence, in Roman's estimation, there is no doubting the knowability of the world. From the position of dialectical idealism, he states,

> The Bible says, "As a man thinketh in his heart, so is he." The thinking makes the doing, the doing does not control the thinking but is controlled by it. Ideas precede action. Sensation precedes motion. What is the universe but a thought of God? "Everything," says a writer, "resolves itself back into an idea. The solid framework of the world, with all its objects of beauty and use, is but the crystallization of God's thoughts." . . . The thought is always prior to the fact. The world has to obey him who thinks and sees in the world. *All the facts of history pre-exist in the mind as laws.*[27] (Italics added)

Granting his thesis, "All the facts of history pre-exist in the mind as laws," then it is Roman's contention that the universe is knowable. Roman's dialectical idealism permits both belief in God and the human capacity to comprehend the world. This idealism evidently reduces historical facts to their corresponding laws, however, existing within the mind. Concurrently, since there are laws of history, which are encapsulated in the mind, it follows that we have the progressive development of philosophical thought. Rather than reoccurring (historical) events signaling inertia, Roman's metaphilosophy allows for growth and development. In the larger scheme, the origins of philosophy indicate a major intellectual development in human culture throughout the world.

Given our overview, it becomes evident that the birth of philosophy—whether in Africa, China, India, or Greece—emerges as a significant break from mythology. The replacement of the authority of the gods as a source of wisdom, began first at the cosmological realm where nature's origin rested not in the supernatural but in nature itself.

Perhaps, this historical reality—surrounding philosophy's origins—explains why Perry dismisses the epistemological worth of philosophy. This grand intellectual departure—from celestial authority—conceptually assaults Perry's notion of "Supreme Power." In divergence, the break from mythological authority, for example, with Thales, opened the door for the elevation of human reason. This sui generis perspective on nature had at its foundation an empirical approach, where the critical observation of nature was sufficient as the very basis for acquiring knowledge of its origins. Knowledge was jettisoned from the constrains of mythology, where wisdom was a property of the gods and human knowledge was subservient to faith in the gods. Philosophy, therefore, represents the secularization of "divine" wisdom and the first form of theoretical knowledge.

In contrast to Perry's thoughts on the matter, we think that Charles V. Roman and Henry T. Johnson would agree with our assessment. Undoubtedly, Roy D. Morrison II provides considerable metaphilosophical insight that offers support for our position. Now we must venture into how African American philosophy—as particular instance of inquiry—is situated within its own specified metaphilosophical parameters.

What is African American philosophy? Metaphilosophical considerations

It should be clear at this point that to advance the notion of African American philosophy inaugurates a crucial and unavoidable metaphilosophical discussion about the nature of philosophy itself. Most importantly, the question "what is African American philosophy?" entails an open challenge to the hegemonic notion that philosophy in its universality was not—in any manner—concerned with ethnic particularity.

In 1976, Drs. Joyce Mitchell Cook (Figure 11), William R. Jones, and Robert C. Williams participated in a historic round table discussion—in Racine, Wisconsin—on the meaning of Black philosophy. These three leading African American philosophers rather cautiously broached the topic and often presented their remarks in an open-ended fashion. (Of course, any philosopher attentive to critical and careful thinking would not resort to facile conjectures.) Instead of hard and sharp pronouncements declaring that Black philosophy had a rather long history, each interlocutor carefully rendered their views on the prospects of Black philosophy.[28]

From their collective viewpoint, Black philosophy was a prospective form of inquiry. While it had legitimate possibility, via critical modes of inquiry, nonetheless, they concluded that history disclosed very little for constructing a sound foundation. The greater emphasis was on future possibilities rather than the past tradition of Black philosophy. Summarily, they did not identify any *historical* body of philosophical literature, suitable for the designation—Black philosophy.

Figure 11 Joyce Mitchell Cook (1933–2014).

The reader may ask, why was this happening? We think, this was due to two key issues. First, there is the problem of *conscious amplification*. By *conscious amplification*, we mean the process of explicitly identifying a specific philosophical school of thought or position. In sum, they could not provide a de facto rubric for labeling "Black" philosophy as an apposite nomenclature for past philosophical thought. The history of African American philosophy remained in the shadows. The reason why they confronted this dilemma, pertains to the next hurdle.

Second, they faced the complexities surrounding the problem of metaphilosophy in its strategic connection with the history of philosophy. The definition and thus naming of philosophy is essentially contained within its history. They did not commit to offering the needed historical overview for discovering the lineaments of Black philosophy. Herein, the metaphilosophical implications affixed to Black philosophy must now come under review.

Our concern about metaphilosophical implications can be summarized with the following questions: First, how does metaphilosophy impinge on the process of defining African American/Black philosophy? Second, what are the specified metaphilosophical parameters adjoined to African American philosophy? Third, how can the concept of *historic form* assist in defining African American philosophy? Does the particularity of African American philosophy imply the negation of the universal nature of philosophical inquiry?

This ensemble of questions functions as a guide for possible avenues of exploration. Granting that metaphilosophy includes the tasks, substance, and scope of philosophy, in succession, the search for definitions is not simply consulting a dictionary of philosophical terminology. Rather it entails posing significant and penetrating interrogations, both of theoretical and historical proportions.[29]

In his groundbreaking essay, "The Legitimacy and Necessity of Black Philosophy: Some Preliminary Considerations," William R. Jones argues,

> In recent years the concept of an ethnic approach to a discipline has emerged. Central to this approach is the self-conscious concern to accent the characteristics of a given cultural, racial, religious, or national grouping and to establish its history, perspective, culture, the agenda, as central as indispensable for the content and method of various disciplines. Black philosophy is a representative of this development.[30]

Here Jones links African American philosophical inquiry to the tortured birth and development of African American Studies. Jones brings into sharp relief how the question of legitimacy is an overriding principle in the defense of what constitutes Black philosophy as a distinctive form of philosophical inquiry. Jones perceptively declares, "As a new entry in the philosophical marketplace, black philosophy finds that it must reply to questions not generally addressed to other neoteric developments. Other newcomers are asking to justify their adequacy and significance. Black philosophy, however, must respond to the prior question of its legitimacy; it must establish its right to exist as an appropriate philosophical position."[31]

Jones argues that Black philosophy is a particular instance of the concrete universality that in fact grounds philosophy in all of its universality. For Jones, the categories of *universality* and *particularity* are not mutually exclusive but instead are *mutually inclusive*. They are *correlative categories*. The defining features of correlative categories is the condition and relation of mutual dependence; you cannot have one category without the other.

Just as there can be no form without content or appearance without essence, we cannot have universality without particularity. The basis for the correlative status of particularity (mutual relation and dependence on universality) is due to the fact that particularity is an *instantiation of universality*. It is immediately clear that particularity as a category is something different from universality. Nevertheless, particularity in its *difference* from universality is concomitantly in dialectical *unity* with universality. The tendency to view the categories of particularity and universality in mutually exclusive terms has engendered intense debates around questions of whether philosophy is universal or particular in substance and method. This has salient importance to discussions centered on the nature of African and African American philosophy in terms of both scope and substance.[32]

By claiming that particularity is grounded by universality, it should be noted that the notion of ground has a dual meaning. Ground in this dual sense means universality is both the *foundation* on which particularity stands and it imposes a *limitation* on particularity. The fact that universality is the ground for particularity implies that universality as content dictates or limits the scope of form as a particular instance. In other words to be a particular instance (form) of something mandates that there is a *something* (the grounds of which are provided by the more general—universal— category) to be "a particular instance of" in each and every case.[33]

Universality without the specific content provided by particularity becomes an arid (empty) abstraction. Consequently, what results when universality is separated from particularity is *abstract universality*. It becomes especially important to make note of this fact about *abstract universality* when human beings come under discussion in philosophical anthropology.[34] When humans are seen as devoid of particularity (particular races, genders, and national identities, for example) then abstract universalism is the result. The often-heard proposition, "I do not see you as Black, I view you as a human being" or the argument, "I do not want to be identified as woman but rather as human" or the claim, "there is only one race, the human race" are all instances of *abstract universality*.[35] The reason why we end up with *abstract universality* follows from the stipulation that one's Blackness or gender is a *particular instantiation* and *constituent expression* of the universal category—humanity.[36] The universality of humanity is a *concrete universality* that embodies the particularity of Blackness.

Our theoretical investigation—up to this point—has already demonstrated that African American philosophy does not boil down to discovering a consensus. *African American philosophy is not a collective worldview or community with a shared epistemology, metaphysics, or philosophical vocabulary.* After all, as we saw in Chapter 1, there are African American philosophers who are materialists, idealists, agnostics, Hegelians, existentialists, phenomenologists, and pragmatists who conceptually dwell within different and oftentimes conflicting discourse communities. Furthermore, careful reading of African American philosophical texts indicate there is considerable divergence on matters of metaphilosophy. The presumption that we have something approximating *the* "African American" metaphilosophical foundations would be far off target. There is no distinctive African American viewpoint on metaphilosophical foundations.

It is important to differentiate "philosophy *and* the African American experience" from the more specified notion of "philosophy *of* the African American experience." The difference here is a qualitative one that is rooted, nonetheless, in a quantitative relationship. The former is more general in scope and is all-inclusive of African Americans without regard for the precise nature of their philosophical works and practices. The latter, in turn, are the identifiable philosophical efforts toward elaborating on the precise characteristics and implications of the African American experience.

This distinction reflects William R. Jones's definition of the scope of African American philosophy. Jones argues that there is a general misguided tendency to focus exclusively on race as the necessary organizing principle of a Black or African American philosophy. This is the presumptive context for the identification of the philosophy of race with African American philosophy proper. Jones persuasively argues, "The experience, history, and culture are the controlling categories for a black philosophy—not chromosomes."[37] For Jones, the concept of African American philosophy encompasses such factors as author, audience, ancestry, accent, and antagonist. He explains,

> The intent appears to be one or more of the following: to identify that the author is black, i.e. a member of a particular ethnic community, that his primary, though not exclusive, audience is the black community, that the point of departure for his philosophizing or the tradition from which he speaks or the world-view he seeks to articulate can be called in some sense the black experience. . . . Special attention must be to "black" as a designation of the antagonist. . . . Accordingly, to call for a black philosophy, from this perspective, is to launch an implicit attack on racism in philosophy, especially in its conceptual, research, curricular, and institutional expressions.[38]

Hence, African American philosophy is simply philosophy that engages the African American experience and condition rather than a case of representing a unitary philosophical perspective, which is shared by all or even most Black people. In this connection, we draw an important distinction between a *Black philosophical perspective* and the *philosophical comprehension of the Black experience*. As John McClendon has explained,

> It is the case that Blackness provides my motivation (for doing philosophy) but not my (philosophical) orientation, that is, my specified philosophical perspective. For me, the issue is not about thinking in Black philosophical terms; rather it is to think philosophically about Blackness. So, therefore, even though I disagree with the Afrocentric notion that one must think in black or African modes of philosophizing, I do not accept William Banner's position that Blackness is outside of the concerns of philosophical thought and investigation. What it means to be Black is a philosophical question and my Blackness cannot be separated from what motivates and informs my philosophical research.[39]

It should be noted that African American philosophers need not (and have not) exclusively engaged the African American experience as an area of inquiry. This is why race is not necessarily *the* organizing principle for African American philosophy. Most importantly, African American philosophy is not limited to the philosophy of race. The philosophy of race is a subfield within the philosophy of African American experience.

Some African American philosophers have addressed the more broadly conceived problem of the nature of values as such or did research in what is the subfield of axiology such as Joseph C. Price, Cornelius Golightly, and Berkeley Eddins. Furthermore, the previously discussed Alain Locke wrote extensively on value theory. Other philosophers confronted problems in the philosophy of science such as the dialectical materialist Eugene Holmes, the idealist Robert T. Browne, in addition to A. J. Kershaw and Edward A. Clarke.

In a similar fashion, we observed how the prominence of dialectical idealism did not, however, result in embracing a monolithic epistemology. Undoubtedly, the idea of a Black epistemology—based on some communal theory of knowledge—would blatantly ignore the history of African American philosophical thought. Our historical overview presented the stark difference between absolute agnosticism and an energetic dialectical idealism, full of the promise about knowing the world.

Even where we uncovered broad consensus—on belief in God— the corresponding philosophical justifications had divergent operative principles. We firmly established that both Henry T. Johnson and Rufus L. Perry fervently held an abiding belief in God. However, we should not lose sight of the metaphilosophical and epistemological chasms separating them were undeniably deep and wide. Now, we come to the proverbial crossroads in this journey for a definition. If philosophical consensus fails as the metaphilosophical parameters for specifying African American philosophy, then our search must continue on a new road.

Let's explore the relevance of *historic form* regarding our definition of African American philosophy. The reader must remember that this notion of historic form served as our category for *the specification of concrete forms* on philosophizing. Thus, over the course of history, we have distinctive philosophical modes of inquiry emerged as concrete forms. Of course, we have already unearthed that the specification of concrete forms is not equivalent with sustaining any consensus in philosophical thinking. The concrete form of African American philosophy is not the same as maintaining broad agreement. If it is not consensus, so therefore, what transpires as the concrete form? How can we move forward in our journey?

Accordingly, we must construct a new set of questions in our expedition toward defining African American philosophy. What we do know is that the specification of concrete forms mandates identifying those philosophical modes of inquiry, which precisely are the historical expression of concrete material and intellectual circumstances. Philosophical inquiry—no matter what—dictates the inspection of the existent material and intellectual context arising from historical circumstances. This mandate is at the crux of the notion—*historic form.*

Next, we must characterize the immediate content of historic forms. The observant student of philosophy must realize that form and content are correlative in nature. There can be no form without content, and no content without form. How do we uncover the content behind historic form? One hint is that the scope of philosophy, given its dynamic character, compels philosophers to select placement regarding the universality or particularity of given historic forms. We observed that Hegel elected to assume universality, while Alain Locke, metaphilosophically, allows for a philosophy of particularity.

In our view, three questions emerge as foremost on the agenda. First, we ask, is philosophical inquiry essentially particular or universal in scope? Second, does the universal character of philosophy, in effect, nullify philosophies of particularity? Lastly, can we identify the historical body of African American philosophic literature, which meets our metaphilosophical criteria of historic form? Let's begin with the last question.

We can undoubtedly establish—on historical grounds—with confidence that African American philosophy is an existent reality. This declaration overtly stands as a valued instance of the concrete universal. The notion of Black philosophy is far from a new idea. The fact is that critical inquiry on Black life involves oppositional categories. Hence, we observed that notions about the "Negro Problem" mandated framing not only dissimilar categories, for example, concepts such as the white problem, but also an entirely different philosophical framework. In accordance with this alternative perspective, the guiding principles for such a framework entails formulating distinctive ideals. As early as 1911, C.V. Roman unequivocally pronounced the following:

> The one great handicap of slavery in this country was the imposition of the white man's ideal on the black man. This cramps the black man at every step of his progress and in many cases is an absolute preventative of any progress whatever. The white man's ideal man is of course WHITE. When the black man consciously, or unconsciously accepts this ideal he has shut himself out of the paradise of earthly achievement.[40]

Roman's observation, "The white man's ideal man is of course WHITE," speaks to how white ideals lead to the dehumanization of Black people. Since the acceptance of white ideals is dehumanizing, the restoration of Black humanity requires Black ideals. Such ideals develop from having Black philosophical perspectives. Roman further elaborates on the need for modes of thinking that enhances Black ethnic group solidarity and progress; even citizenship in the United States should not come at the expense of Black ethnic identity. Visibly, Roman gives voice to the existence of Black philosophy, which is established on Black ideals. Without apology, Roman speaks in distinctively affirmative terms—as a committed Black philosopher.

Even prior to Roman's articulations, Thomas Nelson Baker, in 1906, advocates for upholding, what he terms, the "Black Aesthetical ideal." Although Baker recognizes the universality of ethical ideals, where all humans must not be treated as means to an end; nevertheless, he asserts that aesthetical ideals are established on the particularity of racial integrity. The basic postulate of *racial integrity* controls the process in shaping Black Aesthetical ideals. Baker plainly states,

If race integrity is to be maintained and each race develop its own peculiar racial gifts and thus enrich the life of man on earth—then *our aesthetical ideals of physical beauty must ever be different.* It is in the perversion of the aesthetical sense of physical beauty that the American Negro has struck the lowest depths of racial degradation.[41] (Italics added)

If we correctly understand Baker's premise about Black Aesthetical sensibility, this sensibility can only develop by means of constructing Black philosophical ideals or principles. The heart of the matter is that Baker openly acknowledges that philosophical thinking must be different for Black people. An appreciation of Black beauty requires a distinctive Black Aesthetic. The reader should not neglect that aesthetics form an integral component of axiology. Philosophy of value, Baker argues, is not removed from how racial integrity is philosophically encapsulated as Black ideals. Thus, Black philosophy was on Baker's agenda long before the 1970s.

Clearly, Baker and Roman are open proponents of Black philosophy. Each views Black philosophy as a necessary condition for racial progress. The failure to embrace Black philosophy, they contend, results in Black people remaining under the yoke of white ideological hegemony. In Baker and Roman's view, Black philosophy is the cardinal weapon in the ideological struggle for Black self-determination. With this declaration, they echo the sentiments of Richard T. Greener. Of course, we witness that Greener's pronouncements on the "white problem" extends back into the nineteenth century.

Furthermore, it is translucent that we have more generally answered our last question via the extensive examination of African American nineteenth- and twentieth-century schools of thought. All point to critical—theoretical— inquiry on human problems from the vantage point of the African American experience. While some of this work is more mediated than immediately connected, the entire corpus gains its momentum and vitality from African American material and intellectual culture.

Along with Greener, Baker, and Roman's proclamations on the white problem and Black ideals, we also have the vibrant African American philosophical discussion on the conceptualization of Black progress, mind/ body problem, the philosophy of religion, philosophy of science, ontology, dialectical idealism, dialectical materialism, epistemology, aesthetics, and of course metaphilosophy. All these ventures emerged in the context of African American material and intellectual culture. In effect, we witnessed the concerted philosophical inquiry on the manifold problems confronted by Black people.

Obviously, for instance, dialectical idealism—from the African American standpoint—galvanized the philosophical confrontation with institutional racism, which directs us toward the concrete history of African American philosophy. The African American philosophical tradition shaping dialectical idealism stands in sharp contrast with what we discovered with Hegel. Dialectical idealism, from the African American standpoint, became an instrument in the assault against racism – in both its material and ideological forms. Dialectical idealism served in the defense of Black intellectual capacity and the right to self-determination. On the question of the historical existence of Black philosophy, we have a plethora of supporting evidence.

Moreover, our search for answers is not without some clues on the matter. We previously opened the door with Alain Locke's metaphilosophical suggestions. Metaphilosophical justification, for Locke, does not command that philosophy claim universality as the singular option. From his viewpoint, philosophies of particularity sequentially have metaphilosophical legitimation. In the instances of Greener, Baker, and Roman the overt proclamation of philosophies of particularity is self-evident.

Furthermore, in more general terms, African American philosophy in exemplifying the substance of Black material and intellectual culture encapsulates Black particularity. The historic form of African American philosophy finds its content in particularity. The metaphilosophical justification of African American philosophy—as particularity—merely needs a structure that we can point to that sustains our hypothesis with more explicit terminology. In other words, how can we point to Black philosophy as an identifiable rubric?

Earlier, we witnessed that Alain Locke's deliberation on metaphilosophy implicitly offers the possibility for establishing the needed framework, which could support our *conscious amplification* on the identification of African American philosophy. Since we have clearly demonstrated the presence of this concrete historic form—extending back into the nineteenth century— then our notion of "conscious amplification" requires our in-depth edification. Why suggest the need for adding "conscious amplification" to the discussion? Conscious amplification denotes an identifiable rubric, that is, the assignment of Black/African American philosophy as the definitive nomenclature. *Conscious amplification* is also an overt act or declaration.

When one states, "I am a dialectical materialist," we are witnessing the act of conscious amplification. Yet, the philosopher may very well philosophize from the perspective of dialectical idealism or mechanistic materialism, and not described this work in such terms.

Conscious amplification or philosophical classification—of this sort—is often post facto. Our prior discussion on Du Bois and pragmatism is a prime example. Nowhere in Du Bois's extensive writings does he offer the self-description—pragmatist. The debate over Du Bois's placement within the ranks of pragmatism happened long after the fact. Generally, it is years after the fact that a philosopher is affixed with classificatory descriptors—markers of philosophical placement.

For instance, the idea "Pre-Socratic" would appear as strange to Thales for labeling his place in philosophy. Obviously, the concept of "Pre-Socratic" is not contemporaneous with Thales's lifetime. There is no way Thales went about Miletus claiming he was a likely future—Pre-Socratic thinker. Yet, we discover this designation saliently appears throughout texts on Western philosophy.

Based on our research, neither William D. Johnson nor Henry T. Johnson made public announcements that they were dialectical idealists—let alone engaged in African American or Black/Negro philosophy. Notwithstanding the lack of self-identifying monikers, we would be remiss not to stipulate that they were dialectical idealists. Any other identification would falsely portray their locus in the history of Black philosophy.

Concurrently, our identification of what constitutes African American philosophy cannot rest on the prior absence of conscious amplification. Albeit Thomas Nelson Baker and C. V. Roman are rather unique with their conscious amplification on Black philosophy vis-à-vis Black ideals. We submit that past Black philosophers noticeably engaged in philosophical inquiry, which today would garner the label—African American philosophy. Their concerns from metaphilosophy to axiology were framed in the African American context, often in the shadow of segregation. Many times, these philosophers were combating racism, while philosophically affirming their Black identity and intellectual capacity. There is no other locus for Richard T. Greener's "The White Problem," than African American/Black philosophy.

Nonetheless, there is scarce documentation on attempts at actively constructing the explicit nomenclature—African American or Black/Negro philosophy. Yet, many of the works speak for themselves and ostensibly indicate the presence of an African American philosophical tradition and schools of thought. Our previous discussions on history and its relationship to metaphilosophy are instructive. We unearth that the substance and scope of philosophy is crucially linked to history.

Yet, all philosophies, whether deemed as universal or particular, do not exist in a historical vacuum. If we return to our summation (in Chapter 1) on Aristotle, it is crystal clear that his critique of Plato set the foundation for building a "new" system of thought. What is new or novel depends on what already exists. Philosophy has garnered numerous meanings through its development. The idea of progression in philosophical thinking remains fundamentally a matter of history in association with the definition of philosophy. Rufus L. Perry's metaphilosophical points of contention in juxtaposition to C. V. Roman offer us a clear example of the importance of history. Along the same lines, divergent notions of metaphilosophy have a crucial impact on determining how to define Black philosophy.

With our prior deliberation on metaphilosophy, it was also pointed out that metaphilosophy not only seeks to define philosophy but also prescribes what it should do. In a nutshell, metaphilosophy broadly implies all *normative references* concerning prescriptions about philosophical theory and method. Normative reference involves demarcating what should be *the general tasks* of philosophy and the requisite means to accomplish them.

Concurrently, normative references with respect to *general tasks* are specifically directed at what philosophers must do via their philosophizing. Given this general metaphilosophical principle, how does this apply to our conceptualization on African American philosophers? How are metaphilosophical considerations—on African American philosophy—relevant to the specific tasks of Black philosophers? What is required of them? In the early 1960s, a foremost Black sociologist offered such recommendations for consideration.

In his essay "The Failure of the Negro Intellectual," E. Franklin Frazier argues if African Americans want to obtain any legitimate representation respecting the general scholarly public, then the African American philosopher must meet specific intellectual obligations. Plainly, philosophers must have steadfast commitment for philosophizing from the vantage point of Black life.[42] Frazier did not argue for some form of Black epistemology or standpoint epistemology.

As a result, African American philosophers that merely recite the conventional names in philosophy drastically fall short in carrying out genuine acts of philosophizing. Legitimate philosophizing—from the standpoint of African American philosophy—requires critical scrutiny of the existing conditions pertaining to the African American community. Frazier declares,

> We have no philosophers or thinkers who command the respect of the intellectual community at-large. I'm not talking about the few teachers of philosophy who have read Hegel or Kant or James and memorize their thoughts. I'm talking about men who have reflected upon the fundamental problems which have always concerned philosophers such as the nature of human knowledge and the meanings or lack of meaning of human existence. We have no philosophers who have dealt with these and other problems from the standpoint of the Negro's unique experience in the world.[43]

We must carefully dissect Frazier's statement with attention to his description of Black philosophers vis-à-vis the metaphilosophical aspect concerning the scholarly responsibility of African American philosophers. We have extensively documented that African American philosophers noticeably contributed to all aspects of philosophy. When Frazier penned his pronouncement in 1962—before and during that time—there were a considerable number of Black philosophers actively engaged as public intellectuals (Tables 4 and 5).

Here we present a listing of academic philosophers of African American descent and their dissertation topics. Though not exhaustive, our list is quite extensive. We can see academic philosophers that fully met Frazier's criteria.

Moreover, the impulse for their contributions were directly based on African American material and intellectual resources. In fact, such resources were the raw material for launching philosophical inquiry—as an intellectual instrument—in the immediate struggle against white racism. We have expansively documented such sources in Chapter 1. The academic institutions—HBCU—and scholarly journals that published African American philosophical texts were duly noted. These empirical descriptors are valuable indicators of the concrete locus of African American philosophers.

Now, we must address the second aspect to Frazier's declaration. Namely, Frazier's notion of respect—for Black philosophical work—in the broader intellectual community. The given phrase, "the intellectual community at-large," is no more than the connotation for white intellectuals, then, "what does it mean for Black philosophers to garner respect?" Does Frazier think that white intellectuals "respect" African American philosophers that are attentive to Black concerns? Indeed, can we assume that respect is synonymous with white approval of Black scholarship?

Table 4 Chronological listing: African American doctorates in philosophy and related fields

	Year	Name	Doctoral Institution
1.	1865	Patrick Francis Healy	University of Louvain (Belgium)
2.	1887	John Wesley Edward Bowen	Boston University
3.	1896	Lewis Baxter Moore	University of Pennsylvania
4.	1903	Thomas Nelson Baker	Yale University
5.	1909	Gilbert Haven Jones	University of Jena
6.	1918	James Leonard M. Farmer Sr.	Boston University
7.	1918	Alain Leroy Locke	Harvard University
8.	1921	Willis Jefferson King	Boston University
9.	1933	Albert Millard Dunham	University of Chicago
10.	1933	Marquis Lafayette Harris	Ohio State University
11.	1936	William Thomas Valeria Fontaine	University of Pennsylvania
12.	1938	Charles Leander Hill	Ohio State University
13.	1938	Marc Marion Moreland	University of Toronto
14.	1938	Forest Oran Wiggins	University of Wisconsin
15.	1941	Cornelius Golightly	University of Michigan
16.	1941	John Milton Smith	University of Iowa
17.	1942	Eugene Clay Holmes	Columbia University
18.	1942	Richard I. McKinney	Yale University
19.	1943	Francis M. Hammond	University of Laval (Canada)
20.	1946	George D. Kelsey	Yale University
21.	1947	William A. Banner	Harvard University
22.	1947	Everett F. S. Davies	Columbia University
23.	1947	Winston K. McAllister	University of Michigan
24.	1948	Thomas F. Freeman	University of Chicago
25.	1950	Winson R. Coleman	University of Chicago
26.	1951	Carlton L. Lee	University of Chicago
27.	1952	Broadus Butler	University of Michigan
28.	1958	Wayman Bernard McLaughlin	Boston University
29.	1959	Max W. Wilson	Free University Berlin
30.	1960	Francis Ashe Thomas	Indiana University
31.	1961	Berkley Eddins	University of Michigan
32.	1965	Joyce Mitchell Cook	Yale University
33.	1969	William R. Jones	Brown University
34.	1971	Bernard Boxill	University of California-Los Angeles
35.	1971	Jesse McDade	Boston University
36.	1972	Roy Dennis Morrison II	University of Chicago

Table 4 Continued

	Year	Name	Doctoral Institution
37.	1972	Lucius Outlaw Jr.	Boston College
38.	1974	Leonard Harris	Cornell University
39.	1975	Ernest D. Mason	Emory University
40.	1975	Albert Gene Mosley	University of Wisconsin
41.	1975	La Verne Maria Shelton (Leeb)	University of Minnesota
42.	1975	Robert C. Williams	Columbia University
43.	1976	Charles A. Frye	University of Pittsburgh
44.	1976	George Robert Garrison	State University of New York-Buffalo
45.	1976	John Orville Hopkins	Columbia University
46.	1976	William Horton	State University of New York-Buffalo
47.	1976	Laurence Thomas	University of Pittsburgh
48.	1976	Rudolph V. Vanterpool	Southern Illinois University
49.	1978	Howard McGary	University of Minnesota
50.	1978	Lorenzo Simpson	Yale University
51.	1978	Johnny Washington	Stanford University
52.	1979	Anita L. Allen	University of Michigan
53.	1979	Blanche Radford-Curry	Brown University
54.	1979	Joseph Tolliver	The Ohio State University
55.	1980	Jorge L. A. Garcia	Yale University
56.	1980	Cornel West	Princeton University
57.	1981	Ramona Hoage Edelin	Boston University
58.	1981	Eric Allen Hill	University of Minnesota
59.	1981	Frank M. Kirkland	New School for Social Research
60.	1981	Bill E. Lawson	University of North Carolina-Chapel Hill
61.	1981	Adrian Margaret Smith Piper	Harvard University
62.	1981	James Henry Walker Jr.	Boston College
63.	1982	Tommy L. Lott	University of California-Los Angeles
64.	1982	Maurice Lemont Wade	Stanford University
65.	1983	Stanley Myers Browne	University of Ottawa (Canada)
66.	1984	Robert E. Birt	Vanderbilt University
67.	1984	Kenneth Allen Taylor	University of Chicago
68.	1985	Michael Hardimon	University of Chicago
69.	1985	Adrian Anthony McFarlane	Drew University
70.	1985	Charles Wade Mills	University of Toronto

(Continued)

Table 4 Continued

	Year	Name	Doctoral Institution
71.	1985	Georgette Sinckler	Cornell University
72.	1986	Felmon Davis	Princeton University
73.	1986	Michele Marcia Moody-Adams	Harvard University
74.	1986	Reginald Osburn Savage	University of Wisconsin-Madison
75.	1987	J. Everet Green	Drew University
76.	1987	Joy James	Fordham University
77.	1988	Charles R. Johnson	State University of New York at Stony Brook
78.	1988	Thomas Freeman Slaughter Jr.	State University of New York at Stony Brook
79.	1989	John Peter Pittman	City University of New York
80.	1990	Bobby R. Dixon	Indiana University-Bloomington
81.	1992	Harvey Jerome Cormier	Harvard University
82.	1993	Lewis R. Gordon	Yale University
83.	1994	Janine Jones	University of California-Los Angeles
84.	1994	Barbara Massey McKenney	The American University
85.	1994	Stephen Lester Thompson	City University of New York
86.	1994	Melvin Tuggle	Southern Illinois University at Carbondale
87.	1995	Renee Afanana Hill	University of Virginia
88.	1995	Jacqueline Renee Scott	Stanford University
89.	1996	Arnold Lorenzo Farr	University of Kentucky
90.	1997	Deseia Y. Cavers-Huff	University of California-Riverside
91.	1997	Delia Graff Fara	Massachusetts Institute of Technology
92.	1997	A. Todd Franklin	Stanford University
93.	1997	Barbara J. Hall	University of Arizona
94.	1997	Darrell Moore	Northwestern University
95.	1997	Roosevelt Porter III	Cornell University
96.	1997	Rodney C. Roberts	University of Wisconsin-Madison
97.	1997	Paul C. Taylor	Rutgers University
98.	1998	Jason Damaian Hill	Purdue University
99.	1998	Kevin T. Miles	DePaul University
100.	1998	Tommie Shelby	University of Pittsburgh
101.	1999	John H. McClendon III	University of Kansas
102.	1999	Lionel K. McPherson	Harvard University
103.	1999	Darryl Lamar Scriven	Purdue University
104.	1999	Ronald Robles Sundstrom	University of Minnesota

Table 5 African American philosophers, doctoral institution, and dissertation title

Year	Name	Doctoral Institution	Dissertation
1887	John Wesley Edward Bowen	Boston University	The Historic Manifestation and Apprehensions of Religion as an Evolutionary and Psychological Process
1896	Lewis Baxter Moore	University of Pennsylvania	The Stage in Sophocles' Plays
1903	Thomas Nelson Baker	Yale University	Ethical Significance of the Connection Between Mind and Body
1909	Gilbert Haven Jones	University of Jena	Lotze and Bowne Eline Vergeichuung Ihren Philosophsehen Arbeit (Lotze and Bowne: A Comparison of Their Philosophical Work)
1918	James Leonard M. Farmer Sr.	Boston University	The Origin and Development of the Messianic Hope in Israel with Special Reference to Analogous Beliefs Among Other Peoples
1918	Alain Leroy Locke	Harvard University	The Problems of Classification in Theory Of Value
1921	Willis Jefferson King	Boston University	The Book of Habakkuk from the Standpoint of Literary and Historical Criticism
1933	Albert Millard Dunham	University of Chicago	The Concept of Tension in Philosophy
1933	Marquis Lafayette Harris	Ohio State University	Some Conceptions of God in the Gifford Lectures during the Period 1927-1929
1936	William Thomas Valeria Fontaine	University of Pennsylvania	Concept of Fortune in Boethius and Giordana Bruno
1938	Charles Leander Hill	Ohio State University	An Exposition and Critical Estimate of the Philosophy of Philip Melanchthon
1938	Marc Marion Moreland	University of Toronto	The Theory and Problem of Liberty in New England, 1636-1700
1938	Forest Oran Wiggins	University of Wisconsin	The Moral Consequences of Individualism
1941	Cornelius Golightly	University of Michigan	Thought and Language in Whitehead's Categorial Scheme

(Continued)

Table 5 Continued

Year	Name	Doctoral Institution	Dissertation
1941	John Milton Smith	University of Iowa	A Comparison of Plato's and Dewey's Educational Philosophies
1942	Eugene Clay Holmes	Columbia University	Social Philosophy and the Social Mind: A Study of the Genetic Methods of J. M. Baldwin, George Herbert Meade and J. E. Boodin
1942	Richard I. McKinney	Yale University	Religion in Higher Education Among Negroes
1943	Francis M. Hammond	University of Laval (Canada)	La Conception Psychologique De La Societe Selon Gabriel Tarde
1946	George D. Kelsey	Yale University	The Social Thought of Contemporary Southern Baptists
1947	William A. Banner	Harvard University	Natural Law and Human Rights: A Critical Exegesis of a Theory of Just Law
1947	Everett F. S. Davies	Columbia University	A Plan for Increasing the Effectiveness of Religion in Virginia State College, Petersburg, Virginia
1947	Winston K. McAllister	University of Michigan	The Compatibility of Psychological Hedonism and Utilitarianism
1948	Thomas F. Freeman	University of Chicago	A Study in the Criteria of Effective Preaching through an Analysis of the Preaching of Phillips Brooks
1950	Winson R. Coleman	University of Chicago	Knowledge and Freedom in the Political Philosophies of Plato and Aristotle
1951	Carlton L. Lee	University of Chicago	Patterns of Leadership in Race Relations: A Study of Leadership among American Negros
1952	Broadus Butler	University of Michigan	A Pragmatic Study of Language and Valuation
1958	Wayman Bernard McLaughlin	Boston University	The Relation Between Hegel and Kierkegaard
1959	Max William Wilson	Free University Berlin	Ueber das Kriterium der Verifizierbarkeit und den Begriff des empirischen Beweises unter Berücksichtigung des logischen Positivismus (On the criterion of verifiability and the concept of empirical proof taking into account logical positivism)

Year	Name	University	Title
1960	Francis Ashe Thomas	Indiana University	Philosophies of Audio Visual Education as Conceived by University Centers and by Selected Leaders
1961	Berkley Eddins	University of Michigan	The Role of Value-Judgments in the Philosophies of History of Oswald Spengler and Arnold J. Toynbee
1965	Joyce Mitchell Cook	Yale University	A Critical Examination of Stephen C. Peppers's Theory of Value
1969	William R. Jones	Brown University	Sartre's Philosophical Anthropology in Relation to His Ethics: A Criticism of Selected Critics
1971	Bernard Boxill	University of California-Los Angeles	A Philosophical Examination of Black Protest Thought
1971	Jesse McDade	Boston University	Franz Fanon: The Ethical Justification of Revolution
1972	Roy D. Morrison	University of Chicago	Ontology and Naturalism in the Philosophies of John Herman Randall, Jr., and Paul Tillich
1972	Lucius Outlaw	Boston College	Language and the Transformation of Consciousness: Foundations for a Hermeneutic of Black Culture
1974	Leonard Harris	Cornell University	Racism and the Materialist Anthropology of Karl Marx
1975	Ernest D. Mason	Emory University	Alain Locke's Philosophy of Value: An Introduction
1975	Albert G. Mosley	University of Wisconsin	Perspectives on the Kuhn-Popper Debate—New Directions in Epistemology
1975	La Verne Maria Shelton (Leeb)	University of Minnesota	The Coherence and Historical Pictures of Reference on the Nature of Reference
1975	Robert C. Williams	Columbia University	A Study of Religious Language: Analysis/Interpretation of Selected Afro-American Spirituals, with Reference to Black Religious Philosophy
1976	Charles A. Frye	University of Pittsburgh	The Impact of Black Studies on the Curricula of Three Universities
1976	George Robert Garrison	State University of New York-Buffalo	A Critical Appraisal of William James's Moral and Social Philosophy

(Continued)

Table 5 Continued

Year	Name	Doctoral Institution	Dissertation
1976	John Orville Hopkins	Columbia University	The Social Ethics of Jacques Maritain and Justification of Afro-American Education
1976	William Horton	State University of New York-Buffalo	The Social Philosophy of Marcus Garvey
1976	Laurence Thomas	University of Pittsburgh	Self-Respect and Morality
1976	Rudolph V. Vanterpool	Southern Illinois University	The Social Phenomenon of Sympathy: A Study in Hume's Ethics
1978	Howard McGary	University of Minnesota	Justice and Reparation
1978	Lorenzo Simpson	Yale University	Technology and Temporality: A Critique of Instrumental Rationality
1978	Johnny Washington	Stanford University	Hannah Arendt's Conception of the Political Realm
1979	Anita L. Allen	University of Michigan	Rights, Children, and Education
1979	Blanche Radford-Curry	Brown University	An Unconventional Theory of Progress
1979	Joseph Tolliver	The Ohio State University	Reasons, Perception, and Information: An Outline of an Information-Theoretic Epistemology
1980	Jorge L. A. Garcia	Yale University	Values, Attitudes, and Absolutes in Moral Philosophy
1980	Cornel West	Princeton University	Ethics, Historicism and the Marxist Tradition
1981	Ramona Hoage Edelin	Boston University	The Philosophical Foundations and Implications of William Edward Burghardt Du Bois' Social Ethic
1981	Eric Allen Hill	University of Minnesota	An Investigation of the Problem of the Unity of the Self
1981	Frank M. Kirkland	New School for Social Research	The Bounds of Phenomenology: An Essay on Husserl and Hegel

1981	Bill E. Lawson	University of North Carolina-Chapel Hill	Political Obligations and Oppressed Minorities
1981	Adrian Margaret Smith Piper	Harvard University	A New Model of Rationality
1981	James Henry Walker Jr.	Boston College	The Perception Contrast of the Socratic Theory of Recollection with the Ideas of Husserl's Phenomenology: A Historical Interpretation
1982	Tommy L. Lott	University of California-Los Angeles	Anscombe's Notion of Knowledge without Observation
1982	Maurice Lemont Wade	Stanford University	Passion And Volition in Hume's "Treatise"
1983	Stanley Myers Browne	University of Ottawa (Canada)	The Trustworthiness of Memory
1984	Robert E. Birt	Vanderbilt University	Alienation in the Later Philosophy of Jean-Paul Sartre
1984	Kenneth Allen Taylor	University of Chicago	Direct Reference and the Theory of Meaning
1985	Michael Hardimon	University of Chicago	Individual Morality and Rational Social Life: A Study of Hegel's Ethics
1985	Adrian Anthony McFarlane	Drew University	Toward a Grammar of Fear: A Phenomenological Analysis of the Experience and the Interpretation of Fear as a Propaedeutic to the Study of the Problem of Evil
1985	Charles Wade Mills	University of Toronto	The Concept of Ideology in the Thought of Marx and Engels
1985	Georgette Sinckler	Cornell University	Medieval Theories of Composition and Division
1986	Felmon Davis	Princeton University	Juergen Habermas and the Thesis of Unavoidability
1986	Michele Marcia Moody-Adams	Harvard University	Moral Philosophy Naturalized: Morality and Mitigated Scepticism in Hume
1986	Reginald Osburn Savage	University of Wisconsin-Madison	Law, World and Contingency in the Philosophy of Leibniz

(Continued)

Table 5 Continued

Year	Name	Doctoral Institution	Dissertation
1987	J. Everet Green	Drew University	Kant's Copernican Revolution: The Transcendental Horizon
1987	Joy James	Fordham University	Hannah Arendt's Theory of Power As Communication: A Feminist Critique
1988	Charles R. Johnson	State University of New York-Stony Brook	Being and Race: Black Writing Since 1970
1988	Thomas Freeman Slaughter Jr.	State University of New York-Stony Brook	Toward Preserving the Meaning of the Term "White Masks" in the Title of Frantz Fanon's "Black Skin, White Masks"
1989	John Peter Pittman	City University of New York	Marx's "Capital" and Ethical Theory: A Critique of Fetishism in Bentham and Kant
1990	Bobby R. Dixon	Indiana University-Bloomington	The Master-Slave Dialectic in the Writings of Ralph Ellison: Toward a Neo-Hegelian Synthesis
1992	Harvey Jerome Cormier	Harvard University	William James's Re-conception of Truth
1993	Lewis R. Gordon	Yale University	Bad Faith and Antiblack Racism: A Study in the Philosophy of Jean-Paul Sartre
1994	Janine Jones	University of California-Los Angeles	An Actuality-Oriented Picture of the Notion What Could Turn Out
1994	Barbara Massey McKenney	The American University	Truth and the Social Construction of Knowledge: Logical Fallacies in the Affirmative Action Debate
1994	Stephen Lester Thompson	City University of New York	Meaning and Social Facts: Interpretation in the Black Speech Community
1994	Melvin Tuggle	Southern Illinois University at Carbondale	The Evolution of John Dewey's Conception of Philosophy and His Notion of Truth
1995	Renee Afanana Hill	University of Virginia	Compensatory Justice: A Rawlsian Perspective
1995	Jacqueline Renee Scott	Stanford University	Friedrich Nietzsche's Socrates and the Problem of Decadence

Year	Name	University	Title
1996	Arnold L. Farr	University of Kentucky	*The Problem of the Unity of Theoretical and Practical Reason in Kant's Critical Philosophy and Fichte's Early Wissenschaftslehre, and its Relevance to the contemporary "Rage Against Reason"*
1997	Daseia Yvonne Cavers-Huff	University of California-Riverside	*Cognitive Science and Metaphysics Revisited: Toward a Theory of Properties*
1997	Delia Ruby Graff Fara	Massachusetts Institute of Technology	*The Phenomena of Vagueness*
1997	A. Todd Franklin	Stanford University	*Nietzsche's Perspectivism: A Thesis on Subjectivity*
1997	Barbara Jean Hall	University of Arizona	*On reproduction: Rights, Responsibilities and Males*
1997	Darrell Moore	Northwestern University	*Epidermal Capital: Formations of (Black) Subjectivity in Political Philosophy and Culture*
1997	Roosevelt Porter III	Cornell University	*Music and Metaphysics*
1997	Rodney C. Roberts	University of Wisconsin-Madison	*Rectificatory Justice and Social Groups*
1997	Paul C. Taylor	Rutgers University	*Reconstructing Aesthetics: John Dewey, Expression Theory, and Cultural Criticism*
1998	Jason Damaian Hill	Purdue University	*Creating the Self: Toward a Cosmopolitan Identity*
1998	Kevin T. Miles	DePaul University	
1998	Tommie Shelby	University of Pittsburgh	*Marxism and the Critique of Moral Ideology*
1999	John H. McClendon III	University of Kansas	*Consciencism: The Philosophy Of Nkrumaism*
1999	Lionel Kenneth McPherson	Harvard University	*Special Concern and the Reach of Moral Principle*
1999	Darryl Lamar Scriven	Purdue University	*Theodicy and Resistance: Liberation Trajectories in American philosophy*
1999	Ronald Robles Sundstrom	University of Minnesota	*Rending the Veil: A Critical Look at the Ontology and Conservation of "Race"*

In view of the polemical conditions, surrounding African American philosophical investigation, it continues as highly unlikely that the dominant philosophical establishment would be so inclined in granting approval or respect. The specter of academic racism is part and parcel of this intellectual community. It follows that Black philosophers were not afforded respect and that the quality of their work was not the measure for such judgments. Frazier's verdict—regarding the respect afforded to African American philosophers—is considerably misplaced.

African American philosopher Broadus Butler critically responds to Frazier's verdict:

> Almost all contemporary professional philosophers generally have abdicated their responsibility to profound moral and ethical issues in their theoretical pursuit of the image of the physical sciences and the emulation of the technological model of mathematics. The Negro philosopher, by contrast, who begins as philosopher or theologian like Dr. Martin Luther King and Rev. Fred Shuttlesworth find that he must release his creative genius as a Socratic gadfly to pepper the conscience of a nation with practical demonstrations of how this nation must grow in the difficult learning of abstract and absolute truth. But in this role, he is neither conceived to be nor accorded the title of philosopher—even as Socrates with not a claim philosopher by his contemporaries.[44]

However, Frazier's criteria on legitimate philosophizing has considerable value. This recommendation effectively serves in launching explicit tasks for African American philosophers. Without question "the nature of human knowledge and the meanings or lack of meaning of human existence . . . [in juxtaposition] to the standpoint of the Negro's unique experience in the world" concretely denotes the most crucial task of African American philosophy. A task ably met in the restrictive environment of Jim and Jane Crow and its continuing legacy of institutional racism.

In conclusion, we submit that Drs. Cook, Jones, and Williams would agree with our view that African American philosophy is foremost—a philosophy of particularity. Indisputably, it is exactly the content residing in this historic form—*African American* philosophy. In fact, we have more than adequately demonstrated that it must serve as the crowning foundation—the very rich content—on which future inquiry can discover and embrace as its sustenance. As for our esteemed panel of interlocutors, what they apparently missed was that Black philosophy has a strong anchor in history, with substantial metaphilosophical justification. We submit that the intricate (dialectical) connection of metaphilosophy with the history of philosophy critically remains as the key factor grounding our conclusion.

Notes

1. Annette Imhausen, *Mathematics in Ancient Egypt: A Contextual History* (Princeton: Princeton University, 2016); André Vanden Broeck, *Philosophical Geometry* (New York: Harper & Row, 1987); Beatrice Lumpkin, "Africa in the Mainstream of Mathematics," *Journal of African Civilizations* 2 (1–2) (1982), 101–17; Beatrice Lumpkin, "The Egyptian and Pythagorean Triples," *Historia Mathematics* 7(2) (1980), 68–77; Marshall Claggett, *Ancient Egyptian Science* (Philadelphia: American Philosophical Society, 1989); and Patricia F. O'Grady, *Thales of Miletus: The Beginnings of Western Science and Philosophy* (New York: Routledge, 2016). Although, rather thorough treatment of Thales, we note that this text has Eurocentric bias and views Egyptian mathematics with a despairing eye. A better source for grasping the Egyptian contribution, George Gheverghese Joseph, *The Crest of the Peacock: Non-European Roots of Mathematics* (Princeton: Princeton University, 2011) and the previously cited Imhausen text.
2. Robert T. Browne, *The Mystery of Space* (New York: E. P. Dutton & Co., 1919); William T. Fontaine, "Philosophical Implications of the Biology of Dr. Ernest E. Just," *The Journal of Negro History* 24 (July 1939), 281–90; Charles A. Frye, "Einstein and African Religion and Philosophy: The Hermetic Parallel," in *Einstein and the Humanities*, ed. Dennis P. Ryan (New York: Greenwood Press, 1987); Roy D. Morrison II, "Albert Einstein: The Methodological Unity Underlying Science and Religion," *Zygon* 14(3) (September 1979), 255–66; Eugene C. Holmes, "The Main Philosophical Considerations of Space and Time," *American Journal of Physics* 18(59) (December 1950), 560–70.
3. For works on ancient African philosophy read, Henry Olela, *From Ancient Africa to Ancient Greece: An Introduction to the History of Philosophy* (Atlanta: The Select Publishing Corporation, 1981). Théophile Obenga, *African Philosophy during the Period of the Pharaohs, 2800–330 B.C.* (London: Karnak House, 2000). James P. Allen, *Genesis in Egypt: The Philosophy of Ancient Egyptian Creation Accounts* (New Haven: Yale University, 1988).
4. Read, J. R. Van Pelt, "John Wesley Edward Bowen," *The Journal of Negro History* 19(2) (April 1934), 217–22. For Bowen as a philosopher of personalism, consult, Rufus Burrow Jr., "The Personalism of John

Wesley Edward Bowen," *The Journal of Negro History* 82(2) (Spring 1997), 244–56; and Brian Gann, "John Wesley Edward Bowen," in *BlackPast.org Remembered & Reclaimed* (1855–1933), http://www.blackpast.org/aah/bowen-john-wesley-edward-1855-1933

5. J. W. E. Bowen, "A Psychological Principle of Revelation," *The Methodist Review* 7(5) (September 1891), 727.

6. D. J. Jordan, "The Philosophy of Progress," *The A.M.E. Church Review* 10(1) (July 1893), 119.

7. Eugene C. Holmes, "The Main Philosophical Considerations of Space and Time," *American Journal of Physics* 18(59) (December 1950), 564. Consult, John H. McClendon, "Eugene C. Holmes: A Commentary on a Black Marxist Philosopher," in *Philosophy Born of Struggle.*, ed. Leonard Harris (Dubuque: Kendall/Hunt Publishing Company, 1983), 37–50.

8. Holmes, "The Main Philosophical Considerations of Space and Time," 564–65.

9. Thomas Nelson Baker, *The Ethical Significance of the Connection between Mind and Body* (Doctoral Dissertation, Yale University, 1903), 3–4.

10. James B. Carter, "Wanted-An Idea," *The A. M. E. Church Review* 15(3) (January 1899), 734.

11. Samuel W. Williams, "A. U. Summer School Convocation, July 27, 1954 – Clark College Auditorium," Consult, Box 12, Folder 12, the Samuel W. Williams Collection, Robert W. Woodruff Library, Atlanta University Center, Archives/Special Collections.

12. Wilfred Sellars, *Science, Perception and Reality* (Atascadero: Ridgeview Publishing Company, 1991), 3.

13. Roy D. Morrison II, "Christian Culture and South Africa: Racism, Philosophy and Theology," *The A.M.E. Zion Quarterly Review* 98(1) (April 1986), 5.

14. For works on value conflicts by African American philosophers consult, Alain Locke, "Cultural Relativism and Ideological Peace," in *The Philosophy of Alain Locke: Harlem Renaissance and Beyond*, ed. Leonard Harris (Philadelphia: Temple, 2010), 67–78. Cornelius L. Golightly, "Race, Values, and Guilt" *Social Forces* 26(2) (December 1947), 125–39 and William T. Fontaine, "The Means End Relation and Its Significance for Cross-Cultural Ethical Agreement," *Philosophy of Science* 25 (3) (July 1958), 157–62.

15. Richard T. Greener, "The White Problem," *Lend A Hand: A Record of Progress* 12 (May 1, 1894), 354.

16. Harvard Phi Beta Kappa, Locke also chaired the Howard University philosophy department. For the most recent and extensive biography on Locke read, Jeffrey C. Stewart, *The New Negro: The Life of Alain Locke* (New York: Oxford University Press, 2018).

17. Babacar Camara, "The Falsity of Hegel's Theses on Africa," *Journal of Black Studies* 36(1) (September 2005), 82–96; Olufemi Taiwo, "Exorcising Hegel's Ghost: Africa's Challenge to Philosophy," *African Studies Quarterly* 1(4) (1998), 3–16; and Shannon Mussett, "On the Threshold of History: The Role of Nature and Africa in Hegel's Philosophy," *APA Newsletter on Philosophy and the Black Experience* 3(1) (2003), 39–46. African American philosopher Wayman Bernard McLaughlin's PhD dissertation in philosophy addresses, *The Relation between Hegel and Kierkegaard* (Doctoral Dissertation, Boston University, 1958).

18. Alain Locke, "Values and Imperatives," in *American Philosophy, Today and Tomorrow*, ed. Sidney Hook and Horace M. Kallen (New York: Lee Furman, 1935), 313.

19. Henry T. Johnson, "Philosophy Religiously Valued," *The A.M.E. Church Review* 7(4) (April 1891), 422.

20. Johnson, "Philosophy Religiously Valued."

21. On Augustine's African background read, "Augustine the African," which is chapter 8 in David E. Wilhite, *Ancient African Christianity: An Introduction to a Unique Context and Tradition* (New York: Routledge, 2017). Also read, Luciano Mattei, *Augustine, The Last African Christian Philosopher* (Nairobi: Catholic University of Eastern Africa Press, 1999).

22. Rufus L. Perry, *Sketch of Philosophical Systems* (Privately Printed, 1918?), 1.

23. Kwame Nkrumah, *Consciencism: Philosophy and Ideology for Decolonization* (New York: Monthly Review Press, 2009), 6.

24. Kwame Nkrumah, *Consciencism: Philosophy and Ideology for Decolonization* (New York: Monthly Review Press, 2009), 21–22. John H. McClendon III, "Notes on *Consciencism*: The Epistemological Break and the Notion of Nkrumaism," in *Disentangling Consciencism: Essays on Kwame Nkrumah's Philosophy*, ed. Martin Odei Ajei (Lanham, MD: Lexington Books, 2017), 157–84. Also consult, Stephen C. Ferguson II, "Categorial Conversion in Nkrumah's Consciencism," in *Disentangling Consciencism: Essays on Kwame Nkrumah's Philosophy*, ed. Martin Odei Ajei (Lanham, MD: Lexington Books, 2017), 115–36.

25. Rufus L. Perry, *Sketch of Philosophical Systems* (Privately Printed, 1918?), 1.

26. C. V. Roman, "Philosophical Musings in the By-Paths of Ethnology," *African Methodist Episcopal Church Review* 28(1) (July 1911), 450.

27. C. V. Roman, "Right Thinking the Chief Factor in the Advancement of a Race," *The A. M. E. Church Review* 28(2) (October 1911), 570.

28. Ed Hinshaw, Joyce M. Cook, William R. Jones, and Robert C. Williams, *The Black Philosopher* (Racine, Wisconsin: The Johnson Foundation, 1976). This is a sound recording of the historic exchange. The recording can be found in both the Michigan State University Libraries and the Schomburg Research Center.

29. For a parallel development in African philosophy, see Paulin J. Hountondji, *African Philosophy: Myth and Reality* (Bloomington, IN: Indiana University Press, 1983). See also, Tsenay Serequeberhan, *African Philosophy: The Essential Readings* (New York: Paragon House, 1991).

30. William R. Jones, "The Legitimacy and Necessity of Black Philosophy: Some Preliminary Considerations," *The Philosophical Forum* 9(2–3) (Winter–Spring 1977–78), 149.

31. Jones, "The Legitimacy and Necessity of Black Philosophy," 149.

32. See Paulin Hountondji, "The Particular and the Universal," in *African Philosophy: Selected Readings*, ed. Albert Mosley (Inglewood Cliffs: Prentice Hall, 1995), 172–98; and Jay N. Van Hook, "Universalism and Particularism: African Philosophy or Philosophy of Africa?," *African Philosophy* 12(1) (March 1995), 11–19.

33. On the concept of ground, see Georg Wilhelm Friedrich Hegel, *The Encyclopaedia Logic: Part I of the Encyclopaedia of Philosophical Sciences with the Zusätze*, trans. Théodore F. Geraets, W. A. Suchting, and H. S. Harris (Indianapolis, Indiana: Hackett, 1991), 188–92, 329n9.

34. For a study of abstract universality as it relates to African American Studies see Robert Fikes, "The Persistent Allure of Universality: African American Authors of White Life Novels, 1845–1945," *The Western Journal of Black Studies* 21(4) (Winter 1997), 225–31.

35. For a recent instance of abstract universality in Black popular culture, see Raven Symoné's comments on Season 4, Episode 411 of *Oprah: Where Are They Now?*. This episode aired on October 5, 2014. Symoné stated, "I'm tired of being labeled. I'm an American. I'm not an African American; I'm an American." For a critique of abstract universality, see Langston Hughes, "The Negro Artist and the Racial Mountain," in *The Collected Works of Langston Hughes: Essays on Art, Race, Politics and World Affairs* (Columbia, Missouri: University of Missouri Press, 2002), 31–36.

36. An argument on behalf of the color blind thesis presented by an African American philosopher is Naomi Zack, *Race and Mixed Race* (Philadelphia: Temple University Press, 1993). For a critical appraisal of the color blind thesis read philosopher William A. Banner, "Guest Editorial: Thoughts on a Colorblind Society," *The Journal of Negro Education* 54(1) (Winter 1985), 1–2.

37. Jones, "The Legitimacy and Necessity of Black Philosophy," 152.

38. Ibid., 153.

39. John H. McClendon III, "Act Your Age and Not Your Color: Blackness as Material Conditions, Presumptive Context, and Social Category," in *White on White/Black on Black*, ed. George Yancy (Lanham, MD: Rowman & Littlefield, 2005), 284.

40. C. V. Roman, "Philosophical Musings in the By-Paths of Ethnology," *The A.M.E. Church Review* 28(1) (July 1911), 444.

41. Thomas Nelson Baker, "Ideals, Part 1," *Alexander's Magazine* (September 1906), 28.

42. E. Franklin Frazier, "The Failure of the Negro Intellectual," *Negro Digest* 11(4) (February 1962), 26–36.

43. Frazier, "The Failure of the Negro Intellectual," 31–32.

44. Consult, Broadus N. Butler, "In Defense of Negro Intellectuals," *Negro Digest* 11(10) (August 1962), 43. See Wolfgang Saxon, "Broadus Butler, 75, Ex-Tuskegee Airman and College Leader," *New York Times* (January 13, 1996). For a bibliography of his publications, read Leonard Harris, *Philosophy Born of Struggle* (Dubuque: Kendall/Hunt Publishing Co., 1983), 293–96.

3

The Search for Values:
Axiology in Ebony

Chapter Outline

We examine what African American philosophers have written about axiology, which includes value theory, moral philosophy and ethics as well as aesthetics. We provide a survey of philosophical problems that have emerged from the African American experience such as how do we determine the meaning of "Black is beautiful" and the significance of music in the African American experience. (59)

The *philosophy of value or axiology* remains today an important subfield of philosophy. Axiology involves the study of values and value judgments. By far, the most extensive treatment of any branch of philosophy by Black philosophers has been axiology. In this chapter, we will turn our attention to value theory in addition to aesthetics, moral philosophy or ethics, music, and the philosophy of literature. In the history of philosophy, the formal treatment of value—apart from its ethical and aesthetic forms—is comparably a recent development.[1] Contrastingly, the philosophical study of ethics and aesthetics has a rather long history, extending into antiquity.

Knowledge of value and value of knowledge

Axiology is closely tied to epistemology or the theory of knowledge. In the Western tradition, Socrates was first in claiming that virtue is knowledge, thereby giving ethical value a distinctively epistemological casting. From Socrates's viewpoint, knowledge was the vehicle for grasping virtue, that is, ethical values. Merely acting in accordance with conventional rules of moral conduct, Socrates asserted, lacked the needed justification for ethical actions. He was concerned with the question, how do we *know* if our conduct is virtuous?

From his perspective, tradition, custom, and convention were insufficient in providing the requisite answer. In short, the practical dimension of moral conduct cannot be removed from the philosophical justification of our ethical values. Herein lies the significance of Socrates's philosophical method, that is, persistent questioning of our basic presumptions and assumptions about ethical values. Socrates believed that our incessant queries ultimately lead to knowledge and attainment of the virtuous life. He argued that ignorance was the chief stumbling block to obtaining the virtues necessary to lead the good life. In conjunction, immoral actions resulted from the lack of knowledge. Therefore, Socrates expressly proclaimed that virtue is knowledge.

Plato, the aristocratic pupil of Socrates and his reactionary apologist, gave an ontological dimension to Socrates's epistemology. With Plato, ethical values are not only encapsulated within the Socratic epistemological framework; additionally, they, in fact, ontologically ground the empirical world we inhabit. Plato would designate such encapsulations as Forms or Ideas. Forms or Ideas successively develop from a distinctively self-contained reality. This ontological position is known as *objective idealism*. With objective idealism, Forms or Ideas exist independently without any need for human thinking or perception as their source.

In contrast, *subjective idealism* asserts that perceptual phenomena are dependent on the given perceiver and do not exist in any form as external realities. What we generally consider material objects are, in fact, no more than human/mind dependent phenomena. There are no objects that are "out there" in the world, standing apart from perceiving minds. To be perceived is to attain the status of real existence. Subjective idealism highlights that what is ultimately real are human minds and their attendant perceptions. Therefore, we can conclude that nothing outside of the human mind counts as actually belonging in the world.

Plato's idealism, however, contends that objective Forms/Ideas stand apart from the human mind. Effectively, the Forms or Ideas *objectively exist* within their own self-subsistent realm. One immediate outcome of this presumption is that the origin of the Forms emerges as an unresolved question. Logically, we discern the immediate consequence of Plato's assumption: the Forms are eternal and unchanging.

It follows that this particular ontological scheme also contains what transparently becomes Plato's *theory of change*. Therein Forms are changeless and permanent; yet within the empirical world, all entities correspondingly evolve into existence, transform, and remain constantly in motion. Change thus characterizes a different world than that which the Forms inhabit.

With our examination of values, it is key that Plato assumes that values are unchanging, immutable entities that must be grasped as they are, rather than subject to change to meet fluctuating circumstances and different social needs. What the reader must not overlook is that static values cannot support progressive social change. The social implications of Plato's value orientation, along with his theory of change, explicitly indicate his support for what are essentially reactionary political relations and conservative ideology.[2]

Furthermore, the problem of explaining why and how things change has attracted the attention of philosophers long before Plato. In Western philosophy, Heraclitus and Parmenides are perhaps the two key figures who most actively engage this topic. Parmenides argues that change is only *an appearance* or perceptual illusion. The fundamental reality behind the illusion is that nothing really changes. As Parmenides reasons, the notion of change implies becoming; herein, becoming entails both being and not-being. However, he argues, no entity can be both existent and nonexistent. Either it is or it is not.

In contrast, Heraclitus claims that the only thing permanent is change. All things are in constant flux. By its very nature, the world is in constant motion, change, and development, and this is reflected in the element of fire. Black philosopher Rufus Perry skillfully explains Heraclitus's philosophical conception of fire and how it permeates the notion of change:

> He [Heraclitus] taught that the end of wisdom was to discover the eternal ground principle of things, which is all-pervading and life-giving. This he

called "Fire,"—not what we call fire, but rather a vital energy, perpetually enkindling and extinguishing itself by an inherent, self-regulating principle. The phenomenal world came from this Primal Fire, and even the human soul and the Deity were but its more subtle flames.[3]

The point of contention between Parmenides and Heraclitus is the relation of being and becoming. In ontologically framing how permanence and change can both exist, Plato actually constructs two different worlds, resorting to *dualism*. This contrasts with *monism* that asserts there is only one reality. For monism, being and becoming need not stand as mutually exclusive and hence do not require two opposed realities.

The philosophical puzzle with this particular form of ontological dualism is to account for how two fundamentally different realities can meaningfully function in concrete relation with each other. If permanence belongs to another reality, what sense is there in referring to it in a world where it is absent?

As such, how can change or becoming remain intelligible in a reality where only immutability is possible? How can being and becoming be reconciled if they are mutually exclusive in real (ontological) terms? This problem of dualism is at the heart of Plato's ontology. For Plato, there are two realities—one of being/permanence and another of becoming/change. In what manner does Plato address our previous inquiries? African American philosopher John Milton Smith offers the following insight:

> The character of the world as Plato conceived it was a world divided into two parts, namely, the world of reality and the world of appearance, or in other words, the world of being and the world of becoming. The characteristic traits of the world of being were the eternal, immutable, and unchanging Forms, while the distinctive marks of the world of becoming, were the temporal, divisible, and changing particulars of everyday experience. Whatever degree of reality there was in the world of particulars was due to a certain "participation in" or "partaking of" the universal in the particular or the particular in the universal. Thus, the visible universe exhibits a degree of uniform and eternal law, and a degree of irregularity and change. . . . The value of sense experience as compared with reflective thinking was correspondingly diminished.[4]

Plato's notion of *the* Good occurs as the all-pervasive Form, which arises as the very source of reality. In this connection, the sensible "good things" of the perceptible (material) world continue as ontologically dependent on this chief Form—the Good. Knowing the Good is the path toward achieving goodness, the highest level of ethical life. Here we discover that Plato's attempt to resolve the puzzle of ontological dualism centers on the manner in which we apprehend the world of Forms. What connects the two realities is how we come to know the Forms. Yet, such knowledge cannot be gained by perception or through our common experience. Smith notes,

> For Plato, the ultimate reality was the Form of the Good. It was the cause of all other existences. Because of its subsistence outside of space and time, and because of its immateriality, it could not be apprehended by the senses, but insofar as it partook of the nature of thought, it could be apprehended by finite minds. The senses were confused ideas which had to be brought under subjection to the preexisting (a priori) knowledge of the Forms.[5]

The Form of the Good ontologically stands outside the material circumstances of everyday life. Therefore, the common people—the working masses—are removed from ever achieving the necessary understanding of this immaterial reality. Their station in life determines that they don't have the requisite capacity to apprehend the Good. African American philosopher Charles Leander Hill notes why Plato's conception of metaphilosophy historically points toward elitism:

> The patron saint of the Renaissance thus naturally became Plato. . . . There was a general emphasis on intellectual guidance. Philosophy came to be regarded as the quest for the good life under the guidance of wisdom and reason. This emphasis on intellectual guidance presupposed leisure. A starving man cannot be a philosopher. The intellectuals are elite.[6]

In Plato's world, each class has virtues peculiar and appropriate to it, but the most important point is that true virtue—the Good—is the specific virtue restricted to the few. For Plato, one did not acquire knowledge by empirical means or mere observation. It took reason—a highly developed mind (nous) that transcended the world of sense and ascended to the region of the Forms. Plato's epistemology is best described as *rationalism*, whereby reason supersedes experience as the foundation for knowledge. Concomitantly, Plato rejects "empiricism" because it establishes knowledge based on perceptual experience.

Attendant with obtaining knowledge of the Forms, Plato also locates the very basis for the notion of *freedom* in society in accordance with his ontology of Forms. Freedom was not, in Plato's estimation, a universal principle afforded to all of humanity. Since Plato's notion of comprehending the Good is restricted to a few, freedom, therefore, cannot be established as universal in principle, with respect to the various individuals existing in our material world. For Plato, the distribution of free will is an assignment that differentiates between how various individuals are constituted in terms of individual desire and the unique constitution of the soul. John Milton Smith perceptively states the following:

> In a world as Plato conceived it freedom of the will could hardly be other than transcendental. In The Laws, Plato relates in a myth how God assigned to human souls their respective places in the universe in a manner designed to insure victory of the good over evil: "But the formation of qualities (characters)," Plato says, "He left to the wills of the individuals. For everyone of us is made pretty much what he is by the bent of his desires and the nature of his soul."[7]

Given that "God assigned to human souls their respective places in the universe" in conjunction with individual free will, then it follows with God's help one chooses one's place in society. Those persons who are exploited, those in the most oppressive social conditions, are there by means of transcendental free will. This Platonist transcendental conception of freedom stands antithetical to African American notions of concrete (material) freedom, which we explored in our previous chapters.

Yet, the ideas of Plato and other Greek philosophers directly influenced many who were involved with framing the Declaration of Independence and the United States Constitution. The compatibility of bourgeois notions of freedom and democracy with African slavery, of course, could readily draw upon the principles of Athenian democracy in its immediate conjunction with slavery. Aristotle was quite adamant in his support of slavery, along with suggesting explicit gender restrictions upon the status of citizenship in the Greek city-state.[8]

Nevertheless, African American philosophers affixed a different value orientation to the import of free will and freedom. African American philosopher Angela Davis wisely notes,

> One of the striking paradoxes of the bourgeois ideological tradition resides in an enduring philosophical emphasis on the idea of freedom alongside an equally pervasive failure to acknowledge the denial of freedom to entire categories of real, social human beings. In ancient Greece, whose legacy of democracy inspired some of the great bourgeois centers, citizenship in the polis, the real exercise of freedom, was not accessible to the majority of people. Women were not allowed to be citizens and slavery was an uncontested institution. While the lofty

notions affirming human liberty were being formulated by those who penned the United States Constitution, Afro-Americans lived and labored in chains.

Davis continues her observations,

> The slave who grasps the real significance of freedom understands that it is not ultimately entail the ability to choose death over life as a slave, but rather the ability to strive towards the abolition of the master-slave relationship itself. . . . The slave is a human being whom another has absolutely denied the right to express his or her freedom. But is not freedom a property that belongs to the very essence of the human being? Either the slave is not a human being or else the very existence of the slave itself a contradiction. Of course, the prevailing racist ideology, which define people of African descent as sub-human, was simply a distortion within the realm of ideas based on real and systematic efforts to deny Black people their rightful status as human beings.[9]

With the great body of African Americans emerging from the horrendous experience of slavery and segregation, it follows that most African American philosophers envisioned a world of freedom based on a conception of democracy that included Black people as full participants in the process of political deliberation, that is, granted the right to vote and hold political office. In the aftermath of slavery, Black Reconstruction opened the door to new possibilities on all fronts, including politics, public life, social equality, and freedom of Black artistic expression.[10] Black philosopher Charles Leander Hill perceptively argues the following:

> The quintessence of democracy is the recognition of the moral equality of all human beings, of the equal rights of all human beings, as free and responsible agents, to the opportunity to be, become, and live as a traditional self. Justice has for its ideal end, the progressive discovery and recognition of the right of every normal human being to be treated as a rational self, as a free, self-determining individual. It is with Kant, to regard humanity, whether in oneself or in another, always as an end and never as a means to an end. Justice demands that society be a rational order or community of selves within a kingdom of ends.[11]

Black philosophers Howard McGary and Bill E. Lawson accurately point out that slave narratives as primary resources provide ample evidence of how African American slaves viewed "Freedom." This slave perspective on freedom is philosophically abundant with gems and offers insights into slaves as "moral agents." Obviously, this pivotal concept of moral agents is at the core of Charles Leander Hill's commentary on democracy. In their philosophical text, *Between Slavery and Freedom*, McGary and Lawson note the following:

> Given the brutality of slavery and the assault on the humanity of those held as slaves, it is remarkable that so many slaves were able to emerge from this brutal institution as moral agents. By moral agents, we mean persons who have a sense of right/wrong, good/bad, and who are able to evaluate from a moral point of view their own actions as well as the actions of others.[12]

Because the great majority of African Americans are members of the working class, their aspiration for freedom reflects this class viewpoint. Freedom arises as synonymous with the reaffirmation of African American humanity. For sharecroppers and tenant farmers newly freed from slavery, the clarion calls for "Freedom" were about substantially more than a release from bondage.[13] Ultimately, Plato limited freedom to a few, but Black Marxist philosopher C. L. R. James would argue that "Every Cook Can Govern."[14]

Clearly, the values expressed by the African American mass movement were not in accord with Plato's notion of freedom. Their quest for freedom demanded a qualitatively new social order with a corresponding philosophical perspective that could provide the needed insights for shaping a new future. The problem of values was pivotal in mapping out this new conception on Black life. The old values that sustained and maintained the social order of white supremacy had to be challenged and an alternative viewpoint affirmed.[15]

We have already observed that John Milton Smith presents valuable and critical insights on how Plato structures his ontology in concert with the limits on the attendant notion about freedom. Plato's *transcendental conception of freedom* is far from the conceptualization affixed to the historic quest of African Americans in their fight for freedom. The democratic impulse in the African American struggle for freedom, we will shortly observe, remains absent from Plato's conception of political life. The idea of democracy has no place in Plato's scheme of political relations. Indeed, it transpires as disruptive, specifically regarding the attainment of the Form of the Good or the establishment of ethical living in the Polis.

What value, then, does Plato provide those searching for values that sustain the ideals of freedom from exploitation and oppression? The answer is straightforward. The quest for an alternative value orientation does not mean that studying Plato and other Western philosophers should cease.

Instead, the critical review of the philosophical literature on values becomes absolutely mandatory. Critical examination is far distant from the mere rejection of what one does not agree with or finds repugnant. Philosophical inspection, with the highest level of acute judgment, is the most appropriate standpoint for formulating alternative solutions.

African American philosophers have critically inspected Plato's philosophy along with his notions about freedom. In Plato's view, we have observed, freedom is not something granted to all members of society. Another African American philosopher Winson R. Coleman aptly notes, "It is significant that freedom is introduced in the Republic as one of *the advantages of old age by a wealthy old man*."[16] For the leading role as philosopher, Plato thought that the best candidates were precisely wealthy old men. With wealth, age, and freedom come the capacity for the highest stage of knowledge, knowledge of the Form—the Good. Knowledge of the Good becomes possible because philosophers, with their cultivated minds, could ascend to this contemplative plane of thought, beyond the perceptible region of sensible particulars. Winson R. Coleman further elaborates on the matter of democracy from Plato's standpoint. The definitive impact of the principle of democratic liberty on the exercise of free speech vis-à-vis Plato's concept of political governance is based on the hegemonic rule of knowledge. Coleman states,

> All these things and more are said of democratic liberty, and it is only against the background of a liberty which is reduced to the rule of knowledge that democratic freedom, epitomized as doing and saying what one likes, could appear so utterly despicable, so unjust and so completely irredeemable as it appears to Plato in his description of the democratic state and the democratic man.[17]

Plato claimed that preservation of the Form in the practical world of the city-state could only be maintained if philosophers ruled society. The finest virtues for social life, those that promote the uppermost personal character, cannot be left to *democracy*, that is, rule by the popular masses, consent by the people. This is Plato's main thesis in the *Republic*.

Importantly, Plato's approach to values and knowledge transpires from a definitive class perspective, that is, the aristocracy. Plato's conception of value and knowledge via the notion of "The Good" transforms an adjective into a noun; a virtue becomes the ontological Form that is the solitary province of his ruling class. This class holds political hegemony by means of its superior knowledge of value. The social value of this hegemonic class is precisely its sovereign rule over the very knowledge of value, as retained within "The Good."

Despite his class perspective, Plato opens the door for a dialectical conceptualization of knowledge and value. Therefore, we ask, how are knowledge and value dialectically related? The conceptual reversal of the terms—"knowledge" and "value"—effectively unmasks the dialectical connection of opposite terms. On the one hand, there is *knowledge of value*, and on the other, the *value of knowledge*. The former is immediately rendered as the subject matter of axiology. This is Socrates's primary focus, although framed within the perspective of ethical discourse. The latter brings axiology within the orbit of epistemology. Does knowledge have any worth, and how do we measure the value of knowledge?

Today, it might be self-evident that knowledge is of considerable value. The conceptualization that knowledge has *value* as its essential underpinning transports an axiological mold onto the very pursuit of knowledge. For some philosophers, epistemology is, at root, established on axiological grounds. It follows, this core valuing of knowledge stamps the very process of philosophical inquiry.

The African American quest for establishing an alternative value orientation to white (anti-Black) racism becomes a compelling impulse for the founding of philosophical critique. How can a different set of values shape a qualitatively new orientation toward philosophical inquiry? In what way can this new philosophical orientation and transformation of values sustain the effort to create new prospects for a different conception of freedom?

Given the importance of values in the undertaking of philosophical inspection, it should come as no surprise that Black philosophers historically were attracted to axiology in all aspects. African American philosopher Joyce Mitchell Cook insightfully addresses two key questions. First, how do we measure the value of knowledge? And what significance does axiology offer for the appropriate conceptualization of philosophical analysis itself? Cook astutely observes the following:

> Philosophers continue to debate the primacy of questions of knowledge vs. primacy of questions of values. It seems to me that a strong case may be made for viewing the demand for being reasonable (i.e., producing good reasons for one's beliefs) *as a value* presupposed by the theory of knowledge. Hence, it appears to me that value questions are the basic questions of philosophy.[18] (Italics added)

Cook's thesis, "that value questions are the basic questions of philosophy," locates axiology at the center of philosophical analysis. It also undoubtedly points us in the direction of metaphilosophy. Philosophy in its most essential manner and make up concerns an inquiry based on value questions. While this thesis encompasses the theoretical dimension of metaphilosophy, it is not without crucial, practical results.

In Chapter 2, we explored how metaphilosophy is connected to the practical and theoretical tasks of African American philosophy. We submit that this cardinal principle about the pivotal nature of the value of knowledge extends beyond African American philosophy and concomitantly envelopes the field of African American history. Indeed, the locus of values—and its supplementary impact on knowledge—has significant practical implications on the mode of presentation regarding African American history.

In point of fact, the African American historian Dr. Carter G. Woodson founded "Negro History Week" and the *Negro History Bulletin* because he saw the value of scientific (empirical) knowledge in the popular struggle against racist ignorance and pseudoscientific racism. Woodson, the second African American to earn a PhD in history (from Harvard), accepted what is essentially the Socratic view, namely, if ignorance is what leads to racism, then racism is not something one would pursue or retain, if appropriately educated. In other words, no one is racist by virtue of an educated decision.[19]

Woodson firmly believes that all racist sentiments are expressions of the lack of knowledge. Hence, the accumulation and presentation of facts about the African American experience can substantially assist in overturning the ignorance that derives from systemic miseducation. Woodson adamantly believed that *systemic miseducation* was the basis for racist social relations and practices.[20]

In accord with Socratic thought, Woodson holds to philosophical idealism. From his standpoint, the chief task becomes one of altering social (racist) consciousness for the betterment of race relations. Consequently, this educational approach toward Black history serves as the primary means for transforming racist social relations. The virtue embodied in learning about Black contributions in history subsequently is an exploration of changing dominant value orientations. Misconceived notions about the Black past were the hotbed for the stirrings of racist opinions and correspondingly, racist behavior.

Such misconceptions were detrimental, not only by leading whites to embrace racism but also for leading Black people in turn to embrace negative thinking about themselves. "The Miseducation of the Negro" was one outcome of the racist distortion of the past. Lack of knowledge facilitated distorted value judgments. And systematic education offers the possibility for rectifying such distortions. Without the appropriate education about African American history, the Black person would remain embroiled in reproducing the very conditions that facilitated racist oppression.

In large part, Woodson posits, white supremacy depended on the circumstances of abject ignorance. Holding on to the right values and making the correct value judgments centered on knowledge of the Black past. Woodson explicitly adopted the Socratic conception of how values were intimately linked to knowledge. The value of knowing the facts about the Black past arises as priceless. In Woodson's estimation, knowledge of African American history is an invaluable—indeed the most powerful—weapon in the fight against racism.

On the question of values: The object of philosophical inquiry

The persistent fact that human beings are ubiquitously embroiled with matters about values provokes an ensemble of philosophical questions that appear to be timeless. For illustration, what are values? How do they originate? What precisely grounds values? Are values subjective or objective, particular or universal? How do we determine if values are relative or absolute?

Amid such interrogations, it should not be overlooked that the historical context and material circumstances for these perennial questions are clearly established. Our analysis starts from an examination of the course of human history and its adjoining material ecology. This material environment of human existence comprises being in nature and the emergent social conditions inseparably linked to natural existence. Humans are not only natural beings but also social beings that actively transform nature. What separates humans from other forms of animal life is that humans actively change their natural environment, while other animals merely adapt. Socialized labor—with its attendant social division—emerges as the chief aspect or catalyst of how humans effectively change their natural conditions.

This social conversion of nature is paradoxically an expression of human natural needs; human beings are innately social beings. In the effort to survive and flourish, the transformation of nature mandates the development of social relations, institutions, and practices. For instance, the social division of labor maximizes the collective energy utilized in altering the natural environment. In turn, values that highlight social organization and ethical principles that successively advance the idea of moral duty all assist in crystallizing the social basis of human life. The dominant ethical values concerning moral conduct are ostensibly in direct alignment with social cohesion.

Not only ethical values but all values (as such) command a measure of consciousness, that is, social awareness on the import of the existing social values. Consequently, social consciousness is linked to all forms of valuation, including material values, and thus, social relations require an attendant social awareness that values are the necessary feature of social life. This is at the crux of what we previously identified as *ontological ordering* and *ontological hierarchy*. At root, ontological ordering and ontological hierarchy are socially conscious means toward valuations of human life.

In sum, social existence is the basis for social consciousness, and this principle rests on the philosophical viewpoint of *dialectical materialism*. The materialist dimension consists of the fact that social existence specifically encompasses the material conditions of life. The dialectical aspect denotes that social consciousness is not only the product of socio-natural environment but also actively intervenes to change it. Social existence—the material conditions of life—establishes the objective basis for social consciousness and, thus, enhances our valuations that are congruent with social relations, institutions, and practices.

In contrast, *philosophical behaviorism* argues that consciousness or mind is no more than surrogate language for human behavior, wherein behavior is the resulting *conditioned reflex* to environmental influences. Behaviorism and its auxiliary notion of conditioned reflex effectively remove social consciousness from the equation on the complexity of social existence.[21] Subsequently, philosophical behaviorism is a form of *mechanistic materialism*, which, in effect, constrains the import of values in social life, that is, values as embodied social consciousness.

We submit that with *social existence* emerges *social consciousness*, and this consciousness embodies the prevailing values held within all social relations. Therefore, in accord with our dialectical materialist perspective, the human encounter with nature, that is, the transformation of nature, is not a matter of the instinctive response of adaptation or the behaviorist conditioned reflex, but rather is explicitly *conscious intervention*, which is *social* in character.

With active intervention into the natural environment, there simultaneously occurs the progressive development of social consciousness. The consolidation of social consciousness allows for group solidarity, with its associated forms of collective identity. Subsequently, the values that are attached to collective identity within the given group often assume the highest level amid the existing hierarchy of values.

Social dichotomous relations persisting between notions about "we" and "they" have a long history, which decidedly encompasses the broad range of human development. "We"—the family, tribe, ethnic community, polis, nation, country, race, civilization, and so on—are prevalent throughout the course of history. Designated social groupings are equivalent with human history. The idea of some stage of prehistory, where humans solitarily existed in nature, that is, prior to any forms of social organization, completely lacks scientific merit. Human existence is inherently social in character.

Concurrently, we need not resort to social contract theory as an explanatory device, which details how humans assumed the locus of social existence vis-à-vis nature. The employment of such hypothetical thinking in social/political philosophy amounts to no more than a commitment to sophisticated forms of mythological conjecture—what cultural anthropology terms "etiology." Etiology involves constructing origin myths as explanatory mechanisms that are properly surrogates for presumed nonexistent social facts. In Western philosophy, Thomas Hobbes, John Locke, Jean-Jacques Rousseau, and John Rawls are representatives of this contractarian tradition. Among contemporary Black philosophers, Charles Mills is the leading proponent of contractarianism.

To evade the ahistorical character of contractarianism from Hobbes to Rawls, Mills proposes the concrete history of "The Racial Contract." The purpose of "The Racial Contract" is to disclose how modern (Western) political (power) structures and relations (at the very inception of their formation) incorporated white supremacy as a definitive political system. Concurrently, his conceptual alternative includes a theoretical (philosophical) imperative, namely a reconsideration of contractarianism beyond the constraints of social contract theory to the submerged notion of "The Racial Contract." Against the hegemonic self-conception of modern Western philosophy, Mills argues that racism is pivotal and not merely marginal in the very development of the modern philosophical tradition of contractarianism.

Mills's "racially informed *Ideologiekritik*" of contractarianism is undermined by his acceptance of contractarianism as a heuristic method. While Mills admits that "no single act literally corresponds to the drawing up and signing of a [Racial] contract" by whites, he argues that there was a "set of formal or informal agreements or meta-agreements" which created the "Racial Contract." As Mills notes, "The general purpose of the Contract is always the differential privileging of the whites as a group with respect to the nonwhites as a group, the exploitation of their bodies, land and resources, and the denial of equal socioeconomic opportunities to them. All whites are *beneficiaries* of the Contract, though some whites are not *signatories* to it."[22]

The broader implication of Mills's position is the acceptance of liberal democratic capitalism with the aim of state regulation, but not the eradication of class contradictions. Mills—similar to John Rawls—accepts the inevitability of class inequalities, and both men acknowledge that class inequalities will continue to persist in a just democratic society. Mills claims that the reality is that "for a long time to come we're going to be stuck with capitalism and neoliberalism."[23] Ultimately, Mills's "Black radical liberalism" can't see beyond the horizon of liberal democratic capitalism.[24]

Nonetheless, philosophical speculation about the origins of social relations has generated numerous questions focused on the problem of values. However, whether the analytical focus is directed at social consensus or social conflict—as with Mills's idea of the "Racial Contract"—the substantive issue of values is removed from its material moorings. What is sorely absent from the contractarian tradition is a dialectical analysis on the relation between humans as natural beings and how their social makeup—social life—is bound by the irrepressible requirement of transforming nature. For in the process of this transformation, humans also transform themselves as social beings. This fact of history stands as a universal principle.

Consequently, seemingly timeless philosophical questions about values are, in fact, deeply rooted in basic natural conditions and social (production) relations. In the most concrete sense, human beings are crucially part of nature. We are natural beings with associated needs, a fact affirmed by several of the sciences including astrophysics, geology, chemistry, and biology.

Indeed, the idea that we are made of stardust is a common reference made by astrophysicists and cosmologists.[25] We are well aware that the elements that form the universe are so much a part of our existence that we need them in order to live. From the oxygen that we breathe to other (ingested) elements such as iron, calcium, and magnesium, among others, these elements are essential for life. For instance, Magnesium, a light weight metal naturally produced in stars, possesses both physiological and manufactural importance. Not only is magnesium utilized in producing alloys for use in aircraft, automobiles, and electronics, but it is also vital to a healthy human body.

The National Institutes of Health reports the following: "Magnesium is a cofactor in more than 300 enzyme systems that regulate diverse biochemical reactions in the body, including protein synthesis, muscle and nerve function, blood glucose control, and blood pressure regulation." It is additionally stated that magnesium deficiency can lead to "loss of appetite, nausea, vomiting, fatigue, and weakness. As magnesium deficiency worsens, numbness, tingling, muscle contractions and cramps, seizures, personality changes, abnormal heart rhythms, and coronary spasms can occur."[26] The same element that spreads throughout the galaxy by means of stellar explosions is found on earth, in our bodies and is integral to plant life and the development of photosynthesis.

In many ways, we are clearly a part, however small, of the expansive universe and subject to the same laws of physics and chemistry that govern its motion. Additionally, we are constituent with the various forms of life that have evolved in nature over billions of years. Geology, chemistry, and biology (among other sciences) provide ample evidence of this cardinal fact. Our vital link to nature is *ontologically foundational*, which is irrefutably confirmed by the specialized sciences.

Moreover, as natural beings in the quest of realizing our auxiliary needs, we apprehend such needs by social means. The rudimentary force leading to social relations and institutions, on which human culture is based, immediately develops from the collective (socially engaged) efforts at transforming nature. Natural needs invoke the production of *material values* associated with procurement of our objective (elementary) interests in survival. Put simply, the acquisition of food, clothing, and shelter are natural needs that emerge as objective, human interests. Along with the reproduction of the species, securing rudimentary material needs is most essential in maintaining our existence.

Hence, material needs, which are objective interests, found what we call *material values*. Of all value concerns, the quest to produce *material values* is the most basic for human existence. It reasonably follows that material values are objective in character. Moreover, all human beings come under the purview of material values, which are also universal.

Since material values are both objective and universal, we have answered the question of how values can persist as concurrently objective phenomena with universal entailment. In succession, we have made one step forward in defining what values are. Specifically, they are expressions of human interest, wherein such interest arises from human needs and has an objective character and universal scope.

African American philosopher William T. Fontaine demonstrates that while cultural differences—hence variation in value orientation—persist between innumerable social groupings, there remains a common basis for all humans based on objective and universal principles. Fontaine states,

> It is pointed out that all men have a similar body structure, that individuals of similar temperament are found in all cultures, that prolonged infancy requiring parental care develops common social sentiments, that certain wants and situations are common to men of every culture and that *pan-human needs are the bases of pan human universal values*. . . . The alleged qualitative uniqueness of the minds of persons of different cultures is declared untenable. It is familiar knowledge that the ethical principle of tolerance is particularly embarrassing to certain radical ethical relativists since they actually accord it cross-cultural status.[27] (Italics added)

Therefore, material values are both objective and universal and hence speak to the general character of social life. The fact remains that humans have forged multiple forms of social arrangements with variated cultural formations. Different groups of humanity, both socially and culturally diverse, expand throughout the earth. In concurrence, we discern that sociocultural differences are the substance behind the variance of value orientations that prevail among human groups. And since culture embodies the values of various social groups, cultural differences are an expression of differing value orientations.

One decisive factor accounting for this variation is how social relations of production are distinctively formed in the process of altering nature. Societies where communal ownership of the means of production is dominant give expression to values that are quite different from those values that consist with social relations based on private property via private ownership of the means of production. When the means of production—instruments of labor and the objects of labor—become private property, the owners of such property are in a social (class) position that affords them the capability to exploit those lacking such ownership.

For illustration, African American sharecroppers and tenant farmers in the post bellum period were subject to intense exploitation at the hands of white landowners, or what author Richard Wright refers to as the "Lords of the Land." Obviously, during slavery Black people did not own the means of production. They were actually part and parcel of it. The clash of values, which we earlier documented, is rooted in these conflicting social relations of production. What is good for the "Lords of Capital" is not necessarily good for the working class, any more than what was good for the Southern slaveholder was good for the African slaves.

Work Songs explicitly demonstrate how the objective interests of Black workers were given expression by means of the associated cultural values affixed to this art form.[28] Consequently, the philosophical question "Are aesthetic tastes subjective or objective?" must take into consideration how conflicting (objective) interests enter the picture. In other words, Work Songs are manifestly objective reflections of Black working class values while simultaneously they do not have universal entailment. *It should become evident that objective valuation is not identical with universal values.* Landowners' distaste for Work Songs is consistent with their objective interests. Consecutively, if given aesthetic values can be both particular and objective, then universality need not transpire as the indispensable condition for their founding.

At this interval, the difference between *material values*, which are objective and universal, and *aesthetic values*, which are objective yet particular, explicitly indicates that the answer to the question about the subjective/objective and particular/universal nature of values does not render a simple answer. Differences affixed to *kinds of values* are equally important in our deliberation toward formulating definitions. The complexity of value theory is manifestly subject to careful philosophical examination.

In Western philosophy, Kant is archetypal of the efforts in grounding aesthetic values on universal principles. Thomas Nelson Baker's critical response to Kant's project is most appropriate at this juncture:

It is when men began to know only the human race and ignore all race distinctions and characteristics that art became "an abstract generality of features, and empty charm devoid of character and significance." Kant's transcendental Aesthetic, like his transcendental Ethics, has no practical meaning for the actual life of mankind. There are people so interested in goodness in general that they never do any good thing in particular. Beauty and goodness always express themselves under some particular form and in some particular type. Each particular race on earth implies a race on the spiritual side. . . . Now to see that spiritual beauty of each particular type, each race must be religiously devoted to its own type.[29]

If Baker is correct about the particularity of aesthetic, and more importantly that race distinctions permeate aesthetics, it is therefore quite feasible that we consider affirmative answers to two key questions. Namely, we can answer yes to both: "Is there a distinctive Black perspective on aesthetics?" and "Does the African American artist have a role or duty to play in the advancement of Black liberation?" Baker is most transparent, and he is no less than in the vanguard of advocating for the idea of particularized artistic expression—namely, the Black Aesthetic.

What we have presented up to this moment is not an *a priori* answer to the concerns of aesthetic value, but rather it is our heuristic device for launching an investigation concerning the issue of aesthetic value. Appropriately, instead of closing our deliberations, this heuristic device generates a host of additional questions. For example, what criteria do we use to determine the aesthetic value of Adrian Piper's installation *Art for the Artworld Surface Pattern*, Ellis Wilson's *The Funeral Procession*, Lois Mailou Jones's *Les Fétiches*, Basquiat's *Charles the First*, or Kara Walker's *A Subtlety, or the Marvelous Sugar Baby*? Is it possible to determine if Richard Wright's *Native Son* is aesthetically better than Zora Neale Hurston's *Their Eyes Are Watching God*? Can we determine who is a better singer: Anita Baker, Phyllis Hyman, or Beyoncé Knowles? More broadly, we ask, how is beauty embodied in Black artistic creation, production, and performance?

Black is beautiful: A philosophical investigation of a beautiful problem

There is an ugly history between beauty and Blackness as historian Stephanie M. H. Camp has observed.[30] Let us briefly explore the oft-heard phrase, "Black is beautiful." In light of the sick and twisted history of racism in the United States and the world, how should we evaluate this statement? How does the word "is" function in this statement? From a philosophical perspective, the verb "to be" can have four different descriptive functions, namely, the functions of identity, predication, membership, and existence. Examining these four functions can expand our understanding of the relation between aesthetics and politics.

Spinoza's famous dictum, "all determination is negation," infers that any definition is a negation; to claim a thing "is" something is to simultaneously claim that it "is not" many other things. On the one hand, "Black is beautiful" can be construed as the negation of the assertion that Blackness is ugly. On the other hand, the affirmation of Black beauty ideals could be interpreted as the negation of corresponding white ideals. African American philosopher George D. Kelsey warns against the latter presumption. He states,

> When the claim, "black is beautiful" is made as an affirmation that blackness is an authentic color among the colors of human beings and not a burnt offering to the devil, this is a valuable item of psychological reorientation and education in a world of racist imperialism based on color. But when "black is beautiful" implies that "white is ugly," this is evidence that the old disease has simply been transplanted, for pseudo-species reappears under a color reversal.[31]

If Black and white are thought to be mutually exclusive categories respecting value—particularly in accord with racial designation—then we are confronted with what Kelsey terms as "color reversal." Where before white racism delegated "Black as ugly," now we have the reverse designation, "white as ugly." Kelsey's argument is that such reversal not only fails in initiating qualitative change but also crucially maintains the same core problem.

Perchance, the classic example of color reversal emerges with the political theology of Elijah Muhammad and the Nation of Islam. With its racialized (religious) mythology, the Nation of Islam rendered whites as devils and concurrently the source of evil in the world. If whites by nature are evil, then we have the value judgment that whiteness is inherently ugly.[32]

However, if "Black is beautiful" signifies that we have the negation of the presumption that Blackness is ugly, it follows that this position is in concert with Kelsey's notion that "blackness is an authentic color among the colors of human beings and not a burnt offering to the devil." In contradistinction, Thomas Jefferson made it clear, Black is identical with ugly:

> Whether the black of the negro resides in the reticular membrane between the skin and scarf-skin, or in the scarfskin itself; whether it proceeds from the colour of the blood, the colour of the bile, or from that of some other secretion, the difference is fixed in nature. . . . And is this difference of no importance? *Is it not the foundation of a greater or less share of beauty in the two races?* . . . Add to these, *flowing hair, a more elegant symmetry of form, their own*

judgment in favour of the whites, declared by their preference of them, as uniformly as is the preference of the Oran-ootan for the black women over those of his own species. *The circumstance of superior beauty*, is thought worthy attention in the propagation of our horses, dogs, and other domestic animals; *why not in that of man?*[33] (Italics added)

Consequently, the import of "Black is Beautiful" is explicitly that it represents an assault on the racist dehumanization of Black people. Now, how should we understand the function of "is" in this statement? Is it the "is" of identity, predication, membership, or existence? Since the turn of the twentieth century, philosophers of language have wrestled with "is" propositions. Now we venture into its relevance with regard to the philosophic meaning affixed to "Black is Beautiful." Perhaps this exploration can further assist in our response to Dr. Kelsey's notion of "color reversal."

The "is" of identity is used to assert that a designated item is one and the same entity as some item, as for example in "Muhammad Ali is Cassius Clay." Clearly, the names of Muhammad Ali and Cassius Clay point to the same individual. For those not familiar with Ali's biography, he changed his name from Cassius Clay upon entering the Nation of Islam. Rather than two separate entities, we have one person that embodies the attested nomenclatures at different periods in life. The "is" of identification marks the fact that different forms of nomenclature could readily speak to the same person or entity.

In contrast, the "is" of predication is used to attribute a characteristic or property to a thing, object or person as in "Muhammad Ali is Black." The statement, "Muhammad Ali is a Black person" obviously indicates he is not a white person; Ali is Black rather than white. Transparently, the word "Black" functions as racial descriptor of Muhammad Ali. In alignment with Spinoza's dictum, the very affirmation of Ali's Blackness is the negation of the possibility of his being white. It is important to note that the "is" of predication can effectively work along with the "is" of identification.

If we substitute "Cassius Clay" for "Muhammad Ali" it stands to reason that this person with the name "Cassius Clay" is Black. The "is" of *identification* also indicates that what is true for Muhammad Ali is equally true for Cassius Clay. Simply put, the *racial characteristic of Blackness* is equivalently suitable in each situation. However, we do know that there was another person with the name "Cassius Clay" that was white and not Black. Thus, the statement "Cassius Clay is Black" points to the specific individual that appropriately meets the criteria for such predication.[34]

With the "is" of existence, we are asserting the existence of a certain kind of thing. It remains true that "in 1968, Muhammad Ali was in Columbus, Ohio at the National CORE Convention." Indeed, one of the authors of this text met with him at that place and time. The "is" of existence implies being somewhere and at some time. Likewise, the statement "Muhammad Ali is no longer with us" indicates that today Ali is not present. There is no place or time in which we can now take a photograph with him or convey our gratitude for his magnanimous contributions in advancing Black pride or securing world peace.

However, we can view photographs when he existed and in turn be justified and truly believe that Ali was once an outstanding world figure. While his legacy is undoubtedly a major influence on the world, nevertheless, today he is nonexistent. We have a plethora of assorted documentation along with our memories to sustain us respecting a once existent person. In a nutshell, for something to be, that is, for a person or entity to exist, there is the conditional notion adjoined with being somewhere, at some time. Herein is the value of the "is" of existence.[35]

Furthermore, for the "is" of membership (or class inclusion), we have the proposition, "Muhammad Ali is a Boxing Hall of Famer." Clearly, with this statement, Ali is a member of the Boxing Hall of Fame. He is not identical with the Boxing Hall of Fame as we discerned with the statement, "Muhammad Ali is Cassius Clay." Rather, Ali remains included in the class of those persons that are members of the Boxing Hall of Fame. This exercise in outlining the philosophical complexity over the use of "is" in a proposition leads back to the statement, "Black is Beautiful."

With the proposition, "Black is Beautiful," if it is assumed as a matter of predication, then it directly confronts the racist notion that Black is ugly; for the notion that Black is ugly is based on an absolute principle. As an absolute principle, there is no room for allowing that only some Black people may be ugly or that others may actually be beautiful. From the standpoint of this absolute principle, ugliness is identical with Blackness; hence, we have the "is" of identification. Black and ugly are equivalent, and since Black is a racial designator, we have an outright racist proposition. Anyone who is Black is correspondingly ugly. This is the claim that we observed regarding Thomas Jefferson, which he gave voice to in his deliberations on race and aesthetics.

Black acceptance of this notion is indeed psychologically damaging and harmful. Such harm is why Kelsey explains the need for the "valuable item of psychological reorientation and education in a world of racist imperialism based on color." This harm is directly connected to the subject of aesthetical perspectives within the context of racist social relations. Thomas Nelson Baker notes the following:

> The degradation of the American Negro has been the most subtle and the most pernicious of all the degradation in the world—the perversion of his aesthetical taste which makes him ashamed of his own type—makes him glory in his shame and ashamed of his glory.[36]

C. V. Roman continues along this same line of argumentation and adroitly remarks:

> The hard conditions of discrimination and repression under which Americans of African descent are forced to live have produced a class of individuals that have done untold harm to the race. Whether he has essayed to lead or has been taken as typical and have brought upon us the contempt of other races, the Negro ashamed of his blood or without faith in his race is a nuisance. . . . He *confuses all values* and misrepresent all standards—with the heart of a traitor and the brain of a thief he destroys his own self-respect between the upper millstone of fruitless desire to be white and the nether millstone of senseless dread of being black.[37] (Italics added)

We are fully aware that the philosophical works of Thomas Nelson Baker and C. V. Roman offer a direct challenge to this proposal, "Blackness in its essence is ugly." Furthermore, they amplify the insidious harm of internalized racism within the African American community. By highlighting such deficits, we are able to see why the proposition "Black is Beautiful" suggests a meaningful alternative with respect to a definitive value orientation. With this proposition, "Black is Beautiful," we chiefly discern that ugliness is not a characteristic feature of Blackness.

In a nutshell, ugliness is not a predicate of Blackness, let alone identical with it. Sequentially, there are two important consequences affixed to the proposition that "Black is Beautiful." First, "Black is Beautiful" does not require us to presume that are no ugly Black people. To the extent that there may be ugly Black people, it is not a matter of being Black. Second, "Black is Beautiful" does not entail that "white is ugly." Yet, it follows that while ugliness is not a predicate of whiteness, this does not imply there are no ugly white people.

Consequently, matters concerning humans and the criteria for beauty are effectively removed from any racial determinations. We contend that our method of analysis vis-à-vis the "is" of predication satisfactorily addresses George D. Kelsey's concerns about the associated value judgments surrounding the proposition "Black is Beautiful." Kelsey's admonition about the fallacy of "Color Reversal" is effectually met when "Black is Beautiful" counters the viewpoint that Blackness and ugliness rest on the foundations of the "is" of identification.

Undoubtedly, African American philosophers such as Thomas Nelson Baker and C. V. Roman have adeptly paved the way for a new point of departure. The aesthetics of Blackness is a philosophical subject covering a broad expanse. From literature and cinema to music and sports, the beauty within Black life supplies a tremendous resource for cultural expression as well as philosophical analysis.

Beauty is one of the cardinal notions surrounding the problem of aesthetics and value. The beauty and power of the "People's Champion" is encapsulated with Muhammad Ali's beauty, thus reflected in his ability to "Float like a butterfly" and "Sting like a bee." The aesthetic dimension of African Americans in sports, which Muhammad Ali personified, consists as a rich subject matter for our philosophical examination on aesthetic values.

To paraphrase the Euro-American writer David Foster Wallace, the expression of beauty is not the goal of most competitive sports. However, athletic competitions are often the prime venue for the expression of human beauty.[38] In this respect, the sport arena can be seen as a form of theatre. In sports such as Olympic diving, synchronized swimming and figure skating, aesthetic evaluation is a part of the *telos* of the sport.

Great athletes like Ali can produce beauty in the very motion of their body as they glide through space and time. There simply is something beautiful about the smoothness of Jim Brown, Walter Payton, Barry Sanders, or Adrian Peterson as they skillfully evade tackles and make their way to the end zone. The athletic talent of Laila Ali, Sheryl Swoopes, Cynthia Cooper, Brittany Griner, Althea Gibson, Serena Williams, or Venus Williams is the most sublime expression of beauty. Like a swift and graceful gazelle, Wilma Rudolph, known fondly as "The Black Gazelle," ran with speed and power that was beauty in motion. An unstoppable acrobatic dunk by Dr. J, the sky-hook of Kareem Abdul-Jabbar, the precision of a no-look pass by Magic Johnson or the grace, skill, and flair of Willie Mays are all embodiments of human beauty.[39]

The problem of axiology

Forrest Oran Wiggins (Figure 12) is one of the forgotten figures in the history of philosophy as well as Black intellectual history. One of Wiggins's prime concerns was the relationship of ethics to economics. In 1945, he published

Figure 12 Forrest Oran Wiggins (1907–82).

"Ethics and Economics," in the African American journal *Phylon*. He began this piece on a very interesting note:

> Since the present world war envisages a new type of world with the end of all exploitation of man by man. It is evident that a new type of economic theory must replace laissez faire capitalism; for chief among the promised reforms is the reform of economic life. If "classical" economics no longer meets the demands of a changing economic order, perhaps we can get some suggestions from a representative of the institutional school.[40]

Wiggins's motivation to examine economics was occasioned by his keen interest in ethics, which he knew could not be properly understood apart from economics. Moreover, while his philosophical concern is ethics, Wiggins is decidedly materialist because he relegates ethics to a position intimately connected to economics. Wiggins argues,

> Our interest in problems of economic theory does not stem from the fact that we are economists, but as students of ethics we realize the intimate connection between ethics and economics. While we may with justice maintain that the economic good is subordinate to the moral good, any discussion of the latter which ignores the former is ineffectual—and perhaps dangerous.[41]

Wiggins specifically outlines what links ethics and economics. He states, "This paper purports to examine certain concepts basic to both ethics and economics. The concepts selected for analysis are (1) transactions, (2) interest, (3) scarcity and prosperity, (4) human nature, and (5) value."[42]

Wiggins engages in a critique of John R. Commons's *Institutional Economics*. Here, he primarily explores the philosophical implications of institutional economic theory for value theory. Commons's emphasis on the societal and institutional basis for values proved that he viewed values as objective phenomena in contrast to traditional capitalist economic theories based on subjectivism. This stress on objectivism did not dismiss the subjective side of values but rather took a dialectical view of value.

Wiggins added that for Commons, "Value deals not only with feeling and emotions, but with feelings and emotions aroused objectively by persons and objects, and it is only when these feelings and emotions reach the threshold of action that they become values. Values are not subjective."[43] Nonetheless, Wiggins critically analyzes Commons's alternative theory of value, what he coined as "reasonable value." Reasonable value, for Commons, was not an ideal of *a priori* character but the product of the practical experience of economic, political, and moral conditions. A pragmatic notion, reasonable value accented the expansion of the "institutional personality" via collective action. The core of Commons's reasonable value idealism was to find a practical level where ethical principles could be exercised by an enlightened business stratum which through its own efforts would restrict its self-interest. The failure to reach self-restriction would in turn evoke the control of "collective action" by the nonbusiness sector.

In responding to Commons's "reasonable value," Wiggins argues, "This idealism is so 'reasonable' that it really amounts to nothing more than an empirical generalization. If this criticism be true, then ethical principles can never become law."[44] The failure to elevate ethics to law means the negation of real ethical principles. Wiggins summarized that the reduction of ethics to the practical rather than its elevation to principle, that is, to law, was the contradiction of pragmatism and positivism. Wiggins rejects the notion of "collective action" due to its overlooking the harsh reality of class conflict, political struggle, and so on. He correctly concludes that institutional economic theory with its pragmatic ethics had merely pleaded for an "enlightened capitalism."[45]

In an earlier book review of Joseph Leighton's *Social Philosophy in Conflict*, Wiggins was even more unabashed in his criticism of capitalism. He dismissed Leighton's utopian scheme to reform capitalism by expanding government control of utilities and forming cooperatives. Wiggins commented the following:

> These reforms . . . concern mainly a redistribution of existing property relations without touching the principle of organization (disorganization) of our economic life. But this is the fallacy of all liberal thinking. Professor

Leighton does not touch the basic structure of capitalism. Capitalism is essentially exploitation and the best a liberal can do . . . is to lessen the harshness of struggle. The principles of business are interest and force and neither the one nor the other is a moral force.[46]

As a philosopher of ethics, Wiggins was a discerning critic of capitalism's inability to create the "good life." Conclusively, Wiggins adopts the law of value as a principle resting on ethical considerations. To that extent, Wiggins's philosophical viewpoint is not a thoroughgoing materialism. Yet, we discover Wiggins is not solitary among African American philosophers who discern that the political economic theory of the law of value is important to philosophical inquiry.

Among African American thinkers Reverend J. C. Price presents one of the earliest discussions on value theory. In his 1895 essay, "The Value of the Soul," Price claims that all of nature possesses some degree of value. He states, "Everything from an angel to an atom has some value." Yet, he quickly adds, all things are not commensurate in value. While Price recognizes the law of value is operative in political economy, he maintains that many things are beyond its limits. With phenomena that are subject to the law of value, the magnitude of value is determined by the corresponding amount of labor time. In this respect, Price is committed to an objectivist conception of value. It follows that values—within the purview of labor—are objective, instead of subjective in character. As an objective measure, the law of value permits the uniform identification of various items (commodities) with reference to their worth.

Yet, Price argues that since labor is the source of value, then God's creations are beyond labor's jurisdiction. Since God wills the universe into existence, then he need not labor in creating the world. In this regard, Price departs from the African American tradition captured in James Weldon Johnson's classic poem, *God's Trombone*. Johnson creatively depicts the Black preacher's sermon about how God labored to create the world. Price implicitly undermined this conventional depiction of creation with his notion that God transcends the law of value. Granted the creation of human beings, sequentially is a concern of God's will, therefore, the value of the soul remains priceless. With this essay, Price opens the door on the philosophical subject of value.

It was not, however, until Alain Leroy Locke that we find Black philosophers making considerable inroads into value theory. His prolific production as a professional philosopher range from art, culture, and race relations. It is impossible to review all his writings relating to various aspects of axiology in toto. His writings focused strictly on value theory are limited to six articles, along with his 1917 dissertation—*The Problem of Classification in Theory of Value*.[47] By far, the best introduction to Locke's theory of value is Ernest Mason's dissertation *Alain Locke's Philosophy of Value: An Introduction* submitted to Emory University in 1975.

When Locke wrote his seminal 1935 essay, "Values and Imperatives," pragmatism was reaching its full maturity with John Dewey. Locke was highly critical of pragmatism and chided its reduction of truth to an exclusively empiricist mold. He recoiled from the pragmatic attempt at "making truth too exclusively a matter of correct anticipation of experience, of the confirmation of fact."[48] In its place, Locke sought to establish a relativist conception of truth. For truth and value, in his estimation, were what he termed, "feeling-attitudes and dispositional imperatives of action-choices." Locke resisted the notion of value-free "scientific objectivism," which had come to adorn pragmatic epistemology.

Locke thought this conception resulted from pragmatism's "reaction away from academic metaphysics" and a rather feeble effort at appearing to be scientific. Locke upheld "feeling-judgments" and cast "formal-value judgments" to a secondary role. From his viewpoint, a relativistic truth anchored in feelings was primary. Locke did not deny that human conduct was experiential. However, he wanted to go beyond the realm of experience to affirm the primacy of preference, with preference being the upshot of emotion.

In contradistinction to pragmatism's behaviorism, Locke conceptualized the process of human conduct as one starting with feeling, then moving to preference, which sequentially dictated one's choice of behavior patterns. The serious error of pragmatism was that it not only ignored axiology but also separated emotion from experience. Based on its ancillary empiricism, pragmatism could only proclaim what transpires as the objective character of truth. Locke wanted to integrate values (preferences, feelings) into truth. And if values were intrinsic to truth, then truth was necessarily pluralistic and indeed relativistic, rather than objective.

Locke stated, "To the Poet, beauty is truth; to the religious devotee, God is truth; to the enthuse moralist, what ought-to-be ever tops factual reality."[49] His attack on the objectivist nature of pragmatist's truth concept should not be taken as Locke's intended clarion call for subjectivism or what he termed, "value anarchy." More precisely, this was his philosophical formulation of a system of value classification—a problem he had initially undertaken with his doctoral dissertation at Harvard.

On aesthetics

Aesthetics is concerned both with the study of the beautiful in all its manifold forms and with the elaboration of the nature of art and the process of its development. Art is foremost a creative experience/performance whereby the artist creates an art object that encapsulates and manifests what are determined as underlying elements of beauty. The painting, drawing, photograph, song, play, dance, novel, poem, and sculpture are mediums for the expression of beauty. As early as the period of African slavery, antebellum writers such as Frances Ellen Watkins Harper created literary works that directly challenged the institution of slavery. Harper's standpoint was straight and to the point, namely, aesthetics was founded on the principles affixed to emancipation: "We need men and women whose hearts are the homes of a high and lofty enthusiasm, and a noble devotion to the cause of emancipation, who are ready and willing to lay time, talent, and money on the altar of universal emancipation."[50]

However, in the view of some art critics, the beauty embodied in art objects is removed from such pedestrian elements as political, social, ethical, and economic circumstances surrounding everyday life. In accord with this perspective, the matter of creative impulse is restricted to how the individual artist personally conceives of the artistic project or performance. Likewise, the intended function or aim of the artistic project or performance is purely a matter of the intentions and creative expression of the given artist.

According to this perspective, our earlier treatment of Work Songs would stand as an oxymoron. Since Work Songs as artistic expression would of necessity intend on capturing how the very economic and social circumstances surrounding the process of laboring activity are at base the creative impulse for this art form. Moreover, since a significant number of African American Work Songs are often presented as Freedom Songs, the socioeconomic and political intent of this art form is inconsistent with viewing artistic creation on purely personal inclinations and apart from social intentions and political concerns. Essentially, such critics view art from the angle of an apolitical rendering. Beauty is thus removed from the multifaceted realities of life and, more importantly, artistic production from the objective of changing such conditions.

From this standpoint, the aim of creating the art object or engaging in artistic performance indeed transpires in offering a reprieve from the complexities of social life. It follows that we must embrace the view that art is an entertaining escape from life problems and the aesthetics surrounding our notion of beauty must transcend politics and social problems. Sequentially, the measure of aesthetic value adjoined to art objects is not associated with social issues and political circumstances. The presumption is that artistic value or aesthetics is a pristine experience. Consequently, from this perspective, art sustains itself apart from other features of social life. In other words, art is preeminently an intrinsic value or an end in itself. One important outcome of this assumption is that art is not a means to social ends or more simply put—it is not propaganda. This viewpoint is popularly known as "art for art's sake."

For W. E. B. Du Bois, however, "all art is and must ever be propaganda." The notion of "Beauty" and hence aesthetics is decidedly connected to the overriding concerns of "Truth" and "Right." Concurrently, the Black artist has the role or duty in advancing the broader aims of social concerns, as with Black liberation. In the midst of the Spanish Civil War, Paul Robeson declared at a rally in London, in 1937:

> Every artist, every scientist, [every writer] must decide NOW where he stands. He has no alternative. There is no standing above the conflict on Olympian heights. There are no impartial observers. . . . The battlefront is everywhere. There is no sheltered rear.

He continued,

> The artist must take sides. He must elect to fight for freedom or slavery. I have made my choice. I had no alternative. The history of the capitalist era is characterized by the degradation of my people.[51]

This idea that the Black Aesthetic remained cojoined to Black liberation would be articulated by African American art critics far into the 1970s. Black critic Addison Gayle emphatically proclaims, "The idea that the Black Aesthetic will become simply another literary movement simply misses the point. We are not talking about literary movements in that sense at all. The Black Aesthetic will exist until the liberation of black people is assured, because the Black Aesthetic is as much a political movement as it is a literary movement."[52]

Therefore, given the sociopolitical context of artistic production, Du Bois argues that the freedom of artistic creation is contextualized by the very factors of "Truth" and "Right." Du Bois unequivocally announces,

> The apostle of Beauty thus becomes *the apostle of Truth and Right not by choice but by inner and outer compulsion. Free he is but his freedom is ever*

bounded by Truth and Justice; and slavery only dogs him when he is denied the right to tell the Truth or recognize an ideal of Justice. Thus, all Art is propaganda and ever must be, despite the wailing of the purists. I stand in utter shamelessness and say that whatever art I have for writing has been used always for propaganda for gaining the right of black folk to love and enjoy. I do not care a damn for any art that is not used for propaganda. But I do care when propaganda is confined to one side while the other is stripped and silent.[53] (Italics added)

In his 1926 essay, "Criteria of Negro Art," Du Bois parts company with the "art for art's sake" tradition. In contradistinction, Alain Locke remained the most distinguished African American proponent of this tradition. The definitive biographer of Locke, Jeffrey C. Stewart cites how Locke responded to Du Bois's proposal for art as propaganda. "'The elder generation,' Locke wrote, 'of Negro writers expressed itself in cautious moralism. . . . The newer motive, then, in being racial is to be so purely for the sake of art.'"[54]

As early as 1923, Locke pushed for the notion that Black artists must commit to "art for art's sake." While sympathetic to an African mystique surrounding African American cultural arts, Locke's cosmopolitan sensibilities, nonetheless, desired that Black artistic expression continued without any political admixture. Furthermore, Locke intended for *The New Negro*—his historic text representative of the Harlem Renaissance—as the embodiment of this aesthetic principle.[55]

Du Bois assumed a critical position regarding Locke's aesthetic posture. Du Bois argued that while "Mr. Locke has been newly seized with the idea that Beauty rather than Propaganda should be the object of Negro literature and art," *The New Negro* anthology was far from entirely giving expression to "art for art's sake." Many works in the text were representative of art as propaganda and this fact, for Du Bois, affirmed his stance on aesthetics. Du Bois expressly notes,

If Mr. Locke's thesis is insistent upon too much it is going to turn the Negro Renaissance into decadence. It is the fight for Life and Liberty that is giving birth to Negro literature and art today and when, turning from this fight or ignoring it, the young Negro tries to do pretty things or things to catch the fancy of the really unimportant critics and publishers about him, he will find that he has killed the soul of Beauty in his Art.[56]

Concomitantly, Du Bois declares that works of art could be used to communicate human ideals such as truth and goodness. All artists, especially Black artists, must use truth and goodness toward the creation, preservation, and realization of beauty to help the world recognize and share in an ideal of justice. It follows that Du Bois is critical of how white bourgeois patronage specifically restricted the freedom of African American artists—in the burgeoning Harlem Renaissance—by not allowing the full expression of creativity and unbridled disclosure about the truth surrounding Black life.

The criteria of Black art, Du Bois summons, cannot be relegated to white approval or diluted of its particularity, that is, its rich sources within African American life. He argues,

> The white public today demands from its artists, literary and pictorial, racial pre-judgment which deliberately distorts Truth and Justice, as far as colored races are concerned, and it will pay for no other. On the other hand, the young and slowly growing black public still wants its prophets almost equally unfree. *We are bound by all sorts of customs that have come down as second-hand soul clothes of white patrons.* . . . In all sorts of ways we are hemmed in and our new young artists have got to fight their way to freedom. The ultimate judge has got to be you and you have got to build yourselves up into that wide judgment, that catholicity of temper which is going to enable the artist to have his widest chance for freedom. We can afford the Truth. White folk today cannot.[57] (Italics added)

In a similar vein, Langston Hughes, in his landmark 1926 essay, "The Negro Artist and the Racial Mountain," argues that Black artists have to fight against what he describes as the "Racial Mountain," that is, "this urge within the [Black] race toward whiteness, the desire to pour racial individuality into the mold of American standardization, and to be as little Negro and as much American as possible."[58]

Both Hughes and Du Bois open the door for the elaboration of the philosophy of the Black Aesthetic. Between the late 1960s and the 1970s, the deliberation on the concept of the Black Aesthetic emerged as pivotal among African American artists and art critics. The Black philosopher Ernest Mason has perceptively noted the following: "The philosophy of the Black Aesthetic [is] an inquiry into the experiences and perceptions that black people have of themselves and others."[59] In concert with Mason and Du Bois, Addison Gayle in his 1971 groundbreaking work—*The Black Aesthetic*—remarks how "the dimensions of the Black artist's war against society are highly visible."[60] He cogently adds,

> In order to cultivate an aesthetic sensibility, given an oppressive society, the first prerequisite is that oppression must end; to pay the way for the possibility of an ars poetica, the oppression must end; in more concrete terms, before beauty can be seen, felt, heard, and appreciated by a majority of the earth's

people, a new world must be brought into being: the earth must be made habitable and free for all men. This is the core of the Black Aesthetic Ideology and forms the major criterion for the evaluation of art.[61]

The engagement with aesthetics by African American artists must be contextualized against the background of bourgeois ideology, racism, and class exploitation. African Americans are constantly engaged in a process of coming to self-consciousness, both discovering and creating one's self against the tidal wave of pseudoscientific racism and class exploitation.

The dialectic of class exploitation and racist oppression became the objective basis for some African American intellectuals to embrace Marxist philosophy as the lens for inspecting the question of aesthetics in Black artistic expression. Philosopher Eugene Clay Holmes—along with Richard Wright and Eugene Gordon—ushered in the birth of Marxist literary criticism with a focus on African American literature. In his 1935 essay, "The Negro in Recent American Literature," Holmes (writing under the pseudonym Eugene Clay) offers a stunning class analysis of African American literature. Holmes was very critical of African American intellectuals and their failure to move toward the Left during the depression. He opens with the following:

> Despite the deepening changes occurring in America, most Negro intellectuals have remained indifferent to the increasing leftward movement in American thought. Most of them have continued, undismayed, trying to solve their individual problems within the orbit of capitalism. They have furthermore been unable to understand the real tradition of the Negro people.[62]

Foreshadowing Richard Wright's Marxist politico-aesthetic manifesto, "The Blueprint for Negro Writing," Holmes ties the social origins of the Harlem Renaissance with the "American bourgeoisie [who] had prospered in the re-division of spoils and profits." He argues that a liberal wing of the US bourgeoisie found "new amusements and new thrills" in Black Harlem. This liberal bourgeois element often served as white patrons for Black artists. Holmes critically notes, "These 'new Negroes' prided themselves on the fact that they could act, sing, paint and write as well as their white-skinned patrons. They had arrived."[63]

He further argues that "the salvation of the Negro intellectual lies in his identification with the revolutionary working-class movement throughout the world."[64] Moreover, Holmes highlights the class nature of works by Charles Chesnutt, Paul Laurence Dunbar, Langston Hughes in addition to favorably evaluating the poetry of Sterling Brown and Richard Wright. This latter group of writers utilized the Black working-class experience as the impulse for creative expression.

The folk traditions of the African American proletariat primarily sustain what serve as the core elements of Black artistic culture. In Holmes's analysis, the crisis of capitalism (The Great Depression) was the material foundation for the needed ideological transformation of Black intellectual culture. While Black workers were increasingly moving leftward in political outlook and practice, their intellectual counterparts lagged sorely behind, caught within the snare of petite bourgeois ideology, that is, liberalism remained as their ideological albatross. Holmes not only was in agreement with Du Bois that art served as propaganda but also outlines how the political economy of class contradictions—within bourgeois culture—was the catalyst for Black art in the service of the African American working class and the ongoing fight against imperialism. With Holmes, the philosophy of the Black Aesthetic assumes a definite class content.

Indeed, Richard Wright's 1937 proclamation is quite relevant for our contemporary times as the clarion call that "Black Lives Matter" echoes throughout the world. The rise of state terrorism via police brutality, increased unemployment, homelessness, the dysfunctional character of public schools, and political attacks on civil rights in addition to the decline of social services for the poor and infirmed, along with the repression of working-class organizations are the material realities of present-day capitalism.

Wright's "Blueprint" offers a political aesthetics that has the Black working class as not only the subject of the literary art form but also the primary audience of African American artistic production. The compelling necessity for Black artistic creation and production centers on advancing the lives of the African American working masses against the ever-present conditions of oppression. Wright forthrightly declares the following:

> Every short story, novel, poem, and play should carry within its lines, implied or explicit, a sense of the oppression of the Negro people, the danger of war, of fascism, of the threatened destruction of culture and civilization; and, too, the faith and necessity to build a new world. With the gradual decline of the moral authority of the Negro church, and the increasing irresolution which is paralyzing Negro middle-class leadership, there is devolving upon Negro writers this new role. They are being called upon to do no less than create values by which their race is to struggle, live and die. They are being called upon to furnish moral sanctions for action, to give a meaning to blighted lives, and to supply motives for mass movements of millions of people.[65]

The value of art is no less than the active intervention of the artist into the mass struggles that ebb and flow as a contested fight on a protracted level. This artistic intervention, Wright argues, must come from a given political perspective, an ideological perspective that is founded on the contours of the life experiences witnessed by the Black masses. Wright's class perspective on aesthetics in conjunction with African American mass experiences is highlighted in the following summation:

> We are writers of a minority people whose working class is pushing militantly forward. We have the choice of writing for Negro and white "Society" or for our working class and the cause of social justice it represents. If we choose to stand on the side of social progress, then our artistic expression must shape the (folk-national) aspirations of our people. This necessitates a basic realignment, ideologically and aesthetically, on our part.[66]

In substance, we find that Wright provides a "blueprint" for the relationship between politics and aesthetics. In addition to Holmes, a number of Black philosophers have had an abiding interest in the philosophy of literature. William Fontaine wrote two groundbreaking works: "Toward A Philosophy of American Negro Literature" and "A Study of the Mind and Thought of the Negro as Revealed in Imaginative Literature from 1870 to the Present"[67] and Robert C. Williams published "Afro-American Folklore as a Philosophical Source."[68]

And, lastly, we cannot ignore the contribution of philosopher and novelist Charles Johnson. In his trailblazing book *Being and Race: Black Writing Since 1970* in addition to articles such as "Philosophy and Black Fiction," "Whole Sight: Notes on New Black Fiction," "Where Philosophy and Fiction Meet," and "A Phenomenology of the Black Body," Johnson examine the relationship between Black fiction and philosophy.[69] Through the lens of phenomenology, Johnson argues that fiction is an "interpretive art that deepens perceptual experience."[70] The fictional worlds are "instrumental as a mode for analyzing the appearance (being) of phenomenon in Black life."[71]

The search for objective beauty

Two of the central questions of aesthetics are the following: Are values subjective or objective, particular or universal? How do we determine if values are relative or absolute? If one is a *relativist* about beauty, then beauty is in the eye of the beholder and there are no universal criteria for beauty. Aesthetic preferences are the expressions of the taste of the observer, not an objective evaluation of the aesthetic object. On this view imagine the following, I say, "Kara Walker's *A Subtlety, or the Marvelous Sugar Baby* is a beautiful sculpture. It is such a powerful personification of the relationship between sugar, slave labor and Black women." But you retort, "Kara Walker's *A Subtlety, or the Marvelous Sugar Baby* is a grotesque, neo-coon minstrel show pandering to the white art establishment and collectors. This is a grotesque parody of Black culture by a Black artist who hates being Black." Have we simply reached a deadlock? Should we both just throw up our hands and agree to disagree?

From the relativist angle, you could never be wrong about whether the sculpture is beautiful, nor could I, even if we seem to disagree. We are just expressing our feelings or sentiments. This position is akin to *emotivism*, that is, the metaethical view that ethical sentences do not express propositions but emotional attitudes. As A. J. Ayers argues, statements of value do not have factual meaning; they have an expressive or emotive meaning. Making aesthetic or value judgments is equivalent to saying, "Ouch!" Ultimately, from the standpoint of this radical subjectivist perspective, aesthetic judgments are essentially opinions or subjective preferences which derive from the pleasure we gain from an aesthetic object or experience. So therefore, by implication, there can be no objective judgment of aesthetic value.

If one is a *realist* about beauty, then one holds to the view that beauty is an entirely objective matter. Naturally, we must ask, what does it mean to make objective judgments of aesthetic value? If beauty is objective, how do we make sense of differences in aesthetic taste? Can we claim that certain judgments about artistic beauty are mistaken?

One way to answer these questions is to look at the Greek philosopher Pythagoras. The first principle of Pythagorean philosophy was that all things are numbers. At first glance, this may seem a wild and fanciful proposition. Upon closer scrutiny, we discover that, for Pythagoras, mathematics was the ground of explanation for all phenomena. The Pythagoreans, Aristotle reports, believed "the whole heaven to be a musical scale and a number" (Aristotle, *Metaphysics*, 985b 23). By this Pythagoras and the Pythagoreans meant that what underlined everything in the universe was mathematics, that is to say, the universe was harmoniously ordered and regular and that such ordered regularity was a guarantee of beauty. Beauty arises out of mathematical harmony, order, and regularity. On this basis we can infer that—for Pythagoras and the Pythagoreans—beauty itself was a quantifiable and an objective principle of nature.[72]

One of the significant contributions of Pythagoras is the awareness of the mathematical foundation of music, that is, a relationship between arithmetic and aesthetics. Pythagoras is credited with discovering the mathematical basis to musical intervals—that musical strings at fixed lengths relative to each other produce harmonious sounds, and that the relationship between these is grounded in simple numeric ratios.

Following the example of Pythagoras, a great number of philosophers and thinkers have sought to determine if there is an objective nature to beauty. Are there formal—artistic—properties which are necessary for the aesthetic function of particular art forms? Do the technical components of specified art forms ground aesthetic value or beauty? Should aesthetic taste (judgment) be cultivated such that art appreciation mandates comprehending objective features of the art object or performance? How can we discern what are such features, if they do indeed exist? Do they have universal expression?

With respect to universal expression, Paul Robeson's commitment to and passion for singing "Negro Spirituals," Work Songs, and world folk songs was part of his expressed socialist political ideology and international class solidarity. Robeson argues the following:

> These [African American] songs, ballads and poetic church hymns are similar to the songs of the bards of the Scottish Hebrides, the Welsh bards of the Druid tradition and the Irish bards which inspired Sean O'Casey. They are similar to the unknown singers of the Russian folktales, the bards of the Icelandic and Finnish sagas, singers of the American Indians, the bards of the Veda hymns in India, the Chinese poet singers, the Hassidic sects and the bards of our African forebears.[73]

Here, we can draw parallels with Paul Robeson's philosophy of music.[74] In his autobiography *Here I Stand*, Robeson writes about the commonality of pentatonic chord structures he found in folk music from Africa, Asia, Europe, and North America. He argues the following:

> Continued study and research into the origins of the folk music of various peoples in many parts of the world revealed that there is a world body—a universal body—of folk music based upon a universal pentatonic (five-tone) scale. Interested as I am in the universality of mankind—in the fundamental relationship of all peoples to one another—this idea of a universal body of music intrigued me, and I pursued it along many fascinating paths.[75]

For Robeson, the power of folk music is tied to the pentatonic scale, and hence this structural feature advances an objective grounding—valuation—for the appreciation of this musical form. Along with Robeson, Ramon Ricker observes that pentatonic scales allow for inversions which permit having variant "modes" of expression. Ricker indicates this has been documented in folk music as early as 1911.[76]

The significance of this exploration into the pentatonic scale resides in the fact that conventionally Western music is based on an eight-tone scale; the major scale is structured on the interval of steps such that the mathematical intervals are expressed as whole, whole, half step, whole, whole, whole, half step. The notion of restructuring the octave—eight note sequences—via the pentatonic eliminates the half step in the scale sequence.

For instance, in the key of C, the pentatonic scale would emerge as C, D, E, G, A with C completing the octave. With previous major scale intervals, we would have C, D, E, F, G, A, B, with C completing the octave. Subsequently, Jazz musicians have utilized pentatonic scales for improvisation. Hence, Robeson's earlier insights on folk music and the pentatonic scale actually advances with new scholarship to a broader dimension regarding African American music. Music scholar Ramon Ricker notes,

> Pentatonic scales, as used in jazz, are five notes scales made up of major seconds and minor thirds. Within a scale there are two minor thirds leads in an octave, thus producing the gap. . . . In addition there is no leading tone (seventh scale degree of a major scale) nor, for that matter any half step within the scale. For these reasons, the scales act as chords, and are invertible.[77]

From this notion of pentatonic interval, the idea of "Modal Jazz" develops with Miles Davis and John Coltrane leading the way. Modal music clears the path for a more open and free approach in interpretative performance. Jazz musicologist, Ronald McCurdy explains, "The term 'mode' refers to a scale. In modal forms, improvisations are based on one or two chords played for extended duration. This is not the definition used by classical music theorists; it is, however, the term that jazz musicians and journalists have used to describe modal music."[78]

In view of the Pythagorean notion about mathematical ratio founding the objective feature of beauty, we began our treatment on the pentatonic scale, folk music, and Modal Jazz. This inspection compels us now to move onto the realm of philosophical perspectives on African American music. Does the matter of aesthetics and explicitly the notion of the Black Aesthetic have any relevance, when we transition from literature to music? As an art form, how can we render judgment about the aesthetic value of African American music? Black philosophers such as Alain Locke, Albert Mosley, Roosevelt Porter, John H. McClendon III, and Julius Bailey have examined philosophical issues and problems related to Black music.[79]

Philosophical perspectives on black music

Where must the student of philosophy look to gain an understanding or philosophical perspective on African American music? In what manner is music appreciation culturally specific to a given cultural group and genre of music? How does the African background on African American music enter the picture on the aesthetic quality of Black music? Such questions form the backdrop for our deliberations in this section of our chapter. Let's begin with the African influences on African American music.

The research of African American musicologist Portia Maultsby establishes a conceptual framework for comprehending how Black Atlantic—New World African—music is closely related to African influences. Rather than solely presenting a list of African customs—an empirical (quantitative) indicator that is necessary but insufficient—one must grasp how African traditional forms are qualitatively altered rather than fixed in the new context of transatlantic culture. The notion of African cultural retention is a dynamic process of alteration. The conventional expression or manifest form regarding African customary approaches invariably change, yet the cultural content behind the form may persist in a new manner. The quantitative listing of Africanisms must reside within a framework founded on qualitative analysis.

This qualitative method is extremely valuable for our philosophical inquiry on the African roots of African American music. The continuity of Africanisms in African American music need not require that transformations be absent. Instead, we must examine the nature of such changes with regard to its content and adjoining modes of expression. By means of qualitative analysis, Maultsby demonstrates that although there have been changes in specific African customs and practices, it remains "the concepts that embody and identify the [African] cultural heritage of black Americans have never been lost. The African dimensions of African American music is far-reaching and can be understood best when examined within this conceptual framework."[80]

We should note, in Alain Locke's discussion of Africanism in African American music, he fails to comprehend the important feature of the qualitative aspect of Africanisms. Locke resorts to describing Africanisms with a myriad of loose and a-scientific terms such as "homing instinct," "primitive tropical heritage," and "racial temperament." Concurrently, Locke's ambiguity about African retentions led to declaring that slavery had reduced Black slaves to "cultural zero" as well as (in a contradictory fashion) that "even with the rude transplanting of slavery that uprooted the technical elements of his former culture, the American Negro brought over an emotional inheritance a deep seated aesthetic endowment."[81] James Barnes's summation on Locke's viewpoint on African retention or Africanism is most apropos for our reference: "Despite his petition for scientific scholarship and his status as a leading recognize interpreter of what he termed the African heritage or legacy, Locke was often as ambiguous and enigmatic in terms of his definition as was the theme he was endeavoring to find."[82]

In comparison to Locke, both Du Bois and Robeson have a richer conception of Africanisms and often spoke and wrote of how African American music gave expression to the "Souls of Black Folk." Robeson chiefly notes the following: "Black folk songs exerted a particularly strong influence on American music. The musical culture of the Afro-American originated in the old culture of Africa. The blacks brought with them out of Africa an individual and rich inheritance, numerous beautiful and inspired songs, profoundly unique rhythms and freedom of expression."[83]

Robeson explicitly identifies the Negro Spirituals as rooted in the confluence of African musical culture and the African American creative response to enslavement under the ideological domination of Christianity. In "Songs of My People," Robeson explains to his Soviet reading audience that contrary to how some musicologists in the United States portray the Spirituals as created out of the "influence of English church music, Puritan psalms etc.," the hard facts reveal these as false and "unscientific" assessments. Robeson affirmatively claims that the Spirituals originate out of African slaves' resistance to racist oppression and capitalist exploitation. He further embarks upon the complexity of the aesthetic dimension of the Spirituals:

> These songs reflect a spiritual force, a people's faith in itself and of faith in its great calling; they reflected the wrath and protest against the enslavers and the aspiration to freedom and happiness. These songs are striking in the noble beauty of their melodies, in the expressiveness and resourcefulness of their intonations, in the starling variety of their rhythms, and the

sonority of their harmonies, and in the unusual distinctiveness and poetical nature of their forms.[84]

Black historian Sterling Stuckey advances the Robeson argument about the African influence in African American music and specifically addresses the nature of Work Songs. In congruence with Maultsby's methodology, Stuckey notes that the matter of distinctive African ethnic identity converts into a more generalized Pan-African identity in the course of laboring, within the context of slavery. Therefore, a New World African identity was forged in the circumstances of the slave labor process itself. Starting from this materialist standpoint, Stuckey elaborates,

> As ethnic differences were increasingly subordinated by the force of circumstances, a new form of Africanness centering on the primacy of unity in slavery came to prevail. . . . Work skills, then, were important grounding for a sense of Africanness that was achieved in slavery in ways not achieved in Africa. Under such circumstances, work songs were created of a deeper sense of Africanity than has heretofore acknowledged.[85]

Stuckey and Robeson's observation about the African background to African American music brings forth the question, how do African and European musical traditions differ? Though Robeson talked in terms of the universal expression of folk music, he acknowledges there are differences between musical expressions based on variances between African and European musical cultures. This cultural context for the creative production of African art forms is acknowledged by African philosophers such as Innocent Onyewuenyi. He gives emphasis to the *functional character* of art within the framework of community life:

> African works of art are functional, community-oriented, and depersonalized, unlike Western art which is arbitrary, representative of the values and emotions of the artist, and without reference to the cultural environment and the historical reality.[86]

If this is true of African art forms, then Du Bois's critique of "art for art's sake" gains legitimacy from the standpoint of an aesthetic rooted in African traditional art. In alignment with Onyewuenyi's summation and based on research by Elizabeth Oehrle, African American philosopher and musician Albert Mosley astutely detects,

> Africans make no distinction between composer and performer while Westerners do, Africans make no distinction between audience and performer while Westerners do; Africans make no distinction between professionals

and amateurs while Westerners do; Africans do not typically utilize literacy for music making while Westerners do. Africans emphasize rhythm while Europeans emphasize harmony. Each of these claims offer important issues for consideration and evaluation. . . . Within the African musical tradition, music-making is learned by participation in the community of music-makers rather than in accordance with descriptions generated from music theory.[87]

It is precisely the latter proposition that Mosley highlights is most decisive in evaluating the aesthetics of Black music. Mosley gives greater emphasis to "pedagogical techniques that cultivate tacit responses to felt relationships" which are "foundational to black musical achievement." In contrast to accenting the primacy of literacy in music theory, Black music—African American and African alike—emphasizes that "music-making is learned by participation in the community of music-makers."

One cardinal aesthetic principle for Black music which follows is that the "feeling" evoked by the musical performance has precedence over technical mastery. African American music is not score dependent as often found in Western classical music. The idea of "descriptions generated from music theory" is often expressed via the musical composition as formalized in the written score. Adherence to the written score overshadows the freedom to create via improvisational interpretation. The aesthetics of Black music contrastingly gives greater emphasis on the musician as performer and thus on the musical performance.

With African Americans and the felt response, musical performance is predicated on the notion of call and response, whereby the active participation of the audience is part and parcel of the musical performance. Mosley draws attention to this fact in counter-position to Western classical music. He explains,

> In contrast, Black Atlantic forms (such as spirituals, blues, jazz, R&B, rap, and hip-hop) remained oral, performance-based, and fluid. . . . Historically, music in the African American tradition was performed in conjunction with dance, so that the involvement of the audience was just as important as the involvement of the musicians. This symbiotic and recursive relationship between musician and audience integrated patterns of movement, sound, mood, and attitude. Musicians and audience shared in the active creation of a visual, kinesthetic, and acoustical universe.[88]

The musical performance becomes dynamic and participatory, not formalized based on the hegemonic function of the musical score. From the Western perspective, the audience as passive listeners receive the message conveyed by the musician and created by the composer. With Western classical tradition, "[musical] notation has become the principle medium in which creation and recreation take place, and performers have come to be viewed as simply transmitters of the composer's message."[89]

This presumption in classical Western music relegates the musical performer to a lesser role in generating the message expressed by the music. The matter of the source of musical creativity is vitally linked to the subject of aesthetic quality. Hence the questions, what determines aesthetic quality with regard to music? How can the artist as creative performer establish the basis for the aesthetic quality of music?

It follows that the philosophical problem of aesthetic quality as affixed to music is at the center of our discussion. Does aesthetic quality reside within the musical score or rather in the performance of the music? How can we make the right decision? Is there some objective measure for anchoring our decision on the aesthetic quality of music? African American philosopher and musician Roosevelt Porter III adeptly brings to our attention the following argument:

1 An aesthetic quality which cannot be appreciated as a result of hearing a musical performance is not an aesthetic quality of the musical performance. It follows then that if an aesthetic quality is appreciated as a result of analyzing the score but cannot be appreciated when hearing the performance, that aesthetic quality then belongs to the score and not to the musical performance.

2 As for those aesthetic qualities that are thought to be appreciated by either looking at the score or hearing its performance, these aesthetic qualities actually differ in some aspect from one another.

3 Therefore, appreciating the aesthetic qualities of a musical performance merely by examining the score is impossible.[90]

The relevance of Porter's argument rests on the differentiation and separate consideration of musical score versus musical performance, indicating the pivotal differences concerning judgments on aesthetic quality vis-à-vis African American music. Since African American music—in the context of the Western experience—mandates grasping the concrete aesthetics of Black musical creativity, African American music is better appreciated/judged in terms of performative quality. Judgment on how the music is written (if written at all) is not the compatible measure for discerning its aesthetic quality.

One must hear—if not directly observe—the actual performance of African American musical creativity for discerning its aesthetic quality. Hence, the beauty embodied in African American music is expressed in the performance, which is generally subject to improvisational interpretation. Of course, improvisation is always in conjunction with the very process of performing the music. We should not mystify the improvisational genius of Black musicians. Many Black musicians spend a phenomenal amount of time practicing in order to develop the needed *musical concepts* that frame improvisational creativity. Indeed, it is the innovation affixed to the musical concepts that drive and enrich the substance and scope of improvisation.

The musical conceptualizations of pianist Thelonious Monk, singer Betty Carter, and organist Larry Young, for example, require both critical as well as creative engagement of musical complexity respecting Jazz idioms. Subsequently, their improvisational genius is the product of long hours of practice, of musical knowledge, and of the slow germination and maturity of musical ideas. The maturation of musical ideas leads to extending beyond simply sounding like another musician to attaining one's own voice or signature within the orbit of the idiom.[91]

We must ask, what sets the context for the prominent role of improvisation? The written score must remain an open framework, and this open-ended structuring of Black music delegates the chief responsibility for the creative impulse as derivative from the musician playing the music. The execution and interpretation of the music center on the musician's creative abilities. By the end of the nineteenth century, in addition to the Spirituals, Work Songs, Freedom Songs, and folk ballads, we witness the expansion of the genre of Black music to include Blues, Ragtime, and later the emergence of Jazz. Each of these genres of African American music emphasizes creative musicianship via improvisation. Consequently, aesthetic quality rests primarily in the musician playing the music.

The historical divergence of African American music with Western classical music amplifies the variation respecting conceptions about aesthetic quality. Mosley explicitly notes, "Especially in the nineteenth century, composers of Western classical music began a 'purist' tradition of considering 'their works as discrete, perfectly formed, and completed products' to be performed exactly as the composer indicated on the score."[92]

Given the divergence that we have outlined, the subject of creativity respecting the genre music is a crucial aspect in the matter of aesthetic quality. Substantially, African American musicians best express their originality and innovation within the framework of the African American musical traditions. Of course, African American musicians need not confine their arena of performance to African American music. Yet, at least two very hard questions emerge: what sustains artistic creativity and originality regarding music production and performance? Must the African American musician function within Black musical genres to maximize creative potentiality? Given the restriction of musical score dependency, we discover that a number of Black musicians find the Western classical tradition as restricting with regard to innovation and originality.

Artists such as Paul Robeson made the commitment to performing only music outside of the Western classical tradition. In Robeson's perspective this classical tradition continues to affirm an elitist conception of music. The African American highlighting of content vis-à-vis form—musical performance over the score—undermines the Western classical notion of *perfect form* in music. The dynamic content of the music that develops from the Black working class reflects the material reality of ever-changing conditions of life. Robeson was fully aware that the social dynamics (dialectics) of cultural experiences were the anchor for grounding the content of African American music and musical interpretation.

Generally, the music that emerges from the culture of working people generally and more specifically the African American masses is the social context that grounds music along class lines and which provides the creative space for musical innovation. The musician as artist creates out of a cultural milieu that enriches the musical performance by means of the experiences, which relate to the immediate audience of their works.

This question of creativity is integrally tied to originality, wherein the tradition of African American music stands as an abundant resource for creative expression, from the precise vantage point of musical originality. Pioneering Jazz artist James Reese Europe argues,

> I have come back from France more firmly convinced than ever that negroes should write negro music. We have our own racial feeling and if we try to copy whites we will make bad copies. I noticed that the Morocco negro bands played music which had an affinity to ours. One piece, "In Zanzibar," I took for my band, and though white audiences seem to find it as too discordant, I found it most sympathetic. We won France by playing which was ours and not a pale imitation of others.[93]

African American drummer and musicologist Max Roach accents how Jazz is a creative expression of the indigenous experiences of African Americans, first as Africans on the continent of Africa, then thereafter in the slave trade, slavery, and so-called Black emancipation. While Roach finds the term "Jazz" as an imposed nomenclature, he, nevertheless, digs beyond the label and gives voice to its content. Thus, the creative originality of Jazz is rooted in the African American experience. Roach unequivocally declares,

> "Jazz" is an extension on the African chants and songs. It is an extension of the pain and suffering of those long, and too often, destinationless trips across the Atlantic Ocean, deep in the holes of those dark, damp, filthy, human slave ships.... "Jazz" is an extension of the humiliation suffered by the same human beings while being sold as cattle or produce.... "Jazz" is an extension of the Black man, "freed," who found himself still shackled to the same chain, all shined up, when he unwittingly ventured out into "Their" free world of opportunity and wealth, only to be assaulted, whipped, murdered, and raped some more.[94]

In concert, with our previous deliberation on the aesthetic quality of Black music, Roach asserts that

> "Jazz" is the indigenous music of the indigent Black man and woman. The musical instruments and theories on harmony preceded the Black man in this country, but it was, and is, the Black man's hell on earth, which he sublimated and is sublimating into music, that makes for the aesthetic contribution, "Jazz."[95]

The matter of aesthetic contribution, Roach informs us, is foremost in how Jazz as an expression of Black struggle is linked to the lives of African Americans facing hell in the United States. Hence, as with Du Bois and Robeson, Roach cannot remove the issue of aesthetic contribution from political and social realities. John H. McClendon III outlines the political economic foundation for the very emergence of Jazz as an artistic expression:

> Jazz was incubated and inspired by the new city experience, with its pull into capitalist production and commerce. The Saturday night dance was a cultural space for relief; it encouraged improvisational modes of expression, which offset the drudgery and monotony of hard menial work. *Jazz syncopation is an upbeat response to the downbeat situation of being at the bottom of the social order. The rhythm and cadence of Jazz is a cultural challenge to the repetitive downbeat of measured time over work and life.* It is in this sense that the urban working-class experience is the root and foundation for the creative musical traditions we call Jazz.[96] (Italics added)

Finally, the centrality of capitalist production and commerce cannot be understated when we explore issues of aesthetic quality, originality, and creativity. The political economy of music is a pressing issue for any evaluation of the aesthetic merit of Black music. When the sale of the art object/musical performance is the primary means of distribution then the musical performance is converted into a commodity. The commodification of the art object means that aesthetic quality is subject to being subordinated to an exchange value or price.

Thus, we have the bifurcation of artistic production as creative expression against profit making from the sale of the commodified art object. This bifurcation is generally manifested as the demarcation of the *musician within the community of artists* versus the *performer as participant in the entertainment business.* The aesthetic value of the art object/entertainment utility dichotomy is no small matter in our philosophical appraisal of Black music. A given musician's popularity may very well be based not on aesthetic quality. Rather, popularity could be an expression of an entertainer's marketability, that is, on how well sales dictate the distribution of the musical performance and promotion of the musician.

The more talented artist need not be the most popular or the person receiving the greater monetary reward. After all, capitalism's chief objective is in making profits and not the promotion of aesthetic quality. Hence, we should not ignore the political economy of music when determining who is a better singer: Anita Baker, Phyllis Hyman, or Beyoncé Knowles. The commodification of music and its control by a few major corporations has had a negative impact on the sound that we hear.

The music industry is facing a crisis of profitability as a result of digital streaming platforms like Apple Music, Tidal, and Spotify. Consequently, the business of music has focused on how to reduce the production cost of music and increase profits. One manner in which this has occurred is through increased capital investment in digital recording technologies such as the usage of multitracking, that is, the separate recording of multiple tracks in order to create a song, as opposed to employing session musicians for the production of songs and/or albums. This expresses what Karl Marx refers to as the growth of constant capital relative to variable capital, that is, the rising organic composition of capital.

The capitalist process of the production of music has had a great impact on the aesthetic quality of music in general and Black music in particular. The marketability of hit songs has taken precedent over the promotion of aesthetic quality. In light of the falling rate of profit in the music industry, US journalist John Seabrook reports the following: "Of the 13 million songs available for purchase in 2008, 52,000 made up 80 percent of the industry's revenue. Ten million of those tracks failed to sell a single copy. Today, 77 percent of the profits in the music business are accumulated by 1 percent of the artists."[97] This has led to what some music critics have referred to as the "Death of Music," that is, the lack of musicianship, originality, and creativity in Black music in particular and music as a whole.

Notes

1. For an overview of value theory, see Stephen C. Pepper, "A Brief History of General Theory of Value," in *A History of Philosophical Systems*, ed. Vergilius Ferm (New York: The Philosophical Library, Inc., 1950), 493–503.
2. See Ellen Meiksins Wood and Neal Wood, *Class Ideology and Ancient Political Theory: Socrates, Plato and Aristotle in Social Context* (Oxford: Blackwell, 1978).
3. Rufus Lewis Perry, *Sketch of Philosophical Systems* (Privately Printed, 1918?), 6.
4. John Milton Smith, "A Critical Estimate of Plato's and Dewey's Educational Philosophy," *Educational Theory* 9(2) (April 1959), 110–11.
5. Smith, "A Critical Estimate of Plato's and Dewey's Educational Philosophy," 112–13.
6. Hill, *A Short History of Modern Philosophy*, 17.
7. Smith, "A Critical Estimate of Plato's and Dewey's Educational Philosophy," 114.
8. On Thomas Jefferson, classical philosophy and slavery, see Carl J. Richard, *The Golden Age of the Classics in America: Greece, Rome, and the Antebellum United States* (Cambridge: Harvard University Press, 2009), 154–55, 161, 182–92. Aristotle argues, "But is there any one thus intended by nature to be a slave, and for whom such a condition is expedient and right, or rather is not all slavery a violation of nature? There is no difficulty in answering this question, on grounds both of reason and of fact. For that some should rule, and others be ruled is a thing not only necessary, but expedient; from the hour of their birth, some are marked out for subjection, others for rule. . . . Again, the male is by nature superior, and the female inferior; and the one rules, and the other is ruled; this principle, of necessity, extends to all mankind." Consult, Aristotle, *The Politics of Aristotle*, trans. Benjamin Jowett (New York: Colonial Press, 1900), 4–9.
9. See, for example, Angela Y. Davis, "Unfinished Lecture on Liberation—II," in *Philosophy Born of Struggle: Anthology of Afro-American Philosophy from 1917*, ed. Leonard Harris (Dubuque: Kendall/Hunt Pub. Co, 1983), 130–31.

10. An examination of African American political culture confirms our judgment that most African American philosophers held to the view of full political participation, rather than the statement that all of them held this viewpoint. One specific exception to this rule is Dr. Jerome R. Riley. Riley argues against the notion that the vote should be extended to all Black people as citizens of the United States. In this respect, he agrees with the position taken by Booker T. Washington. For the full examination of his arguments consult, Jerome R. Riley, *The Philosophy of Negro Suffrage* (Washington, DC: Privately Printed, 1897).

11. Charles Leander Hill, "American Democracy," *The Negro Journal of Religion* 6(2) (March 1940), 13.

12. Howard McGary and Bill E. Lawson, *Between Slavery and Freedom: Philosophy and American Slavery* (Bloomington: Indiana University Press, 1995), xxv.

13. W. E. B. Du Bois, *Black Reconstruction* (New York: Harcourt, Brace & Co., 1935). For leftist critiques of Du Bois's *Black Reconstruction*, see Abram Harris, "Reconstruction and the Negro," in *Race, Radicalism, and Reform: Selected Papers of Abram L. Harris*, ed. William A. Darity, Jr. (New Brunswick: Transaction Publishers, 1989), 209–12; Loren Miller, "Let My People Go!" *New Masses* (October 29, 1935), 23; Ralph Bunche, "Reconstruction Reinterpreted: Book Review of W. E. B. Du Bois, Black Reconstruction," *Journal of Negro Education* 4(4) (October 1935), 568–70.

14. C. L. R. James, *Every Cook Can Govern: A Study of Democracy in Ancient Greece* (Highland Park: Facing Reality Pub. Committee, 1956).

15. Also consult, McGary and Lawson, *Between Slavery and Freedom*, particularly chapter 4.

16. Winson R. Coleman, *Knowledge and Freedom in the Political Philosophies of Plato and Aristotle* (Doctoral Dissertation, University of Chicago, 1950), 10–12.

17. Winson R. Coleman, "Knowledge and Freedom in the Political Philosophy of Plato," *Ethics* 71(1) (October 1960), 42.

18. Joyce Mitchell Cook, "On the Nature and Nurture of Intelligence," *The Philosophical Forum* 9(2–3) (1977–78), 289 n38.

19. Carter G. Woodson, *Carter G. Woodson's Appeal*, ed. Darrell Michael Scott (Washington, DC: ASALH Press, 2008). The son of former slaves, Woodson is considered "The Father of Black History." Consult, Pero Gaglo Dagbovie, "Carter G. Woodson (1875–1950)," *BlackPast.org Remembered & Reclaimed*.

20. Carter G. Woodson, *The Miseducation of the Negro* (Grand Rapids: Candace Press, 1996). Originally published by Associated Publishers (1933).

21. For the classic treatment of philosophical behaviorism, consult Gilbert Ryle, *The Concept of Mind* (New York: Routledge, 2009).

22. Mills, *The Racial Contract* (Ithaca: Cornell University Press, 1998), 11.

23. Mills, "Reply to My Critics," in *Racial Liberalism and the Politics of Urban America*, ed. Curtis Stokes and Theresa Meléndez (East Lansing: Michigan State University Press, 2003), 32.

24. For differing interpretations of Mills's Racial Contract, see John H. McClendon III, "Black and White contra Left and Right? The Dialectics of Ideological Critique in African American Studies," *APA Newsletter on Philosophy and the Black Experience* 2(1) (Fall 2002), 47–56; Jorge L. A. Garcia, "The racial contract hypothesis," *Philosophia Africana* 4(1) (2001), 27–42; Kevin Graham, "Race and the Limits of Liberalism," *Philosophy of the Social Sciences* 32(2) (June 2002), 219–39.

25. African American astrophysicist, Neil deGrasse Tyson states, "With Supernovas as the smoking gun. . . . You forge elements heavier than hydrogen and helium in stars, it does the rest of the universe no good unless those elements are somehow cast forth to interstellar space and made available to form planets and people. Yes, we are Stardust." Neil deGrasse Tyson, *Death by Black Hole: And Other Cosmic Quandaries* (New York: W. W. Norton, 2007), 197.

26. NIH, "Magnesium: Fact Sheet for Health Professionals," https://ods.od.hih.gov/factsheets/Magnesium-Health

27. William T. Fontaine, "The Means End Relation and Its Significance for Cross-Cultural Ethical Agreement," *Philosophy of Science* 25(3) (July 1958), 162.

28. As historian Lawrence W. Levine reminds us, "Creating a rhythm for work—issuing instructions which helped laborers to synchronize their efforts, supplying a beat which timed work and controlled body movements—was only one of the functions of song. . . . Work songs accompanied jobs of every conceivable nature because they provided psychic benefits which were no less important than the physical stabilization they afforded. Again and again, black workers have testified to the importance of song in relieving the tedium of work and making the time pass." See Lawrence W. Levine, *Black Culture and Black Consciousness: Afro-American Folk Thought From Slavery to Freedom* (New York: Oxford University Press, 1977), 212. Examples of Black Work Songs: "Rosie," "Lighting-Long John," "I Be So Glad . . . When The Sun Goes Down," Sam Cook's "Chain Gang," Albert King's "Cadillac Assembly Line," and Valerie June, "Workin Woman Blues." See also Nina Simone's vocal presentation and Cannonball Adderly's instrumental performance of "Work Song," John Handy, "Hard Work," Harry Belafonte, "Here Rattler

Here," and "Swing Dat Hammer," along with Paul Robeson, "Water Boy" and "Old Man River." Robeson actually changed the lyrics to the latter song to reflect Black working-class spirit and values.

29. Thomas Nelson Baker, "Ideals, Part 2," *Alexander's Magazine* (October 1906), 40.

30. Stephanie M. H. Camp, "Black Is Beautiful: An American History," *The Journal of Southern History* 81(3) (2015), 675–90.

31. George D. Kelsey, "The Racist Search for Self," *The Journal of Religious Ethics* 6(1) (Fall 1978), 251.

32. Elijah Muhammad argues, "If you understand it right, you will agree with me that the whole Caucasian race is a race of devils. They proved to be devils in the garden paradise and 4000 years later they were condemned by Jesus. Likewise they are condemned today by the great Mahdi Muhammad as the nothing but devils in the plainest language. . . . After the righteous black nation has labored under the wicked rule of the devils for 6000 years, the return to a righteous ruler, under the God of righteousness, the people must be re-organized to live under such government." Elijah Muhammad, *The Supreme Wisdom: Solution to the So-Called "Negroes" Problem* (Chicago: University of Chicago, 1957), 26–27, 38.

33. He further states, "Besides those of colour, figure, and hair, there are other physical distinctions proving a difference of race. They have less hair on the face and body. They secrete less by the kidnies, and more by the glands of the skin, which gives them a very strong and disagreeable odour." Thomas Jefferson, *Notes on the State of Virginia, Queries 14 and 18, 137–43, 162–63* in Philip B. Kurland and Ralph Lerner, eds., *The Founders' Constitution* (Chapter 15, document 28), http://press-pubs.uchicago.edu/founders/

34. The white Cassius Clay was born into a slaveholding family in Kentucky and later became an abolitionist. He assisted in funding the founding of Berea College in Kentucky. However, he was a gradualist respecting the termination of slavery and sought to do so through legal means, that is, by reforming the Constitution rather than the direct assault on the institution. His extensive autobiography can be found online. Consult, Cassius Marcellus Clay, *The Life of Cassius Marcellus Clay: Memoir, Writings, And Speeches* (Cincinnati, OH: J. Fletcher Brennan & Co., 1886). Muhammad Ali's grandfather named his son Cassius Marcellus Clay and in turn Ali's father named him Cassius Marcellus Clay Jr.

35. Charles H. Kahn argues, "The verb 'be' as copula in Indo-European is characterized by two features which are important for the philosophical development. The first I call the *locative*, the second the *durative* aspect. By the locative feature I mean the fact that the verb serves for predication in

general, not only with nominal predicates (predicate nouns and adjectives or participles) but specifically for statements of place, like 'We are in this room.' This locative use seems so essential to the meaning of the verb that we find Aristotle saying that most people believe that whatever is, is somewhere; what is nowhere is nothing: for Greek common sense, a thing cannot really *be* unless it is somewhere. Beginning with Plato, some philosophers will deny the necessity of this connection between being and being in some place. But it has a strong intuitive hold on the Greek feeling about 'what is.'" Charles H. Kahn, "Linguistic Relativism and the Greek Project of Ontology," in ed. Sprung Mervyn, *The Question of Being* (University Park: University of Pennsylvania Press 1978), 31–44. Also consult, Charles H. Kahn, *The Verb "Be" in Ancient Greek* (Indianapolis: Hackett Publishing Co., 2003).

36. Thomas Nelson Baker, "Ideals, Part 2," *Alexander's Magazine* (October 1906), 38.

37. C. V. Roman, *American Civilization and the Negro* (Philadelphia: F. A. Davis Company, Publishers, 1921), 60.

38. David Foster Wallace, "Federer Both Flesh and Not," in *The David Foster Wallace Reader* (New York: Little, Brown and Company, 2014), 939.

39. For a broader treatment of the philosophy of sports and the African Americans experience, consult John H. McClendon III and Stephen C. Ferguson II, *Beyond the White Shadow: Philosophy, Sports, and the African American Experience* (Dubuque: Kendall Hunt Publishing Company, 2012).

40. Forrest O. Wiggins, "Ethics and Economics," *Phylon* 6(2) (1945), 154.

41. Wiggins, "Ethics and Economics," 154.

42. Ibid.

43. Ibid., 160.

44. Ibid., 161.

45. Ibid.

46. Forrest O. Wiggins, "Review of Joseph Leighton's Social Philosophy in Conflict," *Journal of Social Philosophy and Jurisprudence* 6(4) (1940), 377.

47. Locke's six articles are (1) "Values and Imperatives" (1935), (2) "Pluralism and Intellectual Democracy" (1942), (3) "Cultural Relativism and Ideological Peace" (1944), (4) "Pluralism and Ideological Peace" (1947), (5) "Changing Values in the Western World" (1951), and (6) "Values that Matter" (1954). These essays can be found in *The Philosophy of Alain Locke: Harlem Renaissance and Beyond*, ed. Leonard Harris (Philadelphia: Temple University Press, 1991).

48. Alain Locke, "Values and Imperatives," in *American Philosophy, Today and Tomorrow*, 317.

49. Locke, "Values and Imperatives."
50. Harper is quoted in Abby A. Johnson and Ronald N. Johnson, *Propaganda and Aesthetics: The Literary Politics of African-American Magazines in the Twentieth Century* (Amherst: University of Massachusetts Press, 1991), 2–3. Also consult, Frances Ellen Watkins Harper, *A Brighter Coming Day: A Frances Ellen Watkins Harper Reader*, ed. Frances Smith Foster (New York: Feminist Press of CUNY, 1990).
51. Paul Robeson, "The Artist Must Take Sides," in *Paul Robeson Speaks: Writings, Speeches, Interviews, 1918–1974*, ed. Philip S. Foner (Secaucus: Carol Publishing Group, 1978), 118–19.
52. Gayle quoted in Nathaniel Norment Jr., *The Addison Gayle Jr. Reader* (Urbana: University of Illinois Press, 2009), xxxiv.
53. W. E. B. Du Bois, "Criteria of Negro Art," *The Crisis* 32(6) (October 1926), 296.
54. Jeffrey C. Stewart, *The New Negro: The Life of Alain Locke* (New York: Oxford University Press, 2018), 523.
55. For detailed summation of the debate between Du Bois and Locke, read "Beauty or Propaganda," chapter 28 of Jeffrey C. Stewart, *The New Negro: The Life of Alain Locke* (New York: Oxford University Press, 2018). Also consult, Venetria K. Patton and Maureen Honey present a strong summation on Locke's aesthetic principle of "art for art's sake" and his debate with Du Bois in their "Introduction," to Venetria K. Patton and Maureen Honey, eds., *Double-Take: A Revisionist Harlem Renaissance Anthology* (New Brunswick: Rutgers University Press, 2001), xxxv.
56. W. E. B. Du Bois, "Editorial," *The Crisis* (January 1926), 141.
57. W. E. B. Du Bois, "Criteria of Negro Art," in Winston Napier, ed., *African American Literary Theory: A Reader* (New York: New York University Press, 2000), 22–23.
58. Langston Hughes, "The Negro Artist and the Racial Mountain," in *African American Literary Theory*, 27–30.
59. Ernest Mason, "Black Art and the Configurations of Experience: The Philosophy of the Black Aesthetic," *CLA Journal* 27(1) (1983), 2.
60. Addison Gayle Jr., ed., *The Black Aesthetic* (Garden City, NY: Doubleday, 1972), xviii.
61. Gayle Jr., *The Black Aesthetic*, 313. Gayle's employment of the phrase "ars poetica" is a reference to poetic criticism, that is, the art of poetry or more generally literary criticism, which the Roman writer Horace in a letter outlined (around 19 BCE) for what constituted good poetry. The main point is that Gayle argues in supporting an aesthetics, which gives priority to fighting oppression over formalized treatment of literary works that abstract away such realities.

62. Eugene Clay (Holmes), "Negro in Recent American Literature," in Henry Hart, ed., *American Writers' Congress* (New York: International Publishers, 1935), 145.

63. Clay (Holmes), "Negro in Recent American Literature," 146.

64. For excellent treatments of Wright's "Blueprint," see William J. Maxwell, *New Negro, Old Left: African-American Writing and Communism Between the Wars* (New York: Columbia University Press, 1999), 153–78; and Barbara Foley, *Radical Representations: Politics and Form in U.S. Proletarian Fiction, 1929–41* (Durham: Duke University Press, 1994).

65. Richard Wright, "Blueprint for Negro Writing," in John A. Williams and Charles F. Harris, eds., *Amistad 2* (New York: Vintage, 1971), 10–11.

66. Wright, "Blueprint for Negro Writing," 20.

67. William Fontaine, "Toward a Philosophy of the American Negro Literature," *Présence Africaine* 24–25 (1959), 164–76; and William Fontaine, "The Mind and Thought of the Negro of the United States as Revealed in Imaginative Literature, 1876–1940," *Southern University Bulletin* 28 (March 1942), 5–50.

68. Robert C. Williams, "Afro-American Folklore as a Philosophical Source," *Journal of the West Virginia Philosophical Society* (Fall 1976), 1–6.

69. Johnson's 1981 award-winning short story, "Exchange Value," provides a philosophical fable about Karl Marx's account of commodity fetishism. Through the story of two Black working-class siblings Loftis and "Cooter," Johnson weaves an insightful and complex tale about how—in capitalist society—social relations between people taken on the appearance of relations between things. For Marx's discussion of commodity fetishism, see Karl Marx, *Capital: A Critique of Political Economy, Vol. 1: The Process of Capitalist Production* (New York: Lawrence & Wishart, 1976), 76–87. For an interpretation of "Exchange Value," see Linda Furgerson Selzer, "Charles Johnson's 'Exchange Value': Signifyin(g) on Marx," *The Massachusetts Review* 42(2) (Summer 2001), 253–68. For Charles Johnson's presentation of Marx as a sort of Buddhist Dharma socialist, see Charles Johnson, *Oxherding Tale* (New York: Grove Weidenfeld, 1982).

70. Charles Johnson, "Philosophy and Black Fiction," in Rudolph P. Byrd, ed., *I Call Myself an Artist: Writings by and about Charles Johnson* (Bloomington: Indiana University Press, 1999), 83.

71. Johnson, "Philosophy and Black Fiction."

72. For a fuller discussion of this point, see Darren Hudson Hick, *Introducing Aesthetics and the Philosophy of Art* (New York: Bloomsbury, 2017), 2–4, 82–84.

73. Paul Robeson, "The Related Sounds of Music," in *Paul Robeson Speaks: Writings, Speeches, Interviews, 1918-1974*, ed. Philip S. Foner (New York: Brunner/Mazel, 1978), 444.

74. See Harry Targ, "Legacies of the Musical Cultural Front: Robeson, Guthrie, and Seeger," http://ouleft.sp-mesolite.tilted.net/?p=1285 (last accessed November 24, 2014). See also the following articles by Paul Robeson: "The Source of the Negro Spirituals," "Paul Robeson and Negro Music," "Soviet Culture," "Songs of My People," "Some Aspects of Afro-American Music," "The Related Sounds of Music," in Philip S. Foner, ed., *Paul Robeson Speaks: Writings, Speeches, Interviews, 1918–1974* (New York: Brunner/Mazel, 1978), 73–76, 81–82, 136–37, 211–17, 436–39, 443–48; see also Paul Robeson, "A Universal Body of Folk Music – A Technical Argument by the Author," in *Here I Stand* (Boston: Beacon Press, 1971), 115–17.

75. Paul Robeson, *Here I Stand* (Boston, Massachusetts: Beacon Press, 1971), 44.

76. Consult, Ramon Ricker, *Pentatonic Scales for Jazz Improvisation* (Van Nuys: Alfred Publishing Co., 2016), 2. See also Annie G. Gilchrist, "Note on Modal System of Gaelic Tunes," *Journal of the Folk Song Society* (December 1911), 150–53.

77. Ramon Ricker, *Pentatonic Scales for Jazz Improvisation* (Van Nuys: Alfred Publishing Co., 2016), 2.

78. Ricker, *Pentatonic Scales for Jazz Improvisation*, 57.

79. See Alain Locke, *The Negro and His Music* (Washington, DC: Associates in Negro Folk Education, 1936); Albert Mosley, "On the Aesthetics of Black Music," *The Journal of Aesthetic Education* 35(3) (Autumn, 2001), 94–98; Roosevelt Porter III, "Some Peculiarities about Musical Aesthetic Qualities," *The Review of Metaphysics* 48(3) (March 1995), 483–509; John H. McClendon III, "African or American? A Dialectical Analysis of Jazz Music," in Jacob U. Gordon, ed., *The African Presence in Black America* (Trenton, New Jersey: Africa World Press, 2004), 85–114; and Julius Bailey, *Philosophy and Hip-Hop: Ruminations on Postmodern Cultural Form* (New York: Palgrave Macmillan, 2016). Derrick Darby and Tommie Shelby edited a collection of philosophical essays about Hip-Hop music titled *Hip-Hop and Philosophy: Rhyme 2 Reason*. This anthology included contributions by Joy James, Lewis Gordon, Lionel K. McPherson, Stephen Lester Thompson, Kathryn T. Gines, John P. Pittman, Bill Lawson, Rodney C. Roberts, and others. More generally, Paul C. Taylor has written an introductory book which examines problems in philosophical aesthetics, philosophy of art, and Black popular culture titled *Black is Beautiful: A Philosophy of Black Aesthetics* (New York: Wiley-Blackwell, 2016).

80. Portia Maultsby, "Africanism in African American Music," in *Africanism in American Culture*, ed. Joseph E. Holloway (Bloomington: Indiana University Press, 1990), 186–87.

81. James B. Barnes, "Alain Locke and the Sense of African Ancestry," in *Alain Locke: Reflections on a Modern Renaissance Man*, ed. Russell J. Linnemann (Baton Rouge: Louisiana State University Press, 1982), 105.

82. Barnes, "Alain Locke and the Sense of African Ancestry," 104.
83. Paul Robeson, "The Related Sounds of Music," in *Paul Robeson Speaks: Writings, Speeches, Interviews, 1918–1974*, 444.
84. Paul Robeson, "Songs of My People," in *Paul Robeson Speaks: Writings, Speeches, Interviews, 1918–1974*, 212.
85. Sterling Stucky, *Going Through the Storm: The Influence of African American Art in History* (New York: Oxford University Press, 1994), 42.
86. Innocent C. Onyewuenyi, "Traditional African Aesthetics: A Philosophical Perspective," in Albert Mosley, ed., *African Philosophy* (Englewood: Prentice Hall, 1996), 421–27.
87. Albert Mosley, "On the Aesthetics of Black Music," *The Journal of Aesthetic Education* 35(3) (Autumn, 2001), 97.
88. Mosley, "On the Aesthetics of Black Music," 346.
89. Albert Mosley, "The Moral Significance of the Music of Black Atlantic," *Philosophy East and West* 57(3) (July 2007), 346.
90. Roosevelt Porter III, "Some Peculiarities about Musical Aesthetic Qualities," *The Review of Metaphysics* 48(3) (March 1995), 496–97.
91. The authors want to thank Jazz organist Bob "Big Cutty" Bass for his insights on the notion of musical concept as adjoined to improvisational creativity and developing one's own voice or signature. Big Cutty is a leading Jazz organist in the Midwest from Dayton, Ohio. His own body of work extends the tradition of Larry Young, Don Patterson, and Charles Earland.
92. Albert Mosley, "The Moral Significance of the Music of Black Atlantic," 346.
93. James Reese Europe, "A Negro explains Jazz," in R. Waltzer, ed., *Keeping Time: Readings in Jazz History* (New York: Oxford University Press, 1999), 14.
94. Max Roach, "Jazz," in Esther Cooper Jackson, ed., *Freedomways Reader* (Boulder: Westview Press, 2000), 360.
95. Roach, "Jazz," 361.
96. John H. McClendon III, "Jazz, African American Nationality, and the Myth of the Nation-State," *Socialism and Democracy* 18(2) (July/December 2004), 23–4. See also Sidney Finkelstein, *Jazz: A People's Music* (New York: International Publishers, 1988).
97. John Seabrook, *The Song Machine: Inside the Hit Factory* (New York: W. W. Norton & Company, 2015), 15–16.

4

Philosophy of Science:
African American Deliberations

Chapter Outline

Our chapter explores what African American philosophers have had to say about the relationship of philosophy to science, in both its natural and social forms. For instance, we examine the Marxist contributions of Eugene C. Holmes in the philosophy of space and time. And we look at the historical debate on the relationship between epistemology and sociology of knowledge. (59)

As we have noted, philosophy was the first form of theoretical knowledge. Over the course of time, questions that were confined to philosophical speculation have become the province of the physical sciences. Philosophical questions about the *nature of reality* (ontology) have served as the catalyst for scientific questions about the *reality of nature*. From the atom in a void to the relation of form and matter, along with the characterization of change and permanence and even theories of evolution, these objects of philosophical investigation transparently constitute how the seeds for science were historically sowed in philosophical soil. In fact, ancient formulations in political and social philosophy, not to mention ethics, were formative developments which led to what we know as the social sciences today.

The speculative query on the *reality of nature* evolved into probing about *the nature of life*; hence, we have the philosophical infancy of the biological sciences. And with philosophical queries into the *nature of social life*, we have correspondingly the development of social sciences. We would be remiss not to mention the behavioral sciences—such as psychology and cognitive science—have their origins in the philosophy of mind. Historically speaking, what we know is that this process reflects a dialectical progression on how philosophy—as theoretical knowledge—gave birth to the origins of the specialized sciences. Notwithstanding the contemporary separation of science from philosophy, we have what is known as the philosophy of science.

In this chapter, we primarily explore what African American philosophers and scientific thinkers have had to say about philosophical issues in the physical, natural, and social sciences. In far too many anthologies and introductory texts, African American philosophers and scientists are left out of the discussion around the philosophy of science. And, yet, both African American philosophers and scientists have actively engaged in the philosophy of science. For illustration, in the physical sciences we have the work of physicists Robert A. Thornton and Ronald L. Mallett in conjunction with philosophers Eugene C. Holmes and Roy D. Morrison II; in the natural sciences there is biologist Ernest E. Just and philosopher William T. Fontaine; with the social sciences, we have the social scientists Abram Harris and Oliver C. Cox and correspondingly philosophers Cornelius L. Golightly and Carleton L. Lee. Of course, there are other African American scientists and philosophers that are worthy of our attention.[1]

What is the philosophy of science?

What exactly is the philosophy of science? The philosophy of science explores philosophical problems and issues associated with the foundations, methods, theories, and social implications of science. As we noted in Chapter 2, biology and physics are no longer designated as natural philosophy. However, modern-day philosophy investigates biology and physics via the *philosophy of science*. The philosophical investigation of the sciences, of course, is not the same as pursuing the study of biology or physics; it is the employment of a philosophical lens onto scientific subject matter.

Several questions arise within this area: What qualifies as science? What is the nature of a scientific theory? How is science distinct from phrenology, astrology, intelligent design, creationism, and other forms of pseudoscience?[2] What is a law of nature? Are there social laws that apply to the social world? What are the philosophical implications of Einstein's theory of relativity? Does social science use the same methods as natural science? Is there a fundamental difference between the natural sciences and the social sciences? Is history a science? If it is a science, what is its relation to the philosophy of history?[3] Can social scientific inquiry be objective? What is the affiliation between values, ideology, and science? What is the association between the sociology of knowledge and epistemology? What are the ontological limits of religion relative to scientific research? By far, these questions do not adequately cover all the problems and issues that fall within the scope of the philosophy of science. They do provide, however, a general outline for scholarly deliberation.

It perhaps seems self-evident for most of us that the line of demarcation between nature (which is the subject matter of the natural and physical sciences) and human existence as social beings (which is the subject matter of the humanities, social, and behavioral sciences) is rather clear cut. Yet, the scientific conception of this differentiation involves a measure of complexity, involving specific questions about scientific theory and method. The philosopher of science must astutely examine how such theories and methods are concretely applicable. While both neurology and sociology can have human beings as their respective objects of investigation, there remain substantial differences regarding what suitable procedures are associated with relevant modes of scientific inquiry. Hence, the commonality of subject matter is not a defining feature of a given science.

To the extent that the natural and physical sciences examine human life, they function as scientific modes of inquiry by abstracting away from the social character of human existence. In contrast, the social sciences have as their subject matter the very thing that the natural and physical sciences intentionally ignore, namely, the social character of human existence. Therefore, instead of abstracting away from the social character of human existence, the social sciences abstract away the natural and physical features of human beings. Consequently, the social sciences are not concerned with human physiology and anatomy as the biological sciences would.

Yet, we uncover that the behavioral sciences such as cognitive science are often involved in scientific work that brings together the research results from the natural sciences—such as neurology—as well as the social sciences. Furthermore, the referencing of research in social science is quite commonly manifested in the emergence of innovated disciplinary lines. For instance, we have the fields of behavioral ecology and social psychology that straddle the lines of demarcation. One outcome respecting this complexity, regarding disciplinary boundaries, is that the relation between natural and social science has become more transitory, especially with behavioral sciences.

The African American dialectical idealist tradition in the philosophy of science

The relationship of philosophy to science has not escaped the attention of African American philosophers and thinkers over the years. Since the antebellum period, African American thinkers have confronted the many hydra-headed monster of racist ideology. Bathed in the cloth of pseudoscience, racist ideology—as the French philosopher and mathematician Marquis de Condorcet said—sought to "make nature herself an accomplice in the crime of political inequality."[4]

African American thinkers such as Frederick Douglass waged a ruthless struggle in order to "uplift the race" against the rising tide of speciously constructed yet scientifically encapsulated forms of racism. In a speech delivered in 1854, at Western Reserve College, Douglass dismantled the claims of polygenists:

> I propose to submit to you a few thoughts on the subject of the Claims of the Negro, suggested by ethnological science, or the natural history of man. . . . The relation subsisting between the white and black people of this country is the vital question of the age. In the solution of this question, the scholars of America will have to take an important and controling [sic] part. This is the moral battle field to which their country and their God now call them. In the eye of both, the neutral scholar is an ignoble man.[5]

Douglass continues,

> I say it is remarkable—nay, it is strange that there should arise a phalanx of learned men—speaking in the name of science—to forbid the magnificent reunion of mankind in one brotherhood. A mortifying proof is here given,

that the moral growth of a nation, or an age, does not always keep pace with the increase of knowledge, and suggests the necessity of means to increase human love with human learning. The proposition to which I allude, and which I mean next to assert, is this, that what are technically called the negro race, are a part of the human family, and are descended from a common ancestry, with the rest of mankind.[6]

Douglass was not alone as Black critic of polygenism. Black intellectual Martin R. Delany also upheld *monogenism* in opposition to *polygenism*. Based on the idealist presuppositions of biblical texts, Delany posits that all humans come from the same source, that is, God.[7] Consequently, Delany was committed to idealism as the anchor for monogenism. The scientific formulated or materialist conception of monogenism, on the other hand, argued that differences regarding racial features were a matter of environmental influences and all races were members of the human species. Hence, race was not an issue of species differentiation.

The reader may wonder what then is polygenism and who are polygenists? How is polygenism related to the philosophy of pseudoscience and its racist implications? In James Ferguson's penetrating article, "The Laboratory of Racism," he points out,

The polygenists believe that ethnic features were innate and permanent, undergoing no significant modifications through environmental change. . . . They argued that different races were in fact different species and that fecundity between entirely different species was a law of nature. . . . Some polygenists were convinced that certain ethnic communities, notably Africans and aborigines can be excluded from the human species altogether.[8]

David Hume provides one of the first naturalist accounts of polygenism. Richard Popkin keenly observes,

Hume's view was a non-theological form of polygenism, making it a matter of nature rather than God that some species of people have greater intellectual and cultural abilities than others. . . . Hume's naturalistic formulation of polygenetic theory as a way for accounting of black inferiority was taken over by many defenders of African slavery in America and Europe.[9]

The transition from philosophical speculation concerning the naturalistic formulation of polygenetic theory to putatively scientific forms was but a small step. Polygenism found its so-called scientific rationalization with the emergence of human genetics as an academic field of research. Black sociologist Troy Duster remarks, "The core enterprise of the early human geneticists was the search for evidence that there is genetic stratification, i.e., higher and lower forms of life, higher and lower forms of intelligence among population groupings among humans. Physical anthropology and (pre-Boas) cultural anthropology had a near perfect, hand in glove fit."[10]

From their academic start, the landscape of social and behavioral sciences was entrenched in various kinds of research highly supportive of social movements and public policies that affirmed racism. For example, in the nineteenth century, the burgeoning field of biometry, which is the application of mathematical and statistical methods to biological data, was readily employed in the interest of racist social policy. In accord with Duster's analysis, psychologist Robert V. Guthrie in his insightful book *Even the Rat Was White* adeptly exposes how the emergence of psychology as a discipline gave support to the *eugenics movement*, which provided intellectual justification for sterilization laws and, moreover, provided research on how genetic differences could be employed in the pursuit of racial domination. British scientist and one of the founders of biometry Francis Galton—cousin of Charles Darwin—coined the term "eugenics" in 1883. In *Inquiries into Human Faculty and Its Development*, Galton states, "It will suffice to faintly sketch out some sort of basis for eugenics, it being now an understanding that we are provisionally agreed . . . that the improvement of race is an object of first-class importance."[11]

Galton defined eugenics as "the science of improving inherited stock, not only by judicious mating, but by all the influences which give more suitable strains a better chance." He further added, "To give the more suitable races . . . a better chance of prevailing speedily over the less suitable."[12] At the root of the matter, we have the thesis that genetic makeup determines one's social position. Those that rise to the top of the (capitalist) social order do so because they are better suited genetically. Furthermore, race is the vital factor in genetic disposition. Clearly, Galton's eugenics is a sophisticated form of racism which recasts polygenism.

Importantly, Galton's work greatly influenced later contemporary researchers in the twentieth century such as Richard J. Hernstein and Charles R. Murray. As Stephen E. Fienberg and Daniel P. Resnick aptly bring to our view, "The roots of Hernstein and Murray's argument in the *Bell Curve* can be traced to Francis Galton in *Heredity Genius, Its Laws and Consequences*. Galton was the central figure in the founding of the eugenics movement in the study of the relationship of heredity to race and talent."[13] Moreover, scores of African American thinkers attacked the validity and veracity of Richard J. Hernstein and Charles R. Murray's

The Bell Curve, which was published in 1994. Of particular note is the previously mentioned Troy Duster. In 1995, Duster succinctly notes the following:

> Two important conclusions can be drawn from the research on the links between genetics, intelligence, and race. First, nothing new has happened in the last thirty years in genetics at the molecular level. However, there is a considerable amount of funding in genetics, which explains the popularity of Murray and Herrnstein. The second point is that there is something new. . . . What is new is the receptive climate for this formula.[14]

In turn, philosopher Joyce Mitchell Cook confronts this form of "insidious racism," which undergirds genetic arguments about racial differences based on IQ tests.[15] The nature of scientific findings has definite political and ideological implications. African American philosophers have responded to such matters by critically assessing such results. They have not rejected the validity of science; instead they have advanced philosophical interpretation of scientific research in a critical manner.[16]

Previously, a great number of African American thinkers—from the nineteenth century onward—gave voice to the significance of science in its dialectical development. Despite the historical conflict between science and religion, many of these African American philosophers and thinkers viewed science and religion as complementary in character. One glaring example of this dialectical idealist tradition is Black theologian A. J. Kershaw. He argues,

> The term, true Science, is a misnomer, for it implies that there is a false Science, a thing that never was, and never can be. Science, philosophically considered, is a collection of leading truths relating to any subject reduced to a system. Any system that is not absolutely true is not Science, but speculative philosophy; and, of course, this kind of philosophy can do anything and everything.[17]

While Kershaw thinks that science and philosophy are not well-suited, he, however, finds that Christianity (as religious belief system) and science are compatible in their methods and outlook. At the crux of the matter is the notion that systemic absolute truth resides in biblical texts. On the one hand, he believes that religion and science both uphold absolute truth. On the other hand, philosophy falls short of the mark, given that its speculative character can only result in a form of relative truth. Kershaw further remarks, "There never was, there is not, there never will be, a conflict between Science and the Bible, but there is, and always will be an irresistible conflict between the Bible and speculative philosophy."[18]

From the late nineteenth century and on into the twentieth century, African American idealist philosophers found science to be an invaluable part of Black education and critical to the liberal arts orientation. African American philosopher and educator Charles Leander Hill (Figure 13a&b) argues that "The Role of Religion in Higher Education" was not inconsistent with the inclusion of science in the curriculum and indeed complemented it—given that religion was the medium for the dispensation of values. Hill asserted,

> Since the term religion raises the whole problem of value, precisely where does the problem of value stand in relationship to the present status of physical science? This statement is not made with the emotion of one who worships at the shrine of what a philosopher recently called "that false Messiah of the twentieth century—science," but as a concession to those individuals who feel we must forsake pure science and the scientific method whenever we discuss religion in any context whatsoever. I might add here that the term value used to include moral and aesthetic as well as religious values. This is the use of the term value in its generic sense.[19]

Hill argued that the compatibility of science and religion was grounded on an idealist philosophy of science that emerged as a definitive philosophical tradition which we have dubbed as *dialectical idealism*. By "dialectical" we mean that the philosophical conception of reality (ontology) was one that highlighted the dynamic process of motion, change, and development. Reality was not taken as static and fixed and in turn matter was not viewed as mechanical in makeup.

Figure 13a&b Charles Leander Hill (1906–56).

It is important to acknowledge that mechanical materialism is often associated with Newtonian physics, where Newton viewed the physical laws of motion that govern matter as machine-like in character. This viewpoint finds a distinctive replication in the fields of biometry, eugenics, and human genetics more generally; all of which share in the common methodology associated with the mechanical reduction of human social attributions to some rudimentary natural disposition such as genetic makeup. This mechanistic viewpoint leaves little room for the consideration on the problem of value and its association with science.

While Hill gives expression to how values are a necessary feature of both religion and science, nevertheless, the definition of value, from a scientific viewpoint, is not a mundane question. As African American philosopher Cornelius L. Golightly brings to our attention,

> Is it possible to give value a "real" definition in the same way that scientists define cancer or oxygen? A real definition usually subsumes empirical phenomena under a general law or theory and is true or false. When a scientist defines a concept like value, which already has vague and controversial meanings in both conversational and scientific discourse, it cannot be said that his definition is simply true or false.[20]

The immediate implications of Golightly's query become pronounced when we venture into the relation of value to the procedures that outline scientific inquiry. The popular notion that scientific objectivity is synonymous with maintaining a "value free" orientation plays no small part in our deliberation. Indeed, Golightly further adds, "The scientific effort to define value for purposes of theory construction provides an opportunity for observing the process by which a philosophical concept is translated gradually into a scientific concept. Of course this has happened before, e.g., with atom, evolution, memory, self, and emotion."[21]

This distinction between philosophical and scientific concepts—that are by name the same—is crucially important in the philosophy of science. We know the philosophical conception of atom connotes something that remains indivisible—hence the fundamental unit grounding reality—is no longer a precise scientific category. The scientific discovery of subatomic particles, subject matter in the field of quantum physics, obviously reconfigures the very definition of "atom."

In divergence, the philosophical conception of matter is an epistemological category that differentiates how material phenomena ontologically exist independent of any perceiver and is demarcated from sensations, perceptions, and even concepts held in the process of knowing the material world. In contrast, the scientific conception actually examines the physical structure of matter and acknowledges its inexhaustibility. Consequently, the conception of matter is subject to two corresponding and yet cojoined developments, that is, philosophical and scientific comprehension.[22]

Philosophical materialism upholds the viewpoint that the material world (matter) is independent of the knowing subject and is governed by a continual process of cognitive approximation. In contrast, the scientific concept relies on the research that unearths the structural composition of matter. Thus, whether or not quarks are the ultimate units of matter is an open question riding on scientific discovery. However, whatever the structural features of physical matter, philosophical materialism remains consistent with science in upholding that matter (in principle) has ontological autonomy or objective existence.

It is worth noting that few African American philosophers have traveled down the road of philosophical materialism. The philosopher Eugene C. Holmes offers a materialist treatment on the philosophical problems associated with space and time, which we will examine later in this chapter. We should also make note of Black philosopher William Fontaine's examination of Ernest E. Just's research in cell theory, which substantially progresses beyond the popular notion associated with the "struggle for existence" functioning as the governing motif for Darwin's theory of evolution. Fontaine keenly observes what are the materialist implications of Just's research: "For the various philosophical schools of evolutionary naturalism there is a profound message in the recent book of Dr. Ernest E. Just, 'The Biology of the Cell Surface.' The author is a naturalist of naturalists; for years he has sought to validate by scientific experiment the purely naturalistic relationship of the living to the non-living."[23]

William T. Fontaine and Ernest E. Just: The materialist conception of life

Black scientist Ernest E. Just (1883–1941) graduated from Dartmouth College in biology with magna cum laude and Phi Beta Kappa honors in 1903. In 1916, Just earned his PhD from the University of Chicago. As teacher and scholar, Just taught at Howard University, in addition, he conducted research at the Marine Biological Laboratory in Woods Hole, Massachusetts. He was a pioneering and productive scholar, publishing fifty research articles and two books. Our concern in this chapter is his book *The Biology of the Cell Surface* (1939).[24] Just candidly indicates that his method of presentation is designed to reach the general reader:

> Even the most abstract truth needs to be expressed with simplicity and clearness and thus relate itself to everyday human experience. Complexity of expression is often a sign of incomplete knowledge and certainly it is not a *sine qua non* of learning, though there be those who consider profound and erudite that which they can never understand. However cloistered biology may be as a scientific research, as the science of life and having appeal to all men it should make itself articulate beyond its cloistered walls.[25]

Just engages in scientific research in which the supervening problem of philosophical import concerns the question of what connects as well as separates living matter from nonliving matter? For many philosophers and biologists—prior to Just—matter itself was judged as lacking the needed requisites for life, hence the source of life was thought to be immaterial. The immaterial source of life was captured in the theoretical notion of vitalism. Normandin and Wolfe summarily state the following:

> Arguably, all understandings of life in antiquity implied a kind of vitalism. Charting the course of vitalism's history brings us from the classical age (where, on the question of souls and *animas*, we might gesture toward Aristotle, including the way in which his *De Anima* was taken up in early modernity) through the core of mechanizing forces of modern science. . . . While the term vitalism does not enter into actual use until the late eighteenth century, many of the ideas and concepts embodied in the word are as old as medical and biological thought. From the *animas* and *pneumas* of Hippocrates, Aristotle, and Galen to the ethical inducements towards vitalism in the French tradition . . . the idea as a long and multi-faceted history.[26]

The theoretical legacy of vitalism in the biological (life) sciences cannot be understated. Just's research confronts a powerful tradition via his materialist accounting of life. In the field of physiology, right until the late eighteenth century vitalism was the dominant explanatory framework. As Francois Duchesneau notes, "Vitalism has been taken as a general methodological stand in biological science. For vitalists, the phenomena of the living process *sui generis* features that make them radically different from physical and chemical phenomena."[27]

Just starts his treatise on the firm materialist premise that what we know as living matter is crucially linked to all of nature, including the fact of being subject to the laws that govern the physical-chemical processes. Just's opposition to various forms of vitalism becomes immediately transparent. He posits,

> The realm of living things being a part of nature is contiguous to the non-living world. Living things have material composition, are made up finally of units, molecules, atoms, and electrons, as surely as any non-living matter. Like all forms in nature they have chemical structure and physical properties, are physico-chemical systems. As such they obey the laws of physics and chemistry.[28]

Just makes it most apparent that any discussion on living matter must begin on materialist grounds. What we know as living organisms are foundationally linked to nature in the most basic sense of the corresponding laws of physics and chemistry. The unity of living and nonliving matter serves as the theoretical crux for how Just begins his scientific analysis. It stands to reason that what we comprehend as what constitutes life is not something that stands apart from the basic units of physical and natural existence. There can be no life without molecules, atoms, and electrons. In philosophical terms what we acknowledge as the condition of life is ontologically dependent upon physical-chemical processes and their associated laws. Just further adds,

> Would one deny this fact, one would thereby deny the possibility of any scientific investigation of living things. No matter what beliefs we entertain, the noblest and purest, concerning life as something apart from physical and chemical phenomena, we cannot with the mental equipment which we now possess reach any estimate of living things as apart from the remainder of the physico-chemical world.[29]

With this latter proposition, Just makes it most apparent that the very epistemological groundwork for scientific investigation cannot ignore the fact that living things are rooted in nature and are subject to its corresponding laws. If we are to understand the very concept of living organisms, then we cannot afford to overlook the general imperative that surrounds all scientific investigation. Namely, life sciences are fully grounded on the basis of the laws of nature and we cannot in any fashion move away from this fact. Efforts at constructing methodologies that are based on idealist notions—such as vitalism—are then clearly a departure from scientific inquiry.

While Just appropriately pursues the connection between living and nonliving matter, he does not neglect the fact that there still remains a qualitative difference between the two. Mountains and rocks, although quite material, are not living matter. How are we to understand living matter in its difference? Just informs us,

> But although any living thing, being matter, is a physico-chemical system, it differs from matter which constitutes the non-living. . . . The analysis of living things reveals that they are composed of no peculiar chemical elements—instead, they are made up of those most commonly occurring. The difference cannot then be attributed to the elements. To be sure, certain complex compounds, as proteins, carbohydrates and lipins (fats and fat-like substances)—themselves compounded mainly of the commonly occurring elements, carbon, hydrogen and oxygen, and never of rare elements—are peculiar to living matter.[30]

At this juncture, Just confronts how "Wohler's classic synthesis of urea" led some scientists and philosophers to postulate that there existed "some unknown vital principle sets apart the chemistry of living things from that of non-living."[31] In Just's estimation, Wohler's experiment far from offering the confirmation of vitalism, actually did not scientifically (methodologically) justified such conclusions.[32] In alignment with Just on the materialist stance against vitalist (idealist) readings on Wohler, Frederick Engels remarked,

> One thing still remains to be done here: to explain the origin of life from inorganic nature. At the present stage of science that implies nothing less than the preparation of protein bodies from inorganic substances. Chemistry is approaching closer and closer to the solution of this task, but it is still a long way from it. If, however, we bear in mind that it was only in 1828 that Wohler prepared the first organic body, urea, from inorganic materials, and what an innumerable number of so-called organic compounds are now artificially prepared without any organic materials, we shall not be inclined to bid chemistry halt when confronted by protein. So far chemistry has been able to prepare every organic substance, the composition of which is accurately known.[33]

Instead of idealist departures on the differentiation of nonliving and living matter, Just argues, "And yet there is a difference which expresses itself in the chemical make-up of the living thing. It is its organization. The difference with respect to chemistry thus lies in the peculiar combination of compounds which together make a heterogeneous system."[34]

William T. Fontaine keenly grasps that Just in highlighting of chemical organization has some specific insights on the concept of living organism. Fontaine duly notes the following:

> Since life is not found in any such unit as the biogen-molecule, protein, the gene-molecule or the chromatic granule, the two questions remain: What is life and where does one find its most tangible expression? With "*units*" disposed of, life must be sought in the "*organization*" wherein life is at least "contiguous to the non-living." This leads obviously to the protoplasmic organization of the living cell and as already stated to the ectoplasm. The ectoplasm is the most concrete expression of the life-process.[35]

Fontaine recognizes that Just in his primary concern on the organization of ectoplasm effectively opens the door for a thoroughgoing materialism and as well the scientific conception on life removed from various forms of mysticism and idealism. Subsequently, Fontaine declares,

> Now that it is known that ectoplasm is the most concrete organization of the living accessible to the mental equipment of man all truly scientific speculations concerning life origins as well as the cause of evolution must take this as their starting point. Man can know no more about life than life reveals in her most complete manifestation. Dr. Just will not yield to the philosopher's "Will to Believe"; he makes no appeal to a mystical elan vital . . . or originative impulse; he is completely silent about God and is swept by no such extravagances of wishful thinking as C. Lloyd Morgan's "super-personal phylogenetic entelechy."[36]

Hence, we conclude this discussion by returning to Just and his direct commentary on the biology of life. Just boldly brings to our attention in the following summary:

> The evolution-theory constitutes a fundamental postulate of the science of biology and has proved a guiding principle of uncalculable value for biological research. Among biologists exists the almost unanimous verdict that evolution took place. According to the prevailing opinion, the world of living things was evolved from a unicellular organism. It should however be emphasized that this first form of life was not that of some now existing protozoan. The word, Protozoa, literally means first animals; but we should bear in mind that among the Protozoa themselves evolution has taken place. We therefore assume that the first form of life was a simpler unicellular structure than the protozoan.[37]

While affirming the foundational locus of evolutionary theory, Just does not terminate his inquiry with protozoa. Instead he offers the insight that it too was subject to an evolutionary process. In turn, Just concludes that the key factor is in the organization of ectoplasm:

> Thus all forms of behavior by which we recognize that a thing is alive express themselves in response to the environment in the activity either of the ectoplasm itself as in unicellular organisms—or of structures which are rich in ectoplasm. The fineness and nicety of ectoplasmic organization increase progressively in the animal kingdom from the lowest to the highest organisms and thus parallel the course of evolution. This course, from the emergence of life out of non-life to the separation of animals from plants and farther to the unfolding of progressive complexity of animal-form, makes manifest the role and importance of the ectoplasm in evolution.[38]

African American philosophers on Einstein's theory of relativity

Albert Einstein ushered in a revolution in scientific knowledge with the introduction of his theories of relativity. Roy Morrison offers the following insight:

> Einstein's theories of relativity concern the form and character of the laws of nature. Philosophically, one may say that the theories constitute a response to the question whether the laws of nature are relative to arbitrarily chosen coordinate systems—or whether nature's laws are absolute.[39]

Einstein published the Special Theory of Relativity in 1905 and the General Theory of Relativity in 1915. The Special Theory is a special case of general relativity. It could be summarized in the following manner:

1 The laws of physics are the same for all observers in uniform motion relative to one another (principle of relativity).
2 The speed of light in a vacuum is the same for all observers, regardless of their relative motion or of the motion of the light source.[40]

What establishes the Special Theory as "special" is that Einstein, unlike Newton, does not regard space and time as absolute and hence as separate phenomena. The notion of space-time becomes the theoretical basis for comprehending the laws of physics. Events that take place at a certain time for one observer can actually transpire at different times for another. As such, this theoretical conception on space-time has limited application to uniform (constant) velocities with the speed of light—in a vacuum—serving as an absolute principle.

Consequently, there is no fixed frame of reference in the universe, with the exception of the speed of light. Everything (all matter) is moving relative to everything else within the framework of uniform velocity and the speed of light functioning as the foundation for absolute velocity. Significantly, Einstein presumes that space adheres to a flat surface consistent with Euclidean geometry. This theoretical formulation, however, did not adequately explain Newton's laws of motion respecting the question of gravity and planetary motion. It was discovered that gravitational laws respecting the orbit of planets in our solar system were somewhat inaccurate.

Specifically, Newton's calculations regarding the orbit of the planet Mercury were not precise. A hunt followed for two centuries in search of a solution. Esther Inglis-Arkell notes,

> Where people went wrong was looking for objects. Einstein eventually revealed that they should have been looking at space itself. In his theory of general relativity, Einstein showed that mass warps space. This warping didn't noticeably affect planets far from the sun, but Mercury was so close that its strange precession was visible as soon as people started paying close attention.[41]

A decade later Einstein was able to expand his theory of relativity to speak to the problems associated with Newton's conception of gravity. For Newton, gravity is a force that explains matter in motion. While this concept explains the effects of gravity, it does not offer a definition of gravity. Einstein concluded that the impact of massive objects on space-time leads to the curvature of space-time. Thus, his general relativity deals with gravity and has broader application on the measure of planetary motion. Nola Taylor Redd aptly observes, "Einstein then spent 10 years trying to include acceleration in the theory and published his theory of general relativity in 1915. In it, he determined that massive objects cause a distortion in space-time, which is felt as gravity."[42]

At its core, general relativity began with the equivalence principle, that is, gravity and inertia are one and the same. In more technical language, the states of accelerated motion and being at rest in a gravitational field (e.g., when standing on the surface of the Earth) are physically identical. Standing on the earth's surface, relative to an inertial frame is a state of rest, while simultaneously this involves the earth in its motion as it orbits the sun and rotates on its axis.

But, what have African American thinkers had to say about the philosophical significance of Einstein's theory of relativity?[43] Roy D. Morrison observes that many people mistakenly associate Einstein's theory of relativity with relativism. Einstein's theory, Morrison observes, is

> afflicted by a most unfortunate misnomer—a kind of semantic tragedy that perpetuates the myth that Einstein regarded everything as relative. The situation is compounded because in some quarters the term, "relative," is identified with that which is private, pluralistic, and subjective. . . . According to Einstein, the propagation of light and its absolute velocity are not subjective, or idealistic, or mathematical realities. . . . In any case, Einstein's science and his relativity theories do not relativize or subjectivize our knowledge. Instead, Einstein's contributions provide monumental reinforcement for the principles of invariance and of objectivity.[44]

Morrison brings out the epistemological mistake of moving from Einstein's theory to erecting the idea of the relativity of our knowledge into a general principle of knowledge. By offering a subjectivist reading of the "relative state of the observer," people miss the materialist implications of the theory of relativity.

The African American philosopher of science and physicist Robert A. Thornton was one of the first to recognize the general impact that Einstein's theory of relativity had on formal instruction in the philosophy of science. He engaged Einstein in many discussions—both in person and through written correspondence—about the relationship between science and philosophy. In a letter to Thornton in 1944, Einstein wrote the following:

> I fully agree with you about the significance and educational value of methodology as well as history and philosophy of science. So many people today—and even professional scientists—seems to me like someone who has seen thousands of trees but has never seen the forest. A knowledge of the historic and philosophical background gives that kind of independence from prejudices of his generation from which most scientists are suffering. The independence created by philosophical insight is—in my opinion—the mark of distinction between a mere artisan or specialist and a real seeker of truth.[45]

While a number of African American philosophers held to a religious orientation that was ontologically founded on dialectical idealism, they nevertheless maintained a keen interest in and some were actually quite receptive to Einstein's theory of relativity, finding it to be consistent with their respective religious beliefs. However, this general tendency to uphold scientific advancements and yet at the same time adhering to dialectical idealism had its philosophical import in a propensity to adopt an anti-realist ontology in the philosophy of science.[46]

When we enter the twentieth century, we have Robert Tecumtha Browne's seminal text *The Mystery of Space*, published in 1919. Brown was one of the first philosophers of science to analyze Einstein's theory of relativity from the perspective of dialectical idealism. Among the institutions where Browne served on faculty was at Samuel Huston College, a historically Black college. Browne was also a member of the American Negro Academy founded by the African American philosopher and theologian Alexander Crummell. Browne was invited to present a paper on Einstein's theory of relativity before the Academy in 1920.[47]

Despite lacking the formal credentials as philosopher, Browne's stature in the field was duly noted in the *Negro History Bulletin*, started by Dr. Carter G. Woodson. The journal noted Browne's contributions to the field of philosophy:

> The outstanding production of the Negro in this field is a work of mathematical philosophy produced by Robert T. Browne. . . . Mr. Browne was born and trained in the South. He made his way to New York City where he underwent further development in school and in scientific and philosophical circles. At the time that the world was concerned with abstruse problems as the fourth dimension and relativity which have been so extensively elaborated by Einstein, Browne plunged into the discussion. His book covers such theories as hyperspace movement, the non-Euclidean geometry, dimensionality, and the fourth dimension.[48]

The conception of fourth dimension emerges from Einstein's notion of space-time continuation. Given space and time are a continuum and space is three dimensional, then time effectively becomes a fourth dimension. Browne rejected the idea of fourth dimensionality and remained a staunch critic and ardent opponent of Einstein's theory of relativity. Browne was actually a vital part of a larger adversarial movement that at base was a countermovement concerning the philosophy of science. Milena Wazeck explains,

> This counter-discourse questioned the axioms of modern physics and simultaneously asserted specific demands on what constitutes science. It denied the status of a theory of physics to the theory of relativity and provided niches for devalued knowledge and alternative systems of recognition. This counter-discourse was apparent not only in a content dimension in the narrow sense in the form of the existence of other bodies of knowledge,

but also in a strategic dimension–that is, in amalgamations, networks, and counter-measures against the marginalization of these bodies of knowledge.[49]

Browne's idealism expressed in *The Mystery of Space* pointed to a psychic dimension of reality, where consciousness was a vital principle to the very composition of the universe. Browne describes the universe accordingly:

> The universe is a compacted *plenum*. It is chock-full of mind, of life, of energy and matter. These four are basically one. They exist, of course, in varying degrees of tenuity and intensity and answer to a wide range of vibrations. Together, in their manifestation of action and interaction, in their *dynamic appearance*, if you please, they constitute space. If these were remove with all that their existence implies there would result in condition of spacelessness in which no one of the appearances which we now perceive would be possible. Even sheer extensity would be non-existent.[50]

In the assumption that consciousness was the norm of space determinations, Browne concludes, "We are so fashioned, in the entirety of our being, that some part of us is exactly congruent with some part of every sphere of possible actions and interest in the kosmos, and therefore, each of us has being or consciousness of a kind that is keyed to and registering in the totality of such spheres."[51] Browne demarcates what are two forms of consciousness. There is the notion of consciousness that is brain dependent that derives from sensation and then we have intuitive consciousness, which is supersensuous. The latter, he argues, is a priori (free from sensuous experience) and functions on a higher plane of thought. Browne subsequently argues,

> Consciousness alone fixes the apparent limits of life; it also determines the state of our knowledge of life. And thus when the Thinker is confined to any stage of reality and congruent degree of consciousness it appears that what he there finds is ample for all of his purposes. . . . It is only when he is able to raise consciousness to a point where he can contact higher realities that he becomes aware that there are higher stages in which his consciousness may manifest.[52]

Browne's idealism stands in opposition to the materialist implications of Einstein's theory. Consequently, in 1921, Browne joined forces with a scientist of significant theological proclivities, the Swedish engineer Arvid Reuterdahl. As one of Einstein's leading antagonists, Reuterdahl believed that he had importantly preceded Einstein on such questions as the space-time continuum and that the concept of ether was not a real physical entity in the configuration of the universe. Reuterdahl thought that the ether concept was too materialist and hence detrimental to how God was a cardinal factor in the makeup of the universe. On such theistic presumptions, it followed,

> Reuterdahl claimed the unification of space and time for himself and thought that he had anticipated the theory of relativity in his concept of "Space-Time-Potential." Reuterdahl's "scientific theism" constituted the theoretical framework for "Space-Time-Potential." It was based on the assumption that the universe was a "unitary, interacting, rational, purposive, and teleological system." Reuterdahl identified various levels of reality in this system (physical, psychic, etc.) that could ultimately be traced to the existence . . . of God.[53]

Together Browne and Reuterdahl constituted the leadership of the US branch of the Academy of Nations. As the secretary general, Browne engaged in organizing with the aims of establishing an international grouping which efforts were toward the promotion of spiritualist/occult interpretations of reality. Wazeck brings the following to our attention:

> They had met in May 1921 when Browne approached Reuterdahl in a letter emphasizing the necessity of acting educationally in order to remedy the chaos in the area of knowledge for which the Einsteinian theory of relativity was particularly responsible in Reuterdahl's opinion. Browne's attention was probably drawn to Reuterdahl through a press report about one of Reuterdahl's lectures on religious topics. The AoN was intended to remedy the current complexity in the knowledge systems. [Browne states] "The Academy of Nations will function in the unification and co-ordination of systems of knowledge, thus procuring the development of a synthesized body of knowledge as against the highly specialized condition now existing."[54]

Wazeck continues,

> In addition, it was to be a world tribunal for deciding scientific and philosophical controversies and one of its prominent content goals was, "Discovery, investigation and dissemination of truth." The struggle for truth and the defense of "correct" science and world view were at least as important for the members of the AoN as the struggle against the theory of relativity.[55]

Clearly, Brown's engagement in the philosophy of science, while spurred by Einstein's theory of relativity, had broader implications in viewing science from the standpoint of philosophical idealism. Therein, Browne's commitment to philosophical idealism via the occultist rendering of science is a significant chapter in this African American tradition. As the first African American to publish a work in the philosophy of mathematics, Browne would pave the way for others trained in science to attempt at forging the unity of science with religion.[56]

Later, we discover that this dialectical idealist method is exercised in an explicit manner with Marquis Lafayette Harris's 1933 doctoral dissertation "Some Conceptions of God in the Gifford Lectures, 1927–1929." Harris (Figure 14a&b) was the first African American to earn a PhD in philosophy at The Ohio State University. Prior to working on his doctorate, he was a professor of physics at Claflin College during 1930–31. His background as a physicist facilitated in completing the dissertation. Harris undertook a comparative examination of the relationship of philosophy to science via the conception of God in the philosophies of Arthur Eddington, J. S. Haldane, Alfred North Whitehead, and John Dewey as presented in the Gifford Lectures.[57]

It should be noted that Arthur Eddington was a key player in the experimental confirmation of Einstein's General Theory. Nonetheless, from a philosophical standpoint, Eddington was an idealist. Harris brings the following to our attention: "Eddington has done much by way of astrophysics to support the doctrine of a spiritual reality. Perhaps it is not beside the point to say that is scientific investigations have made more use of the doctrine of cosmic relativity, and has demonstrated its plausibility, than any other work of science."[58]

Figure 14a&b Marquis Lafayette Harris (1907–66).

Harris's concern for Einstein's Theory of Relativity comes by way of his treatment of Eddington. He cogently states,

> Eddington's entire system of thought centers around the Doctrine of Relativity. Such a view is elucidated in and corroborated by his Gifford Lectures. Here one finds such doctrine paramount. It is extended into every facet of experience, whether "subjective" or "objective." Such being the case he begins his system of philosophy with a refutation of the absolute existences of classical or Newtonian physics.[59]

Without any critical judgment on Eddington's philosophical idealism, Harris summarily states that Eddington's ontology is founded on the idea of universal mind:

> This world is a universal mind or Logos which forms the background outside of the cyclic schemes of physical science upon which the latter depends. It is in this wise that Eddington accepts the validity of the "matter-of-factness" of the new science on the one hand and at the same time appeal to the subjective factor and the so-called secondary qualities of classical physics in an aesthetic and mystical interpretation of reality, on the other. Faced with the inevitable dualism which such a position presents, his only recourse is an intellectual Spiritualism as a ground of cosmic unity.[60]

Following Browne and Harris, there were other African American philosophers engaged in the philosophical treatment of Einstein as well as made inquiry into the philosophy of space and time. The most prominent philosophers include the names of Roy D. Morrison II, Charles A. Frye, and Eugene C. Holmes.

Morrison develops a humanist (non-transcendent theistic) methodology to Einstein's theory yet his interpretation remains idealist. His book *Science, Theology and the Transcendental Horizon: Einstein, Kant and Tillich* offers a challenging discussion of the limitations of human knowledge (or what Morrison refers to as the "Transcendental Horizon") through an examination of Einstein, Kant, Paul Tillich, Neils Bohr, and Werner Heisenberg. He concludes that critical philosophy is necessary to mediate the tension between religion and science. Morrison argues that there is a methodological unity underlying Einstein's approach to religion, philosophy, and science. Consequently, Einstein offers us "a profound but nondogmatic religiosity that is highly compatible with scientific method, with critical philosophy, with a humanistically oriented ethic, and with the human need for a sense of ultimacy."[61]

Frye argues for an idealist view of Einstein's theory by means of a connection to African philosophy. In his "African Religion and Philosophy: The Hermetic Parallel," Frye claims,

Einstein's work suggested that there is no absolute standard for time and no solid objects. There are only energy fields interconnecting processes or relationships. Relationships are the source of consciousness. Relations seems to permeate all of creation, with apparent correspondence between events on every plane of being. (For example, the sentient force that is Mars as planet, is also the imagery of and the physical "fact" of iron, the color red, and musical tone c, the number 3, and the mythic figure, i.e. psychological state, characterized by passions and activity.)[62]

With Frye's idealist interpretation, the concept of energy is rendered as immaterial. Consequently, energy and consciousness as immaterial phenomena are judged as basic to what pertains to material facts about the nature of reality. Thus, the planet Mars becomes no longer a real (physical) object of our solar system but instead a "sentient force" reducible to some kind of psychological state. This idealist interpretation is inconsistent with how Einstein seeks to comprehend the world in terms of the laws that govern matter in motion.

The crux of Frye's error is a philosophical misconception, resting on equating energy as an immaterial entity and thus congruent with consciousness. The equation, $E = MC^2$, explains the equivalence of energy to matter; it is not explaining a relationship between consciousness and matter. Energy, for Einstein, is matter of a specific form and open to observation by way of mathematical description and physical observation.

Eugene C. Holmes on the problem of space and time

Eugene Clay Holmes (Figure 15) stands as an anomaly within the history of African American philosophers of science. Working in the tradition of dialectical materialism, Holmes's work on space and time is more consistent with Einstein's own ontological viewpoint.[63] Let's turn to an examination of Holmes's work on space and time.

Holmes was not the typical "ivory tower" philosopher. As a member of the Communist Party USA, he sought to unite the scientific world outlook of dialectical materialism to the practical struggle for Black liberation and socialism. Holmes's entire academic career was at Howard University, where he taught for thirty-eight years in the Department of Philosophy. He followed his mentor Alain Locke as chairperson of philosophy and held this position

Figure 15 Eugene Clay Holmes (1905–80).

for eighteen years, retiring with emeritus status in 1970. During his tenure at the "Capstone of Negro Education," Holmes played a seminal role in the life of Howard's Black Left. He was instrumental in building a chapter of the National Student Union in addition to a faculty union at Howard. Along with Abram Harris, Ralph Bunche, E. Franklin Frazier, William Alpheus Hunton, Harold Lewis, Eric Williams, and Doxey Wilkerson, he was involved in a left critique of capitalism, racism, and bourgeois scholarship. While, no doubt, there were Black left scholars at other Black colleges and universities, for example, Oliver C. Cox at Lincoln University (Missouri), Howard was the only institution which had a substantial nucleus of Marxist oriented intellectuals. This chorus of left voices from Howard would represent for the first time in African American intellectual history what would approximate a distinctive school of thought. We say approximate because in comparison with the Frankfurt School of Critical Theory it would never reach a level of systematic and institutional form.[64]

While Holmes's early philosophical work was focused on aesthetics, his philosophical focus shifts in the 1950s—perhaps, as a result of the rise of McCarthyism—to the philosophy of science. During this period, Holmes held firm to Marxism and gave voice to a defense of a materialist ontology within the orbit of the philosophy of science. His work on the highly complex topic of space/time displayed his mastery of higher mathematics, physics, and the history of philosophy. Holmes's writings on the topic of space and time numbered three articles: (1) "The Main Philosophical Considerations of Space and Time," in the *American Journal of Physics*; (2) "The Kantian

Views of Space and Time Reevaluated," in *Philosophy and Phenomenological Research*; and (3) "Philosophical Problems of Space and Time," in the leftist journal *Science and Society*. The objective of each of these articles was to confirm materialism's opposition to various idealist philosophical formulations related to the conceptualization of space and time. Given space restrictions, our focus will be on Holmes's essay, "The Main Philosophical Considerations of Space and Time."[65]

Holmes begins by observing that it was not too long ago when "space and time or space/time were not thought of as having real existence."[66] The exceptions were certain materialists, such as Galileo Galilei, Pierre Gassendi, and René Descartes among others. However, in the materialism of Francis Bacon, Thomas Hobbes, and Joseph Priestly, "space and time were taken for granted." It was the agnostic Immanuel Kant who sought to scrutinize the philosophical significance of space and time, only to render them as *a prior* intuition. The categories of space and time are central components of his subjective idealist epistemology. Neo-Kantians have not moved beyond the muddle of Kant's agnosticism and idealism. Ernest Mach, Richard Ludwig Heinrich Avenarius, Hermann Cohen, Paul Natorp, Karl Pearson, and Henri Poincare ultimately became positivists of some sort. Holmes adds that their contemporary counterparts are Moritz Schlick, John von Neuman, Rudolf Carnap, Bertrand Russell, and to an extent Alfred Whitehead.[67]

It is noteworthy that Holmes recognized philosophical continuity of this reactionary trend. On the one hand, it explicitly anchors his own work in the tradition of V. I. Lenin; for Lenin had subjected the former group to a scathing critique in his *Materialism and Empirio-Criticism*. On the other hand, Holmes had anticipated the need for a Marxist-Leninist analysis of the latter group, a task that was also undertaken by Maurice Cornforth in *Science versus Idealism*, which was published in 1955, five years after Holmes wrote, "The Main Philosophical Considerations of Space and Time."[68]

The emergence of geometry in Egypt (Africa) was used as an example by Holmes for historical evidence to support his argument. He states, "No consciously theoretical notions about space were supported until men learned that such theories had practical purposes."[69] Geometry, in turn, developed in Egypt in response to the objective problems of agricultural production and the flooding of the Nile River. Yet, the general level of science and the limits of scientific work were a reflection of the determinate development of the productive forces (Bronze Age) and production relations (class/caste structure) of Egypt. The aim of science narrowly became control and prediction. However, the mixture of theology with science was the product of the relations between clerk and priest.

The Ionian philosophers (the first materialists in the Western—European—world) were not circumscribed by production to the degree of their Egyptian forerunners. The Ionians advanced to a more abstract conception of space. In part, Holmes reveals that this advancement was due to the progressive evolution of the productive forces from bronze to iron instruments. The Marxist philosopher Theodore Oizerman, we might add, points out that the division of labor resulting in the separation of mental and manual labor, gave a relative independence to theory in Ionia. Relative independence from production meant a great possibility for abstract, theoretical thought.[70]

Theories developed by Ionian philosophers were a substantial aid toward a materialist cognition of reality. Democritus's atomistic materialism, for example, was naïve and speculative, yet it gave us a notion of matter (the atom) and of space (the void). Holmes indicates that Democritus saw time as objectively real but viewed it separated from matter. Time, for Democritus, was absolute and metaphysical.[71] In Holmes's view, some materialists of the seventeenth century, like Gassendi, not only were influenced by Democritus but merely parroted the pioneering materialist. Gassendi was a materialist for whose philosophy the ideas of Democritus, Lucretius, and Epicurus were central. Gassendi's notion of the relationship of space to time was initially the same as his materialist progenitors, that is, a conception of space and time as disunited.

Holmes believed Renè Descartes was more important for the development of a clear idea of space and time than Gassendi. For Holmes, the importance of Descartes's mechanical materialism lies in his notion of space as "the property of material bodies in extension."[72] According to Holmes, Descartes had not seen, however, the unity of space and matter, that is, space as the mode of matter's existence, but identified matter with space.

Holmes, by giving greater weight to the philosophy of Descartes over Gassendi, we contend, failed to see that the contribution to materialism made by Gassendi was the very basis of Gassendi's criticism of Descartes. Although Holmes did recognize the dualism of Descartes's philosophy, namely, that it was idealist in its epistemology but materialist in regard to physics, he did not go far enough to recognize that Descartes's metaphysics was precisely what Gassendi attacked.

Karl Marx and Frederick Engels, the founders of dialectical materialism, in their work *The Holy Family* remarked,

The metaphysics or the seventeenth century represented in France by Descartes, had materialism as its antagonist from its birth. The latter's opposition to Descartes was personified by Gassendi, the restorer of Epicurean materialism. French and English materialism closely related to Democritus and Epicurus. Cartesian metaphysics had another opponent in Hobbes. Gassendi and Hobbes triumphed over their opponents long after their death.[73]

Holmes's summation of Isaac Newton's mechanistic materialism is instructive. Holmes brings into focus how mechanical materialism can collapse into idealism. On an epistemological plane, Newton (along with Galileo and John Locke) held to agnosticism. He separated qualities available to perception from properties of matter, which Newton thought could not be known. (Of course, this agnosticism would find full measure in Immanuel Kant's "thing-in-itself." Newton's mechanical materialism had deprived matter of intrinsic motion; thus, matter remained inert. Additionally, Newton separated matter from space and time. Thus, the catalyst for mechanical motion became the "prime mover"—God. Also, space was seen by Newton as the "sensorium of God.")

In his classic study, *The Metaphysical Foundations of Modern Physical Science*, the esteemed philosopher of science Edwin A. Burtt explains Newton's position on "sensorium" accordingly:

> Absolute space is the divine sensorium. Everything that happens in it, being present to the divine knowledge, must be immediately perceived and immediately understood. Certainly, at least, God must know whether any motion is absolute or relative. The divine consciousness furnishes the ultimate center of reference for absolute motion. Moreover, the animism in Newton's conception of force perhaps plays a part in the premises of the position. God is not only infinite knowledge, but also Almighty Will.[74]

Nonetheless, the mechanical physics of Newton was raised to the level of a worldview, that is, mechanistic materialism. However, to the degree that Newton had advanced materialism, we must distinguish his physics from his metaphysics, as was necessary with Descartes earlier. Holmes did not grasp this fact and consequently missed the import of Newton's role in the history of materialism.

Because Kant's conception of space and time was consciously developed from Newtonian physics (and Euclidean geometry as well), Holmes's treatment of Kant is extremely important. Holmes argues, "Kant raised the philosophical problems of space and time to their highest metaphysical–idealist expression."[75]

In countering Hume's skepticism based on the empirical source of knowledge, Kant grounds his epistemology in subjectivity. Space and time were conceived by Kant as intuitive constructs, as subjective forms of sensibility that were *a priori*, that is, logically prior to and a condition of experience (perception).

For Kant, Holmes notes, the infinity of space and time was not a reflection of the unity of material reality but something imposed on experience intuitively. Holmes goes on to say, Neo-Kantian philosophers "were just as concerned as Kant with the problems generated by regarding space and time as modes of thought or as reflections of objective reality."[76]

But then Holmes (incorrectly) identifies Mach and Avenarius (two leading Neo-Kantians) as "materialist" philosophers that disguise" their materialism under the cover of "empirio-criticism." Yet, Holmes contradicts himself, for he states, "Mach regards consciousness and sensation as the ultimate elements of the world . . . he regarded space and time as subjective consciousness, conditioned by sensation." Holmes further states that this was "an idealist operation performed by mechanical materialism upon physics by destroying any vestige of an independent reality which had been preserved by Kant's noumena."[77]

The central confusion in Holmes's argument, namely, that Mach was a mechanical materialist, lies precisely in his attributing to Mach, Kant's dualism. Kant, by arguing for the existence of "noumena," that is, the "thing-in-itself," was pointing to materialism. Yet, by denying the knowability of "noumena" and making time and space subjective categories, Kant was decidedly an idealist. Kant's critical philosophy was an effort to merge two irreconcilable opposites, materialism and idealism. Mach and Avenarius, by rejecting Kant's thing-in-itself, were in fact negating the materialist side of Kant's ontology. They were upholding Kant's idealism by way of what Lenin described as a right critique of Kant.

Lenin accurately states, "Mach and Avenarius reproach Kant not because his conception of the thing-in-itself is not sufficiently realistic, i.e., not sufficiently materialistic, but because he admits its existence. That is, Kant is reproached not because he refuses to deduce causality and necessity form objective reality, but because he admits any causality and necessity in nature at all."[78]

A left critique, a materialist analysis (mechanical or dialectical), would have accentuated the opposite side, that is, noumena, the objective, material side of Kant's philosophy. Hence, Holmes erred in assigning mechanistic materialism as the source of the incorrectness of Mach and Avenarius. Their position was at base idealist and their subsequent conception of space and time was rooted in a reactionary, rightist interpretation that went beyond Kant's dualism directly to idealism.

Holmes returns to the correct philosophical path when he emphatically supports Marx, Engels, and Lenin in their defense of materialism. Specialized sciences, physics, geometry, and mathematics, all confirmed the dialectical materialist thesis that the universe is matter in motion and that space and time are intrinsically tied to matter as its mode of existence. Thus, "space and time are objectively real forms of existence." Space and time are understood as existing in unity.[79]

Holmes argues, "Before there could be any new contribution to the study of the physical nature of space, there had to come into being revised or new geometries."[80] This "new" geometry (or geometries) significantly altered the Euclidean conception of space. The fixed and seemingly immutable character of spatial relations in Euclidean geometry was in fact the basis for Kant's subjective and intuitive notion of mathematics. Holmes explains, "The Euclidean geometry had become established as the Platonist philosophy of logical and mathematical harmony, with its emphasis on unswerving and invariant relations."[81] The advent of non-Euclidean geometries meant "geometrical axioms have value and retain validity only in the event that they mirror definite, actual properties of real space."[82] The new geometries along with field theory changed the classical notion of physics regarding space and time. Einstein's theory changed the classical notion of physics regarding space and time; Einstein's theory of relativity limited the applicability of Newtonian physics and erased absolute space and time. Instead, as Holmes stated, "Einstein referred to the absolute character of the space-time continuum."[83]

Space and time were inseparable and motion (velocities) was calculated relative to a relationship of different coordinate systems and not on the "perception of the observer or his subjective qualities."[84] Holmes correctly asserts that dialectical materialism is compatible with the objectivity of the theory relativity, the eternality of time, and the infinity of space/time.

Holmes concludes his essay by explaining that theory of relativity supports the Law of the Conservation of Mass and Energy, that is, the indestructibility of matter and energy and their mutual transformation. Unfortunately, he does not elaborate on how this verifies dialectal materialism's demand that the unity of the world consists in its materiality. And, thus how the dialectical conception of matter denies the necessity for divine intervention by God or a first cause to explain the development of the nature. Such a summation would have cast in bold relief the revolutionary implication of dialectics for the emergence of a consistent materialist ontology in correspondence with the historical development of science. Yet, Holmes's contribution to the philosophy of science was his militant defense of the materialist philosophical tradition. He stood as the only professionally trained Black philosopher, of this period, to apply dialectical materialism to an analysis of space and time.[85] Following in the tradition of Marx, Engels, Lenin, Du Bois, and J. D. Bernal, philosophy for Holmes was not an esoteric exercise or the juggling of words.[86] The role of philosophical exposition was not a mere act of gaining professional recognition but more significantly philosophy was an ideological weapon in the battle for liberation. Moreover, Holmes attempted to bring philosophy into the orbit of Black intellectual inquiry and the working-class struggle.

Normative values, social reality, and social activism

Social scientist and social scientific inquiry are frequently accused of violating Hume's law. According to David Hume and all of his progeny, it is logically inadmissible to derive a value judgment from a factual proposition or statement. There is a logical gap between "is" and "ought," factual and value statements. The fact/value divide was later reconstituted in Immanuel Kant's notion of pure and practical reason. Hume's philosophical children went on to argue that the social sciences should be exactly like the natural sciences in that value judgments are not welcomed. Science as a value-free undertaking cannot be tainted by moral, political, or class interests of any sort; it should be a neutral undertaking.

What are the implications of sticking to Hume's law? Normative values and judgments are pushed outside the realm of social scientific inquiry. This empiricist view, as Charles Taylor observes, means that "scientific findings are held to be neutral: that is, the facts as we discover them do not help to establish or give support to any set of values; we cannot move from fact to value."[87] Yet, as Charles Taylor astutely informs us, all explanatory frameworks—within the realm of the social sciences—give expression to a particular value position. For instance, in neoclassical economics the explanation of profit is in terms of marginal efficiency of capital. From this we are lead to the value judgment that profit is a fair return to capitalists. On the other hand, the explanation of profit put forward by Marxism gives us the judgment that profit is an undeserved appropriation of workers' surplus labor by capital.

The point is not that values reign supreme over facts. Rather, social scientific inquiry is not just descriptive in nature, that is, letting the facts speak for themselves. It involves the interpretation of the facts and assessing the value implications of the interpretation offered. Objectivity should not be confused with neutrality; neutrality means that one takes no position on an issue. As Joyce Mitchell Cook observes, in regard to the view that Black people are intellectually inferior to whites: "It is possible to appraise the issues with disinterest, even though I fail to see how any black person, myself included, can be without a vested interest in the final resolution of the IQ controversy."[88] Having a vested interest in discovering the objective truth does not mean that the quest for objectivity and objective knowledge is necessarily sacrificed. If a belief—for example, Black people are intellectually inferior to whites—*is* known to be false, then, it makes no sense to deny that people *ought* not to believe it.

In "Ethics and Moral Activism," the philosophical activist Cornelius Golightly (Figure 16) attempts to show how the philosopher of ethics can have an impact on the practical affairs of public life *qua* philosopher without politicizing philosophy.[89] However, he does note that the philosopher of ethics is also a citizen and thus can become involved as a citizen. He argues, "This is nothing more than citizen activism by a citizen who is well informed."[90] Golightly's research on normative ethics and the social sciences brings to our attention that the social sciences are not value neutral. Moreover, the quest for objective knowledge does not require value neutrality. This point can be illustrated by looking at the role of Black social scientists in the fight against Jim Crow racism.

Figure 16 Cornelius Golighty (1917–76).

Beginning in the 1930s the social psychologist Kenneth B. Clark in collaboration with his wife Mamie K. Phipps Clark conducted studies on the damage of segregation on children's self-perception. As part of their research each child was presented with two dolls. Each of the dolls was identical in every way except for skin color and hair texture. One doll was white with yellow hair, while the other was brown with Black hair. After observing these descriptive facts of the dolls, each child was asked to make value judgments about the dolls. Which doll would they prefer to play with? Which one did they consider to be the nice doll? Which one looks ugly? Which one is beautiful? The experiment demonstrated a clear value preference for the white doll among all children in the study. The Clarks' doll experiments would later become foundational to several school desegregation cases, including *Briggs v. Elliott* (1952), which was later combined into the famous 1954 Supreme Court case *Brown v. Board of Education*. The conclusions drawn from the Clark studies by the Supreme Court demonstrated the normative consequences of social scientific inquiry. In contrast to the logical positivist view, we can and do derive value judgments from factual (descriptive) statements; that is, we derive ought from is. Ultimately, the question is not whether the social sciences are value-free. Rather, the question is whether we have an objective (scientific) view of values.

In "Social Science and Normative Ethics," Golightly investigates how intentional normative statements in social science are helpful in answering questions in value theory—an area which is usually confined to the interests of philosophers. He asserts that social sciences prior to the twentieth century were the outgrowth of moral philosophy, and as such were "highly normative and teleological."[91]

Twentieth-century social science, in reaction to the "ethical theory and hidden bias" of social science in the nineteenth century, sought to formulate a value-free social science. With the advent of social planning and social criticism as branches of social science, intentional normative statements and thus value theory increasingly became the subject of scientific investigation rather than philosophical speculation. Golightly welcomes this development and sees the possibility for the field of values to completely become the subject of social science. However, he cautions that a review of intentional value judgments in social science reveals considerable advancement in ethics but not in value theory.

He then makes a distinction between judgments (or propositions) of normative ethics and ethical theory. Normative ethics are evaluative judgments concerning whether something is good or bad, right or wrong.

Ethical theory constitutes the set of propositions on which normative ethics rests. They are value predicates or first principles and are ultimate in nature. The relationship between the two approximates the relationship between essential and instrumental values. The possibility for a scientific approach to value is grounded in the fact that normative ethics or instrumental values are open to empirical verification.

Golightly studies Gunnar Myrdal's *American Dilemma* as one of the social scientific works that employ the use of normative ethics. Myrdal's condemnation of caste (segregation and discrimination) is based on the notion that the denial of "liberty and equality" restricts democracy for Black people. But Myrdal further claims that the value premises he utilized are not absolute and others may be valid alternatives. He argues that as a social scientist he must distinguish between the "analysis of morals" and "analysis in morals." Golightly sees in Myrdal's distinction the same point he had made in separating normative ethics from ethical theory.

Golightly thinks that the inroads made by social science in regard to normative ethics could eventually open the door to a scientific methodology in value theory. He concludes, "The problem for social sciences is to discover or formulate universal value principles which are verifiable in some sense within the framework of established scientific procedures."[92] His subsequent research (too extensive to explore here) was to expand on this effort and value theory. Of particular note, Golightly's essay, "Value as a Scientific Concept," is his elaboration of a classification of values. With regard to the formulation of a classification of values, Golightly and Locke stand alone among African American philosophers.

On a more critical note, Black sociologist Oliver C. Cox, however, has a penetrating critique of Myrdal and significantly advances beyond Golightly on the issue of values in social science research, particularly race relations research. Cox declares, "Myrdal conceives of his problem, that is to say of race relations in the United States, as 'primarily a moral issue of conflicting valuations' and of his 'investigation' as 'an analysis of morals.'"[93]

Cox's argument is premised on the thesis that Myrdal's two volumes of the *American Dilemma* are no more than idealist mysticism. Essentially, Myrdal's treatment of values rests on an idealist conception that removes racism and race relations from their materialist foundation in capitalism. Cox states,

> They [the two volumes] bring to finest expression practically all the vacuous theories of race relations which are acceptable among the liberal intelligentsia and which explain race relations away from the social and economic order. The theories do this in spite of the verbal desire of the author to integrate his

problem in the on-going social system. In the end the social system is exculpated, and the burden of the dilemma is poetically left in the "hearts of the American people," the esoteric reaches of which, obviously, may be plumbed only by the guardians of morals in our society.[94]

Ultimately, Myrdal's ideological mystification seeks to hide the realities of racism, race relations, and class conflict beneath the mystical veil of the American creed.

Epistemology contra sociology of knowledge

Ideas, beliefs, philosophies, and doctrines grow out of particular material conditions. As we demonstrated in Chapter 1, there is a dialectical relationship between philosophical texts and social context. For instance, political conditions in the Athenian city-state form the backdrop for Plato's philosophical works. And imperialism serves as the political ecology for Kwame Nkrumah's *Consciencism*. However, the social context of ideas should not be reduced to the epistemological content of ideas. As Terry Eagleton succinctly notes, "Ideas are internally shaped by their social origins, their truth value is not reducible to them."[95] Epistemology vis-à-vis the sociology of knowledge is concerned with the nature of knowledge or understanding what is the substance (content) of knowledge. It is concerned with the justification of beliefs and what constitutes truth.[96]

Following Karl Mannheim, William T. Fontaine engages in the sociology of African American thought. He begins by arguing that the "social situation . . . determines the origin and development of his attitudes, feelings, and plans of action."[97] As such, African American social thought is "socially determined" by "sociopsychological factors such as resentment, aggression, rage and the desire for equality." Fontaine argues that there is a correlation between the "defense psychology" of Black intellectuals and their opposition to the "thought patterns, concepts and techniques of the democratic-liberal-scientific Weltanschauung."[98] As Fontaine explains,

> The mind of the Negro scholar is fundamentally the same as any other. It is a historical phenomenon, existent in and subject to the influences of its epoch. It both conditions and is conditioned by its social position. As a Negro, the scholar has faced discrimination against his race, and his

experiences consciously and unconsciously have engendered psychoses centering around fear, rage, repression, aggression, security, status, and equality. As undergraduate and graduate student, he learns that certain kinds of knowledge lend support to race discrimination.[99]

Fontaine brings to our attention the importance of the social context of knowledge. The social context of knowledge is important because it provides a means for uncovering the objective, material conditions for the genesis of certain forms of thinking and action. Although Fontaine is a precursor to the movement for a "Black Social Science," he does not usher in a full-fledged relativity of truth.

From the beginning of the Black Studies movement, Black activists and scholars were forced to grapple with a range of philosophical questions related to the social sciences. This debate often took the form of critiquing the ideological presuppositions of the social sciences. Some Black theorists argued for the need to develop a Black perspective and method of social scientific investigation, that is, a Black Social Science.[100] Roy D. Morrison called for a "Black Enlightenment." Joyce Ladner declared "The Death of White Sociology" and Robert Staples wrote *The Introduction to Black Sociology*. Staples would write that "the purpose of Afro-American sociology is to study Black life and culture which when seen from a new Black perspective can serve to correct myths about Afro-Americans found in sociological literature."[101] Sociologists such as Nathan Hare, Abdul Alkalimat, and Delores Aldridge would also come to play a seminal role in the development of the "Black Social Sciences."[102] These frameworks were the precursors to Molefi Asante's "Afrocentric Idea." With Asante, we are told the following: "Social science in the West is imperialistic, the disciplinary justification for expansion."[103]

One of the pitfalls of this trend was to identify social experience with theoretical reflection, that is, the sociology of knowledge with epistemology. To conflate the *sociology of knowledge* and *epistemology* is to confuse the genesis of thought with its validity and veracity. This view is also known as the genetic or *ad hominen* fallacy. This identification is given full expression in Patricia Hill Collins's *Black Feminist Thought: Knowledge, Consciousness and Politics of Empowerment* published in 1990.

Collins's framework gives primacy to lived experience as the foundation of epistemology. One of the central points that Collins makes is that the social (material) conditions of Black women's lives, which inherently involves respectful and caring interaction with the physical world on a daily basis, provides a basis for an epistemology, "unique angle of vision," that is less oppressive and more caring.[104] Unfortunately, Collins presents no empirical evidence to support her claim that when Black women do scientific inquiry the substantive results are more "objective," that is, a more objective reflection of material reality. Here the anti-realist implications of Collins's position should be evident.

The perspective that experience is sui generis of theory is a philosophical error rooted in empiricism; the timeworn—yet popular—view that "I lived it so I know it" is an expression of vulgar empiricism. Here Collins identifies social experience with theoretical reflection, wherein sociology of knowledge is identified with knowledge proper. A description of immediate social experience is only, at best, phenomenalist and does not disclose the underlying essential social relations giving rise to immediate experience. A scientific—that is, materialist—epistemology, on the other hand, requires the mediation of theory, in order to understand our immediate social experience. Our immediate experience will not disclose that the sun is the center of our universe or the existence of subatomic particles.

The weakness of empiricism (and positivism as a form of empiricism) is that it begins with the legitimate notion that knowledge starts with experience and comes to the more general conclusion that knowledge is limited to experience. Our critique of empiricism should not be seen as the rejection of what is a legitimate pursuit in the natural and social sciences, that is, the undertaking of empirical scientific inquiry. Rather, it is a critique of empiricism. Empiricism is not identical to engaging in empirical work. Just as living under capitalism does not necessarily make one a capitalist, engaging in empirical research does not necessarily make one an empiricist.

Moreover, Collins denies the existence of an objective reality and, consequently, discards the idea of objective truth. For Collins, in order to gain a greater perspective on truth, an account must be taken of all partial truths, including those which attach to the interests of the oppressor. She argues,

> Each group speaks from its own standpoint and shares its own partial, situated knowledge. But because each group perceives its own truth as partial, its knowledge is unfinished. Each group becomes better able to consider other groups' standpoints without relinquishing the uniqueness of its own standpoint or suppressing other groups' partial perspectives.[105]

So instead of objective truth, grounded in material reality, we have a notion of truth founded on consensus. Consequently, this broader truth derives from various partial truths as situated knowledges. Collins seems to suggest it is only by means of the aggregation of partial perspectives and hence partial truths are we thus able to embark upon the path to wider truth. We, in turn, must embrace this wider truth, which is born of consensus, in lieu of the fact that for us there is no real possibility in obtaining objective truth itself. How can any standpoint, from this perspective, ever be wrong? Here the bugbear of relativism raises its head.

On closer scrutiny we find embedded in Collins's presupposition grave political implications. Philosophically, we have no more than a subjectivist form of relativism. In the tradition of Mikhail Bakhtin's "dialogism," Hill Collins posits each subject has a partial truth that must be respected and recognized by all concerned. Therefore, it follows the oppressed ought to acknowledge the fact that their oppression is not the whole (objective) truth. Perhaps in the tradition of Hegel's *Phenomenology*, Collins implicitly desires to make known to us that the oppressor (as much as the oppressed) is the real victim in an oppressive relationship. If this is not her implicit intention, it is certainly the explicit implication contained in her conception of truth.

This subjective relativism, founded on a part/whole dichotomy, simply reduces to the following proposition: "Just as the oppressor does not have an objective claim to the truth, so it is for the oppressed." The truth of oppression intrinsic to slavery, for example, cannot be gathered only from the slave's standpoint. Hill Collins's rejection of the slave narrative's propriety to objective truth is constituted in her aim to establish truth on the grounds of *intersubjectivity*. Consequently, we discover a significant philosophical implication of political import, when *objectivity* gives way to *intersubjectivity* then *subjective relativism* reigns supreme.

On this account the slave narrative must be adjoined with the slave master's narrative in order to acquire the greater truth. The slave master brings partial truth, which complements the perspective of the slave narrative. Hence, the slave must be just as open to the master's partial truths as the slave master must be of the slave's. For this is an entrenched imperative inextricably tied to Hill Collins's notion of truth resulting from consensus.[106]

Such an epistemological position ushers in nothing less than a politics of compromise. Ostensibly the suggestion is a most debilitating political proposal, namely, pursue the politics of recognition. Moreover, the upshot of this epistemology of dialogical truth is not a politics of liberation but an ethics of reconciliation between the oppressed and the oppressors. In ideological terms, we are left with inept liberal moralism serving as a surrogate for a political struggle guided by revolutionary theory and scientific epistemology.

Notes

1. African American physicist Robert A. Thornton corresponded on the philosophy of physics with Albert Einstein beginning in 1944 and continued for nearly a decade. See Don A, Howard, "Albert Einstein as a Philosopher of Science," *Physics Today* (December 2005), 34. Also consult, Robert Ewell Greene, *Robert A. Thornton, Master Teacher: Scholar, Physicist, Humanist* (Fort Washington: R. E. Greene, 1988); Ronald L. Mallett (with Bruce Henderson), *Time Traveler: A Scientist's Personal Mission to Make Time Travel a Reality* (New York: Basic Books, 2009); Also consult, Amber Esping, *Epistemology, Ethics, and Meaning in Unusually Personal Scholarship* (Cham, Switzerland: Palgrave Macmillan, 2018), especially chapter 4, "Theoretical Physics: Building a Time Machine to Save My Father." Eugene C. Holmes, "The Main Philosophical Considerations of Space and Time," *American Journal of Physics* 18(9) (December 1950), 560–70; Ernest E. Just, *The Biology of the Cell Surface* (Philadelphia: P. Blakinston's Company, 1939); Roy D. Morrison, *Science, Theology, and the Transcendental Horizon: Einstein, Kant, and Tillich* (Atlanta: Scholars Press, 1994); William T. Fontaine, "Philosophical Implications of the Biology of Dr. Ernest E. Just," *The Journal of Negro History* 24(3) (July 1939), 281–90; Abram L. Harris, "Economic Evolution: Dialectical and Darwinian," *Journal of Political Economy* 42(1) (February 1934), 34–79; Oliver C. Cox, *Capitalism as a System* (New York: Monthly Review Press, 1964); and Cornelius L. Golightly, "Value as a Scientific Concept," *The Journal of Philosophy* 53(7) (1956), 233–45. Also read Golightly's review "Science: Its Method and Its Philosophy by G. Burniston Brown" *Philosophy of Science* 20(1) (January 1953), 83. Carleton L. Lee, "Toward a Sociology of Black Religious Experience," *The Journal of Religious Thought* 29(2) (Autumn–Winter 1972), 5–18.
2. Perhaps one of the most confusing matters for the beginning student in philosophy of science is comprehending the difference between science and pseudoscience. What we mean by pseudoscience is captured in the following statement: "A pseudoscience is a body of belief or practice advertised or sold as science without being as such. . . . Pseudoscientists either do not conduct any research at all . . . or that conducted flawed

research. . . . In either case, when sincere, they are gullible and on the whole impervious to criticism. They fail to comply to what Merton called 'organized skepticism.'" See Mario Bunge, *Finding Philosophy in Social Science* (New Haven: Yale University Press, 1996), 205.

3. On the matter of the philosophy of history, Earl E. Thorpe remains the foremost scholar among Black historians and within the ranks of philosophers there is Berkeley B. Eddins. See Earl E. Thorpe, *The Desertion of Man: A Critique of Philosophy of History* (Baton Rouge: Ortlieb Press, 1958). See also, Jerry Gershenhorn, "Earl E. Thorpe and the Struggle for Black History, 1949–1989," *Souls* 12(4) (2010), 376–97. Berkeley B. Eddins, *Appraising Theories of History* (Cincinnati: Ehling, 1980).

4. Quoted in Stephen Jay Gould, *The Mismeasure of Man* (New York: W. W. Norton & Co., 1981), 21.

5. Frederick Douglass, *The Claims of the Negro Ethnologically Considered* (Rochester: Lee, Mann & Co., 1854), 3, 5.

6. Douglass, *The Claims of the Negro Ethnologically Considered*, 10.

7. Martin R. Delany, *Principia of Ethnology: The Origin of Races and Color with an Archaeological Compendium of Ethiopian and Egyptian Civilization, From Years of Careful Examination and Enquiry* (Philadelphia: Harper & Brother, 1879), 9.

8. James Ferguson, "The Laboratory of Racism," *New Scientist* 1423 (September 27, 1984), 19. Polygenists were far from a marginal or fringe grouping in the United States scientific community. Noted Harvard zoologist Louis Agassiz was one of its chief proponents. Read Milford H. Wolpoff and Rachel Caspari, *Race and Human Evolution* (New York: Simon & Schuster, 1997). See especially the section on, "Polygenism, Society, and Politics," which is in chapter 4. Also, consult chapter 3, "Polygenism, Racism, and the Rise of Anthropology."

9. Consult Richard H. Popkin, *The Third Force in Seventeenth-Century Thought* (Leiden: Brill, 1992), 65–66.

10. Troy Duster, "What's New in the IQ Debate," *The Black Scholar* 25(1) (Winter 1995), 25.

11. Francis Galton, *Inquiries into Human Faculty* (London: Macmillan and Co., 1883), 423.

12. Quoted in David J Galton and Clare J Galton, "Francis Galton: and Eugenics Today," *Journal of Medical Ethics* 24(2) (April 1, 1998), 99. Also consult, Sir Francis Galton, *Hereditary Genius: An Inquiry into Its Laws and Consequences* (New York: Appleton & Co., 1870).

13. Stephen E. Fienberg and Daniel P. Resnick, "Re-examining the Bell Curve," in Bernie Devlin, Stephen E. Fienberg, Daniel P. Resnick, Kathryn Roeder, eds, *Intelligence, Genes, and Success: Scientists Respond to The Bell Curve* (New York: Springer Science+Business Media, 1997), 5.

14. Troy Duster, "What's New in the IQ Debate," *The Black Scholar* 25(1) (Winter 1995), 29–30. For other Black responses to *The Bell Curve*, see *The Black Scholar* 25(1) (1995), 2–46. For a response from a Black evolutionary biologist, see Joseph L. Graves and T. Place, "Race and IQ Revisited: Figures Never Lie, But Often Liars Figure," *Sage Race Relations Abstracts* 20(2) (1995), 4–50.

15. Robert V. Guthrie, *Even the Rat Was White: A Historical View of Psychology* (Boston: Allyn and Bacon, 2004). Joyce Mitchell Cook, "On the Nature and Nurture of Intelligence," *Philosophical Forum* 9 (1978), 289–302.

16. One exception would be Cornel West who endorses the postmodern rejection of science and more generally "the bland universality, glib generality, and monotonous uniformity of the Enlightenment." See West, *Prophesy Deliverance!: An Afro-American Revolutionary Christianity* (Louisville: Westminister John Knox Press, 1982), 28, 32, 61–62. See also Cornel West, "The New Politics of Cultural Difference," in Russell Ferguson, ed. *Out There: Marginalization and Contemporary Cultures* (New York: New Museum of Contemporary Art, 1990), 19–36.

17. Kershaw, "Evolution," 429.

18. Ibid., 434. In contrast to Kershaw, the German phenomenologist Edmund Husserl views philosophy as identical to science, the lawful nature of reality, the encompassing nature of philosophy as well as having a commitment to idealism. Speaking on Husserl, Dermot Moran argues, "Sciences as such, for Husserl, are always focused on the sphere of essential validity, the necessary laws and structures governing the realm of phenomena they study. Phenomenology [philosophy], similarly, is to be a science of pure essences. It must extract from a merely contingent, factual features of our experience in order to isolate what is essential to all experiences of that kind." See Dermot Moran, *Introduction to Phenomenology* (New York: Routledge, 2000), 132.

19. Charles Leander Hill, "The Role of Religion in Higher Education," 1–2 Charles Leander Hill Papers Wilberforce University (Folder 39).

20. Cornelius L. Golightly, "Value as a Scientific Concept," *The Journal of Philosophy* 53(7) (1956), 234.

21. Golightly, "Value as a Scientific Concept," 234. Also consult, Cornelius L. Golightly, "The James-Lange Theory: A Logical Post Mortem," *Philosophy of Science* 20(4) (October 1953), 286–99. Golightly in this essay addresses William James's psychological theory of introspection as a theoretical basis for emotion. Golightly comments, "James, who was more philosopher than experimental psychologist, believed that analytic description of the mind was the necessary scientific method for psychology. Introspective analysis of mental activity was orthodox

British empiricism with a history that ran from Hobbes through Locke, Berkeley, Hume, and James Mill. James utilized this empiricist or analytical method to criticize certain aspects of the current German 'experimental' psychology." Consult, p. 287.

22. On the distinction between philosophical and scientific concepts, see V. I. Lenin, *Materialism and Empirio-Criticism* (Moscow: Foreign Languages Publishing House, 1972), 127, 269–70.

23. William T. Fontaine, "Philosophical Implications of the Biology of Dr. Ernest E. Just," *The Journal of Negro History* 24(3) (July 1939), 281.

24. Kenneth Manning, *Black Apollo of Science: The Life of Ernest Everett Just* (New York: Oxford University Press, 1983).

25. Ernest E. Just, *The Biology of the Cell Surface* (Philadelphia: P. Blakinston's Company, 1939), viii.

26. Sebastian Normandin and Charles T. Wolfe, eds., *Vitalism and the Scientific Image in Post-Enlightenment Life Science, 1800–2010* (New York: Springer Science+Business Media, 2013), 6.

27. Francois Duchesneau, "Vitalism in the Late Eighteenth-Century Physiology: The Cases of Barthez, Blumenbach, and John Hunter," in William F. Bynum and Roy Porter, eds., *William Hunter and the Eighteenth-Century Medical World* (New York: Cambridge University Press, 2002), 259.

28. Ernest E. Just, *The Biology of the Cell Surface* (Philadelphia: P. Blakinston's Company, 1939), 1.

29. Just, *The Biology of the Cell Surface*.

30. Ibid., 1–2.

31. Ibid., 2.

32. Ibid.

33. Consult, Frederick Engels, *Dialectics of Nature* (Moscow: Progress Publishers, 1974), 127.

34. Just, *The Biology of the Cell Surface*, 2.

35. William T. Fontaine, "Philosophical Implications of the Biology of Dr. Ernest E. Just," *The Journal of Negro History* 24(3) (July 1939), 285.

36. Fontaine, "Philosophical Implications of the Biology of Dr. Ernest E. Just," 286.

37. Just, *The Biology of the Cell Surface*, 354.

38. Ibid., 360.

39. Roy D. Morrison II, *Science, Theology and the Transcendental Horizon* (Atlanta: Scholars Press, 1994), 301.

40. See Wikipedia contributors, "Theory of relativity," *Wikipedia, The Free Encyclopedia*, https://en.wikipedia.org/w/index.php?title=Theory_of_relativity&oldid=835363827 (accessed June 27, 2018). For the nonscientist there are a number of fine texts available to assist one in understanding Einstein's theory of relativity. See Nigel Calder, *Einstein's*

Universe (New York: Wings Books, 1982); Eric Chaisson, *Relatively Speaking* (New York: W. W. Norton & Co., 1988); Wesley C. Salmon, *Space, Time and Motion: A Philosophical Introduction* (Minneapolis, MN: University of Minnesota Press, 1980); and Albert Einstein, *Relativity: The Special and General Theory* (New York: Bonaza Books, 1961). For a materialist treatment of Einstein's theory of relativity, see Robert Steigerwald, "Materialism and the Contemporary Natural Sciences," *Nature, Society and Thought* 13(3) (2000), 279–323.

41. Esther Inglis-Arkell points out, "The precession of the orbits is accounted for by Newton's laws of motion. As astronomers charted the progress of the planets, they conformed agreeably to predictions based on those laws of motion. All except one. Mercury's orbit made its round faster than predicted. It didn't race ahead. The precession was 93 percent accounted for, but no one could adequately explain that last seven percent." Read Esther Inglis-Arkell, "The 200-Year-Old Mystery of Mercury's Orbit — Solved!" *Physics*, https://io9.gizmodo.com/the-200-year-old-mystery-of-mercurys-orbit-solved-1458642219. More recently the research of physicist Clifford Will indicates that Einstein General Theory indicates additional effects concerning Mercury. For explanation of this finding read, Emily Conover, "Einstein's General Relativity Reveals New Quirk of Mercury's Orbit," *ScienceNews*, https://www.sciencenews.org/article/einstein-general-relativity-mercury-orbit

42. Nola Taylor Redd "Einstein's Theory of General Relativity," Space.com (November 7, 2017), https://www.space.com/17661-theory-general-relativity.html

43. Fred Jerome and Rodger Taylor, *Einstein on Race and Racism* (New Brunswick, New Jersey: Rutgers University Press, 2006). This book captures the relationship that Einstein had with African American working people in Princeton's Black community. In addition, Jerome and Taylor examine Einstein's political relationship with W. E. B. Du Bois, Marian Anderson, Paul Robeson, and many other Black intellectuals.

44. Roy D. Morrison, "Einstein on Kant, Religion, Science, and Methodological Unity," in Dennis P. Ryan, ed., *Einstein and the Humanities* (New York: Greenwood Press, 1987), 51, 54.

45. Einstein quoted in Don A. Howard, "Einstein as Philosopher of Science," *Physics Today* (December 2005): 34.

46. The dialectical idealist tradition has generally been associated with the German Enlightenment. See Ludwig Heyde, "The Unsatisfied Enlightenment: Faith and Pure Insight in Hegel's Phenomenology of Spirit," in William Desmond, Ernst-Otto Onnasch, and Paul Cruysberghs, eds., *Philosophy and Religion in German Idealism* (New York: Kluwer Academic Publishers, 2004).

47. See Robert Fikes, Jr., "The Triumph of Robert T. Browne: The Mystery of Space," *APA Newsletter on Philosophy and the Black Experience* 6(2) (Spring 2006), 10–13.

48. Read "Negroes in the Field of Philosophy," *The Negro History Bulletin* 2(9) (June 1939). 76, 80. On Browne and the American Negro Academy, consult, Alfred A. Moss, *The American Negro Academy: Voice of the Talented Tenth* (Louisiana State University Press, 1995). Also see Fikes, Jr., "Postscript: The Triumph of Robert T. Browne: The Mystery of Space."

49. Milena Wazeck, Einstein's Opponents: The Public Controversy About the Theory of Relativity in the 1920s (New York: Cambridge University Press, 2014), 8.

50. Robert T. Browne, *The Mystery of Space* (New York: E. P. Dutton and Company, 1919), 107.

51. Browne, *The Mystery of Space*, 167.

52. Ibid., 198.

53. Wazeck, *Einstein's Opponents*, 167.

54. Ibid., 250.

55. Ibid., 250–51.

56. Furthermore, Browne's works in the occult would eventually lead to creating his own organization. For a detailed discussion on Browne's engagement in the occult, see Matt Marble, "The Hermes of Harlem: Harlem Esoterics and the Secret Life of Robert T. Browne," *Abraxas* (No. 6, 2014). Also consult, the informative video by Carolyn Wilkins's given in the four part series, titled, "The Mystery of Robert T. Browne," https://www.youtube.com/watch?v=krJoVIj48Rk

57. Harris's interest in the philosophy of Alfred North Whitehead was by no means atypical among African American philosophers. During the 1930s and 1940s, Richard McKinney also worked on Whitehead. After Richard McKinney finished his work for the Bachelor of Divinity, he then completed the Master of Sacred Theology in the philosophy of religion from Newton in 1937. His S.T.M. thesis topic was *The Cosmology of Alfred North Whitehead and Its Bearing on Religion and Theology.* Albert Millard Dunham (who studied with Whitehead at Harvard) wrote his 1931 MA thesis at the University of Chicago on *Whitehead's Philosophy of Time*, and we have Cornelius Golightly's 1941 University of Michigan PhD dissertation, *Thought and Language in Whitehead's Categorial Scheme.*

58. Marquis Lafayette Harris, *Some Conceptions of God in the Gifford Lectures during the Period of 1927–1929* (Doctoral Dissertation, The Ohio State University, 1933), 3–4.

59. Harris, *Some Conceptions of God in the Gifford Lectures*, 8.

60. Ibid., 9–10.

61. Roy D. Morrison, "Albert Einstein: The Methodological Unity Underlying Science and Religion," *Zygon* 14(3) (1979), 255–66.

62. Charles A. Frye, "African Religion and Philosophy: The Hermetic Parallel," in Dennis P. Ryan, ed., *Einstein and the Humanities* (New York: Greenwood Press, 1987), 65–66.

63. Robert T. Browne, *The Mystery of Space: A Study of the Hyperspace Movement in the Light of the Evolution of New Psychic Faculties and an Inquiry into the Genesis and Essential Nature of Space* (New York: E. P. Dutton and Company, 1919). Read Frank L. Mather, ed., *Who's Who of the Colored Race* (Chicago: Frank Lincoln Mather, 1915) and Alfred A. Moss, *The American Negro Academy* (Baton Rouge: Louisiana State University, 1981). Roy D. Morrison, *Science, Theology and the Transcendental Horizon: Einstein, Kant and Tillich* (Atlanta, Georgia: Scholars Press, 1994). Charles A. Frye, "Einstein and African Religion and Philosophy: The Hermetic Parallel," in *Einstein and the Humanities*, ed. Dennis P. Ryan (New York: Greenwood Press, 1987).

64. See Alan M. Wald, *Exiles from a Future Time: Forging of the Mid-Twentieth-Century Literary Left* (Chapel Hill, NC: University of North Carolina Press, 2002), 84–86. Indeed, as the decade of the 1940s moved along the left-wing faculty began to lose crucial members from its ranks. Alphaeus Hunton left Howard and joined W. E. B. Du Bois and Paul Robeson on the Executive Board of the Council on African Affairs. Doxey Wilkerson resigned from Howard to become a full time worker for the Communist Party of the United States (CPUSA). In the case of Abram Harris and Ralph Bunch not only did they leave Howard, they also moved away from the Left. Bunche worked actively in the service of imperialism. As a faculty member at the University of Chicago, Harris embraced the liberal reformism of John Stuart Mill.

65. The most extensive exegesis of Holmes's space/time research has been done by a former student of Holmes, Percy E. Johnston, *Phenomenology of Space and Time* (New York: Dasein Literary Society, 1976). However, this work is flavored with esoteric and useless verbiage and lacks a consistent dialectical materialist outlook.

66. See Eugene C. Holmes, "The Main Philosophical Implications of Space and Time," *American Journal of Physics* 18(9) (December 1950), 560. For a treatment of the relationship of Egyptian to Greek philosophy, see Henry Olela, "The African Foundation of Greek Philosophy," and L. Keita, "The African Philosophical Tradition," both in *African Philosophy: An Introduction*, ed. Richard A. Wright (Washington, DC: University Press of America, 1979). Additionally, consult Edward P. Philip's "Can Ancient Egyptian Thought be Regarded as the Basis of African Philosophy?," *Second Order* 3 (1974).

67. Philip, "Can Ancient Egyptian Thought," 560.

68. Lenin's *Materialism and Empirio-Criticism* appears in Lenin, *Collected Works*, vol. 14 (Moscow: Progress Publishers, 1972); and Maurice Cornforth, *Science Versus Idealism* (New York: International Publishers, 1962).

69. Holmes, "The Main Philosophical Considerations of Space and Time," 561.

70. Theodore Oizerman, *Problems of the History of Philosophy* (Moscow: Progress Publishers, 1973), 81–84.

71. Holmes, "The Main Philosophical Considerations of Space and Time," 561.

72. Ibid., 561–62.

73. Karl Marx and Frederick Engels, *The Holy Family* in Marx and Engels, *Collected Works*, vol. 4 (New York: International Publishers, 1975). For Lenin's conspectus on *The Holy Family*, see Lenin, *Collected Works*, vol. 38 (Moscow: Progress Publishers, 1972), 19–51. For a more recent Marxist discussion on the materialist critique of Descartes, see Howard Selsam, *Philosophy in Revolution* (New York: International Publishers, 1957), 94–95.

74. Edwin A. Burtt, *The Metaphysical Foundations of Modern Physical Science* (London: Routledge & Kegan Paul, 2003): 259.

75. Holmes, "The Main Philosophical Considerations of Space and Time," 563.

76. Ibid., 563–64.

77. Ibid., 564. For Lenin's critique of Kant, see Lenin, *Collected Works*, vol. 38, 91–92, 100, 108–09, 112–13.

78. V. I. Lenin, *Materialism and Empirio-Criticism* in *Collected Works*, vol. 14, 97. His full exposition is in section 1, chapter 4, 194–204, subtitled "The Criticism of Kantianism from the Left and the Right."

79. Holmes, "The Main Philosophical Considerations of Space and Time," 564–65.

80. Ibid., 565.

81. Ibid.

82. Ibid.

83. Ibid., 566.

84. Ibid., 566–67. Also see Albert Einstein and Leopold Infeld, *The Evolution of Physics* (New York: Simon and Schuster, 1961), 177–208. For more recent dialectical materialist philosophical critiques of classical physics and the "revolution" in physics, see V. Ia. Pakhomov, "Contemporary Physics," and "Lenin's Conception of Objective Truth," *Soviet Studies in Philosophy* 9(1) (Summer 1970), 70–80; also see M. E. Omel'ianovskii, "The Conception of Dialectical Contradictions in Quantum Physics," in John Somerville and Howard Parsons, eds., *Dialogues on the Philosophy of Marxism* (Westport, Connecticut: Greenwood Press, 1974), 116–39.

85. This is not to imply that white professional philosophers were any different in their attraction to Marxism-Leninism. Notable exceptions are John Somerville, Howard Selsam, and Howard L. Parsons.

86. For a more extensive discussion of the relationship of Marxism to the philosophy of science, see Helena Sheehan, *Marxism and the Philosophy of Science: A Critical History. Vol 1, the First Hundred Years* (Atlantic Highlands, NJ: Humanities Press, 1984).

87. Charles Taylor, "Neutrality in Political Science," in *Readings in the Philosophy of Science*, ed. Michael Martin and Lee C. McIntyre (Cambridge: MIT Press, 1994), 548.

88. Joyce Mitchell Cook, "On the Nature and Nurture of Intelligence," *Philosophical Forum* 9 (1978), 290.

89. When Golightly was hired at Olivet College in 1945, he became the first black philosopher permanently hired to teach at a white institution in the twentieth century. Golightly was soon followed by black philosophers, Forest O. Wiggins (University of Minnesota) and Francis M. Hammond (Seton Hall) when both were employed in 1946, and William T. Fontaine at the University of Pennsylvania in 1947. For biographical information on Golightly, see Richard B. Angell, "Memorial Minutes: Cornelius Golightly, 1917–1976," *Proceedings and Addresses of the American Philosophical Association* 49 (1975–76), 158–59.

90. Cornelius Golightly, "Ethics and Moral Activism," *The Monist* 56(4) (October 1956), 586.

91. Cornelius Golightly, "Social Science and Normative Ethics," *The Journal of Philosophy* 44(19) (September 1947), 506.

92. Golightly, "Social Science and Normative Ethics," 516.

93. Oliver C. Cox, "An American Dilemma: A Mystical Approach to the Study of Race Relations" *The Journal of Negro Education* 14(2) (Spring 1945), 132, Consult note 2.

94. Cox, "An American Dilemma," 132.

95. Terry Eagleton, *Ideology: An Introduction* (New York: Verso, 1991), 108.

96. For an overview of epistemology as a subfield of philosophy, see Louis P. Pojman, *What Can We Know? An Introduction to the Theory of Knowledge* (Belmont, CA: Wadsworth/Thomson Learning, 2001). See also Christopher Norris, *Epistemology* (London: Continuum, 2005).

97. William T. Fontaine, "The Mind and Thought of the Negro of the United States as Revealed in Imaginative Literature, 1876–1940," *Southern University Bulletin* 28 (March 1942), 6.

98. William T. Fontaine, "An Interpretation of Contemporary Negro Thought from the Standpoint of the Sociology of Knowledge," *The Journal of Negro History* 25(1), 7.

99. William T. Fontaine, "'Social Determination' in the Writings of Negro Scholars," in *Philosophy Born of Struggle: Anthology of Afro-American Philosophy from 1917*, ed. Leonard Harris (Dubuque, IA: Kendall/Hunt Publishers Co., 1983), 90.

100. See Jesse McDade, "Towards An Ontology of Negritude," *Philosophical Forum* 9(2–3) (Winter–Spring 1977–78), 161–68; Roy D. Morrison, "Black Enlightenment: The Issues of Pluralism, Priorities and Empirical Correlation," *Journal of the American Academy of Religion* 46(2) (June 1978), 217–40; Amiri Baraka, "A Black Value System," *Black Scholar* 1(1) (November 1968), See also, Nagueyalti Warren, "Pan-African Cultural Movements: From Baraka to Karenga," *The Journal of Negro History* 75(1–2) (Winter–Spring 1990), 16–28; and Vernon J. Dixon, "African-Oriented and Euro-American Oriented World Views," *Review of Black Political Economy* 77(2) (Winter 1972), 119–56.

101. Robert Staples, *Introduction to Black Sociology* (New York: McGraw-Hill, 1976), 21. For a Marxist critique of Staples's *Introduction*, see John H. McClendon III, "Black Sociology: Another Name for Black Subjectivity," *Freedomways* 20(1) (Spring 1980), 53–59.

102. See, for example, Floyd McKissick, "The Way to a Black Ideology," *The Black Scholar* 1(2) (December 1969), 14–17; Vivian Gordon, "The Coming of Age in Black Studies," *Western Journal of Black Studies* 5(3) (Fall 1981), 231–36.

103. Asante, "The Ideological Significance of Afrocentricity in Intercultural Communication," *Journal of Black Studies* 14(1) (September 1983), 5. We do find that Asante's view of the social sciences as "imperialistic" does not necessarily extend to the natural sciences. Asante is willing to concede that the natural sciences provide us with universal truths. For instance, he seems to believe in the truths of quantum mechanics. See Asante, *The Afrocentric Idea* (Philadelphia, Pennsylvania: Temple University Press, 1987), 11.

104. Patricia Hill Collins, *Black Feminist Thought: Knowledge, Consciousness, and the Politics of Empowerment* (Boston, Massachusetts: Unwin Hyman, 1990), 25. All references are to the first edition.

105. Collins, *Black Feminist Thought*, 236.

106. Hill Collins does not reference Hegel's *Phenomenology* nor for that matter Mikhail Bakhtin's "dialogism" as a source for her ideas. Our comments rest on the commonalties. For treatment of Bakhtin see Michael Holquist, *Dialogism: Bakhtin and his World* (New York: Routledge, 1990). Hegel's *Phenomenology* has had considerable influence on African American intellectual history and the discussion of slavery. A short list would include William Ferris, Charles Leander Hill, Martin Luther King Jr., Eugene C. Holmes, and C. L. R. James.

5

Mapping the Disciplinary Contours of the Philosophy of Religion:

Reason, Faith, and African American Religious Culture

Chapter Outline

We provide a survey of the philosophy of religion as it relates to the African American experience. We look at the relationship of philosophy of religion to the psychology of religion. We provide an overview of issues tied to historical criticism and the epistemological status of faith as it relates to the African American experience. (58)

"In the name of Jesus," African slaves were brought to the New World. Not only was Christianity used as an ideological justification for capitalist slavery but the slave ship *Jesus of Lübeck* literally brought slaves to the Americas, on the behalf of Queen Elizabeth. In the Americas, under the brutality of capitalist slavery, the religions of Africa came into conflict with Christianity. Traditional African beliefs, Islam in conjunction with African styles of worship, forms of ritual, systems of belief, and fundamental perspectives were adapted to form a New World African religious consciousness. As Albert J. Raboteau notes, "At least in some areas of the Americas, the gods of Africa continued to live—in exile."[1]

Is it the case that this New World African religious consciousness reflected the complete hopelessness of African slaves in light of the blind forces of capitalism? Given what seemed like endless days and nights of toil under the lash of slavery, some slaves accepted their lot in life as inescapable, perhaps even ordained by God or Allah. They may have resigned that God's reasons for why things are as they are should not be questioned. However, other slaves pondered the question, is God a white racist? Or perhaps, they reflected on the spiritual, "Didn't my Lord deliver Daniel and why not every man?" At the heart of the latter questions is the issue of theodicy. Theodicy is concerned with how to explain God's actions (or inaction) in light of the continued existence of evil. Why would God allow for Black oppression and exploitation under the yoke of capitalist slavery? Is God on the side of Black people? What good is a religion that allows for human suffering? Are there rational grounds for holding to religious beliefs beyond just faith? These questions bring us to some of the central issues of the philosophy of religion.

In this chapter, we map the contours of the philosophy of religion as it relates to the African American experience. Given the limitations of space, our treatment of the philosophy of religion has its entire point of reference directed on Christianity. Despite the historical influence of Christianity on African American culture and life, the reader should not assume that all African Americans are Christian; there are African American humanists, atheists, Muslims, Jews, and practitioners of traditional African religions such as Yoruba. Our discussion of the philosophy of religion is applicable to Al-Islam or Judaism as components of African American religious culture.

Philosophy of religion and psychology of religion

The philosophy of religion is foremost an academic discipline which requires scholarly rigor and critical deliberation. The philosopher of religion in reading and interpreting religious texts is not hindered by religious commitment and associated faith claims, which ultimately give expression to religious belief. In the case of the first-time philosophy student with religious convictions, psychological impediments attached to religious belief may result in a reluctance toward engaging with the philosophy of religion. Consequently, the religiously oriented student pursuing such work may, in turn, view these requirements with a measure of trepidation, if not skepticism. Why are trepidation and skepticism potentially circumstances that can be encountered with studying the philosophy of religion?

Imagine the beginning philosophy student with religious convictions who is given the task of rationally assessing Karl Marx's critique of religion.[2] It is unlikely that they will find Marx's critique of religion as refreshing; they are likely to experience a sense of trepidation and skepticism. For Marx, religion is the emotional expression of idealism, and idealism is the philosophical expression of a religious worldview. Marx sought to uncover the social basis for religion and faith from the standpoint of philosophical materialism. For Marx, religion offers solace in light of the real pain that people face in their everyday life. However, religion—similar to opium—produces a sense of euphoria and offers the illusion of happiness in the afterlife; a dreamworld of never-ending happiness, "the city of the living God," a land flowing with milk and honey with streets paved in gold. Thus religion stands in the way of an objective comprehension of politics, society, and social relations. Moreover, religion prevents the possibility of a cognitive ethical theory vis-à-vis a religious morality based on faith and/or divine commands. These are the ideas expressed in the often-quoted essay that Karl Marx wrote in 1844:

> *Religious* distress is at the same time the *expression* of real distress and also the *protest* against real distress. Religion is the sigh of the oppressed creature, the heart of a heartless world, and the spirit of spiritless conditions. It is the *opium* of the people.[3]

Here the function of religion is to serve as a painkiller in a world full of pain, a world of oppression and exploitation. As Angela Davis explains, "It is true indeed that real wants, real needs, and real desires can be transformed into impotent wish-dreams via the process of religion, especially if things appear to be utterly hopeless in the world. But it is also true that these dreams can revert to their original state—as real wishes, real needs to change the existing social reality."[4] Hence, only social revolution will produce social conditions in which religious illusions are made unnecessary.

Now, we think that most people that have religious convictions are usually born into some type of religious culture, with appropriately suited forms of social networking.[5] It follows that the matter of religious identification is firmly linked to an assumed personal (basic) identity, perhaps within some religiously influenced community. Furthermore, it also involves adopting a generalized viewpoint on the world, which derives from the espoused religious standpoint, concomitantly anchored in a specific religious culture and life style. This combination of religiously based personal identity and worldview transpires as an all-encompassing psychological influence on the respective believers. As Black philosopher Roy D. Morrison informs us, this religious worldview functions as a comprehensive (cultural) guidance system: "A guidance system is always a dynamic constellation of ideas, methods, constructs, symbols, value judgments and deeply entrenched psychological connotations. Elements of it may be highly invisible because of its essentially psychological locus. However, the behavioral consequences are empirically objective and often photographable."[6]

The reader should not ignore the fact that the psychology of religion is a distinctive area of scholarly concern; its abiding influence on the pedagogical complexities surrounding the learning process—attendant with the philosophy of religion—cannot be ignored. Since the philosophy of religion is within the purview of the academic discipline of philosophy, then one's psychological orientation respecting religious beliefs is not grounded on the same principles. Consequently, one's religious identification can prove to be more than just a rational mode of cognitive comportment. Frequently what becomes transparent is the added dimension of significantly affective (emotional) bearings on the placement of religious convictions. Therefore, the starting point for the religious believer is often far removed from any academic inspection of the basic presumptions that inform one's religious beliefs. As Jason Long notes, "The reasons given for belief are driven not by rational thought and reasoned argumentation, but by psychological factors that maintain what society has given the religious believer through indoctrination." Hence, religious identification primarily assumes a *lived experience* without critical scrutiny.[7]

Additionally, we discover that on rare occasion certain philosophers were also psychologists. Among the number of scholars located in both fields of study include Harvard professor William James and Black philosopher/ psychologists Drs. Gilbert Haven Jones (Figure 17) and Francis M. Hammond. Given the Jim Crow barriers in both professional philosophy and psychology facing Jones and Hammond, they were exceptional Black philosophers of the twentieth century.

Gilbert Haven Jones was born and reached adulthood during the period of consolidation of what W. E. B. Du Bois called the "Color Line." One

Figure 17a&b Gilbert Haven Jones (1881–1966).

striking result is that his entire professional career was limited to teaching at the following HBCUs: St. Augustine Collegiate Institute (Raleigh, North Carolina), Oklahoma Colored Agricultural & Normal University (renamed Langston University in 1941), and Wilberforce University. Despite the restrictions of academic racism, Jones was an important pioneer among Black philosophers on several accounts. His book *Education in Theory and Practice* (1919) was not only the first—written by a Black philosopher—in the field of philosophy of education. He also boldly presented a philosophical (dialectical) materialist approach to the subject matter. Jones argues,

> Everything in the organic and inorganic world, the bee, the flower, the stone, has its moment of beginning, its period of growth and development, it's season of flower and fruition, his hour of death and decay and finally its faithful process of dissipation and disintegration. The mental life so far as his earthly existence is concerned in its relations with body, undergoes apparently the same process. It's susceptibility to educational processes and educational influences lies in the fact that it is imperfect from the start and its power of manifestation, but from the beginning one possesses the power of taking on an enlarging form subject to the growth of its place of abode, the body, and to the influence of the environment.[8]

Jones's explicit dialectical materialist stance is a remarkable step in light of the fact that the dominant tendency among African American philosophers was dialectical idealism during this time.[9] Additionally, Jones was the first

African American scholar—holding a doctorate—to teach psychology at a higher educational institution. Among his professional associations, Jones was also a member of the Association for the Advancement of Psychological Research.[10]

Jones's dissertation *Lotze und Bowne: Eine Vergleichung Ihrer philosophischen Arbeit* (Lotze and Bowne: A Comparison of Their Philosophical Work) examined two of the key founders of Personalism. Jones's dissertation was also the first work, by a Black philosopher, in the field of religious philosophy. Borden Parker Bowne was crucially important to the advancement of Personalism in the United States and acknowledged the seminal influence of the German philosopher and logician Rudolf Hermann Lotze on his thought. Recently, in his intellectual biography of Lotze (2015), William R. Woodward cites Jones's dissertation on this very point about Lotze's considerable influence.[11]

Of course, we are faced with the question, what is Personalism? Black Personalist scholar Rufus Burrow appropriately notes the following:

> Personalism holds that reality is personal and that persons are the highest-not the only-intrinsic values. It is a type of idealism which maintains that PERSON is the supreme philosophical principle-that principle without which no other principle can be made intelligible. It is the view that the universe is a society of interacting and intercommunicating selves and persons with God at the center. The term personalism was first used by the German theologian Friedrich Schleiermacher in 1799, although he did not develop it philosophically. . . . Personalism was made a going concern in this country by Borden Parker Bowne (1847–1910), who came to be known as "the father of American Persona."[12]

We should point out there is the particular case of Dr. John Wesley Bowen, who preceded Gilbert Haven Jones into the ranks of Personalism. Bowen was an African American theologian and religious philosopher. Rufus Barrow keenly brings to our attention that

> John Wesley Bowen . . . was the first African-American academic personalist, i.e., the first to actually study the philosophy of personalism in the classroom, and with Bowne himself! Indeed, Bowne was still in the first stage (i.e., the objective idealism stage) of his movement toward personalism when Bowen earned his seminary degree at Boston University and then entered the doctoral program. Although his academic advisor was Henry C. Sheldon, he was most influenced by the latter's teacher and friend, Bowne.[13]

Bowen is not only a seminal figure in the ranks of Personalism but also one of the first to explore the scholarly region of the psychology of religion. As for Personalism, it would later emerge as a prominent school of thought among Black religious philosophers from J. Leonard Farmer Sr., Willis Jefferson King, and Howard Thurman to Martin Luther King and Rufus Burrow.[14]

Francis M. Hammond (Figure 18) received his PhD from Laval University in Quebec, Canada, in 1943. After teaching at the HBCU institutions of Xavier University (New Orleans) and Southern University, Hammond was not only on the faculty of the Philosophy Department at Seton Hall University but also was chair of the department from 1946 to 1951. Hence, Hammond was the first Black philosopher to assume such rank at a white institution. Moreover, he also became chair of the Psychology Department, at the same institution, serving from 1952 to 1955. This was also the first time for a Black psychologist to hold such a position.[15]

Hammond did graduate study in psychology with Professor Albert Michottee at the University of Louvain and his doctoral dissertation was on a topic covering both philosophy and psychology. His dissertation, *La Conception Psychologique de la Societe chez Gabriel Tarde*, was a critical focus on Gabriel Tarde, the pioneering French social psychologist, sociologist, and theorist of criminology as well as nemesis of Emil Durkheim. Critical of the Cartesian influences on Durkheim, Tarde sought to map out a distinctive path via what Tarde scholar Terry Clark identifies as "Spontaneity."[16]

Figure 18a&b Francis M. Hammond (1911–78).

Additionally, Hammond was a member of the American Psychological Association and assumed the role of consulting social psychologist relating to industrial and social problems from 1951 to 1955. Hammond often received invitations to lecture within the framework of the psychiatry of religion. Nonetheless, a white colleague at Seton Hall questioned Hammond's qualifications for the appointment as chair to the psychology department. Importantly, Hammond was a scholar in both the philosophy of religion and the psychology of religion.[17] While our review of Jones and Hammond brings to light the disciplinary connections of philosophy of religion to psychology of religion, the fact remains that one's psychological disposition can prove to be detrimental in grasping the former.

Method of investigation: Academic study versus devotional study of the Bible

So, therefore, the philosophy of religion as an academic discipline requires scholarly methods for its inquiry. Of course, religion itself is not an academic pursuit, rather it is—among other things—a belief system that does not mandate any scholarly comprehension. Morrison observes, "In religion humans seek not merely reality but that which is envisioned as ultimate reality, god or in different categories the power which generates the cosmic order and intelligibility that we have been able to discover."[18]

As academic inquiry, the philosophy of religion engages in the critical examination of religious beliefs. Conventionally, in divergence, Christian educational programs—such as Bible study—are primarily devotional rather than academic in nature. African American biblical scholar Michael Joseph Brown accurately points out,

> Bible study as it is conducted in the average church often has to do with what I call "self-help" religion. That is, many people come to Bible studies not to hear what the text is saying, but to reaffirm themselves and their faith perspective. . . . The aims of parish Bible study are devotional and geared towards personal improvement. These are very important goals for people aspiring to live productive religious lives, but these are not the goals of the academic study of scripture.[19]

Devotional study of the Bible has a rather protracted tradition within African American religious culture. For example, during slavery, we unearth that African American writer Jupiter Hammon recommended to the community of slaves that it focus exclusively on studying the Bible. Furthermore, he commanded that those that were literate should teach the illiterate how to read the Bible. Hence, Bible study, from Hammon's standpoint, is essentially a communal project. In no uncertain terms, he declares,

> Those of you who can read, I must beg you to read the Bible; and whenever you get the time, study the Bible; and if you can get no other time, spare some of your time from sleep, and learn what the mind and will of God is. . . . If there is no Bible, it would not matter whether you could read or not. Reading other books do you no good. But the Bible is the word of God, and tells you what you must do to please God; it tells you how you may escape misery, and be happy forever.[20]

Foremost on Hammon's philosophical agenda is the question of the ethical conduct of the slave vis-à-vis the slave master. In his critique of Hammon's position, religious studies professor Anthony Pinn astutely demonstrates that Hammon is prey to a theodicy that affirms slavery as justifiable, if not commendable. In effect, Hammon argues that slavery is the manifestation of divine punishment and that slavery actually functions as an opportunity for African Americans to begin the needed preparation for greater things in heaven. While some may have argued that Hammon's "philosophy was born of struggle," its substance is emphatically accommodationist.[21]

The divine punishment argument as an explanation of African American oppression has a long history extending from Hammon and others in the eighteenth century right up until the twenty-first century. Philosophers William R. Jones (*Is God a White Racist?*) and Stephen C. Ferguson II ("Teaching Hurricane Katrina: Understanding Divine Racism and Theodicy") provide important critiques of African American theistic conceptions of reality and history. Ferguson aptly remarks, "While religion has been at the center of the African American experience, substantive philosophical issues about theodicy, the epistemological nature of religious beliefs, and even creationism have been avoided."[22]

In addition, without critical reflection, Hammon presumes that the Bible is the means to comprehending the will of God. Thus, while lacking any rational demonstration, he assumes God's existence, purely as a matter of faith. For both Hammon and Michael Joseph Brown, the process of devotional Bible study is principally an engagement within the given community of faith. It follows that religious affiliation is a matter of making a pledge of faith. While it is permissible that anyone can make some kind of pledge of religious commitment, however, not every person is academically equipped to undertake work in the philosophy of religion. The philosophy of religion requires more than a declaration of faith. The reader should keep the following in mind: "When two disagree on some philosophical matter, the only avenue of progress open to them is to consider and evaluate arguments on both sides. Therefore, philosophical inquiry must be critical and logical if any gain is to result."[23]

Thus, we ask, what is most essential for academic preparation and scholarly mastery? The philosophy of religion as academic discipline involves mastery of a particular set of tools respecting the process of critical thought based on logical reasoning. One aspect of logical reasoning—that plays a large part in philosophical thinking—is the primary concern for the rational justification for our beliefs and this involves the validity and soundness of arguments. At minimum, our arguments must withstand the test of rational assessment. A rational (deductive) argument must have validity, if not soundness. What then constitutes a sound argument and how can validity be determined? Put simply, "A deductive argument is said to be sound when the premises of the argument is true and the argument is valid. Saying an argument is valid is equivalent to saying it is logically impossible that the premises are true and the conclusion is false."[24]

It follows that the philosopher of religion engages in the academic study of religion. Consequently, on assuming the role as philosopher of religion, one need not hold to any religious affiliation or allegiance. However, critical attention to the validity affixed to justifications that are provided by means of theological claims, with respect to specific religious beliefs, stands as the paramount concern. The rational assessment of religious beliefs—without theological allegiances—marks one of the defining features of the philosophy of religion.

In contrast, the religious devotee is a member of a faith community and shares in a common allegiance grounded on articles of faith. Even the study and interpretation of biblical texts are positioned on the basis of the shared vision associated with a given faith community. Black biblical scholar Brad Braxton states,

> When contemporary Christian communities read the Bible they also make a faith claim that is more explicitly *theological*. These communities believe that as they read the Scriptures bequeathed to them by Christian history God *may*

speak fresh words of Revelation. The Scriptures are not the word of God *per se*, but the Scriptures possess the potential to become the word of God as they are read faithfully and creatively under the auspices of the Holy Spirit.[25]

Such an approach to reading the Bible is far from an academic procedure. The academic study of the Bible presumes there is an objective content to given texts resulting from authorial intent and sociohistorical context. Herein Michael Joseph Brown's earlier insight is most helpful, the student of devotional study ultimately fails "to hear what the text is saying," via the pursuit to "reaffirm themselves and their faith perspective."

Evidently, Braxton's suggestion remains essentially an affirmation of the *devotional approach* to biblical study. In line, this method is dependent upon the presumption that faith is the guiding principle. Since Braxton adjoins faith claims to theology, the question arises, if a faith claim is "more explicitly *theological*," what, therefore, is the meaning of theology? As well, how does theology differ from philosophy?

Theology is chiefly concerned with outlining the meaning of the God concept, that is, defining the nature of God and explicitly indicating representative features of divine existence, such as the character of divine attribution, along with delineating God's relationship to human beings as well as the universe at-large. There is also the theological requirement of providing the defense and propagation of Christian doctrines and traditions. This latter function, within Christian theology, is conventionally referenced as *apologetics*.

Moreover, Christian theology makes faith (in God's existence) pivotal to its pursuit in understanding the full meaning attached to the God concept. Theologians Howard Stone and James Duke comment, "All Christians are theologians. It's not that they are born that way or decided one day to go into theology. It's a simple fact of Christian life: their faith makes them theologians, whether they know it or not, and it calls them to become the best theologians they can be."[26]

Given our exploration into the definition of theology, it should be clear to the reader that the implied meaning of Braxton's reference to "theological" points to how faith becomes a pivotal factor in the study of biblical texts. For the devout believer, without the element of faith, the Bible ceases to have any meaningful value. Certainly, this presumption is preeminently expressed as a theological claim. In short, the import of biblical texts resides in the theological orientation of the reader and not in extracting meaning from the text itself.

The matter of religious beliefs: Historical criticism contra faith commitment

The academic assessment of the Bible—prominently outlined with the historical critical method—cannot rest on faith-based presuppositions, such as the Bible representing the inspired word of God. Correspondingly, the philosophy of religion is quite compatible with the academic approach founded on the *historical critical method*. Both the philosophy of religion and the *historical critical method* jettison any reliance on the inspired locus of biblical texts, which are based on theological decisions guiding the process of historical analysis. In David Law's book *The Historical Critical Method: A Guide for the Perplexed*, he appropriately notes how historical critics academically approach the subject of the Bible. One crucial element is their critical take on the presupposition that the Bible is the inspired word of God:

> Although some scholars have indeed rejected the notion of inspiration, it is probably more accurate to say that historical criticism is methodologically indifferent to the question of the inspired status of the Bible. The question is put to one side, "bracketed out" and plays no role in the historical critic's examination of the text. Historical critics tend to leave God as the author or inspirer of the Scriptures out of consideration and treat the Bible as a historical work, or a collection of works, to be interpreted by means of historical methods appropriate to all historical works.[27]

Along similar lines, Edward Krentz aptly observes the following:

> An appeal to the canon, a carefully circumscribed body of literature, does not settle the question of *sources* for biblical history. The boundaries of the canon are not the boundaries of *the source material for Israelite or primitive Christian history*. . . . In short, the question of sources is as open in biblical history as in history in general. The canon represents a *theological decision, not a decision concerning historical methods or sources*.[28] (Italics added)

Krentz insightfully brings to our attention how biblical texts—as canon or the designated religious texts afforded the status of Scripture—themselves are the product of theological decision. Such texts are not constituted as empirically verifiable sources that explain the past history of biblical texts or for that matter history writ large. Those religious texts that are afforded canonical status as Scripture assume such a position by way of theological decision. The acceptance of what is considered as the genuinely inspired word of God rest on faith and not scrutiny of the historical process associated with canonization.[29]

In this latter respect—canonization as a matter of theological decision-making—Braxton fundamentally agrees with Krentz. Braxton conveys,

> Religious, or more specifically theistic texts are produced when persons attempt to codify their experiences with God in language. This process of codification, however, does not in and of itself catapult these religious texts to the status of "Scripture." Scriptures are religious writings that a community deems to be reliable mediators of "an encounter with the transcendent." In spite of the large numbers of religious texts that ancient Israel and early Christianity compose, the history of canonization of both the Jewish and Christian Bibles demonstrates that not all "religious writings" in these religious movements were elevated to the status of Scripture.[30]

In contrast to Krentz, Braxton is still faced with the problem of explaining how the contemporary Christian may establish that such Scriptures are historically valid. Did the process of canonization get it right as to what texts were selected? How can the present-day student of the Bible know? Braxton's answer is unequivocal, "Contemporary communities that appeal to Scripture are affirming their faith in the essential correctness of our religious forebears' decision concerning which texts most helpfully articulate the contours of Christian faith."[31]

Quite explicitly, Braxton must turn to faith as the overriding principle anchoring his method of biblical study. Academic methods of examination and interpretation of biblical texts are not restricted by theological concerns. Likewise, along such lines, the philosophy of religion shares this precise orientation toward biblical texts specifically and religion as belief system more generally. Theological encumbrances are not allowable as core features within the philosophy of religion nor for that matter with the historical critical method.[32]

At this juncture, we return to the question, how does theology differ from philosophy? In accordance with our thesis, African American theologian J. Deotis Roberts suggests for our deliberation the following demarcation:

> Theology is a study about God and about man's nature and destiny. It includes man's relationship to God and to his fellow man. Christian theology treats these concerns in the context of Christian affirmations. Both philosophy and theology are concerned with ultimate questions. Whereas the philosopher may relate these presuppositions broadly look to all religious experiences, a theologian must apply his faith-claims narrowly in his own theological circle.[33]

While Roberts outlines the differences between philosophy and theology, he, nevertheless, does not provide the substance behind theology and philosophy with respect to a definition of religion. To address that matter, we must return to Roy D. Morrison and his critical assessment of both philosophy and religion. As for religion, Morrison clearly states,

> I define religion as a cluster of values, symbols, myths, rituals, and commitments through which humans nurture their sense of mystery, awe, and transcendence, explain the meaning of their lives in the scheme of things, establish the foundations of morality, and provide grounds for hope in the future. Religion affords interpretations of reality which at times, from a scientific perspective, may do violence to reality—and to human integrity; nevertheless these interpretations help believers to ward off the terror of history and to grope toward some particular kind of meaning.[34]

If the main purpose of theology is to affirm religious beliefs, then scientific knowledge need not come within its scope nor guide what it is in substance. All that matters is the affirmation of religious faith and/or religious beliefs. In comparison, Morrison defines philosophy along divergent lines:

> By philosophy I mean an intellectual activity in which the thinker conducts an inquiry into the basic value judgments, attitudes, categories, postulates, and the logic of the various special sciences, including those of philosophy itself. Therefore I am speaking of critical philosophy. Also I designate five major branches of philosophy: epistemology (the study of knowledge), metaphysics (the study of universal or pervasive categories and functions in thought and in external reality), semantics (the study of communication, meanings, and the relevant logic systems), aesthetics, and ethics.[35]

What substantially comes into play with Morrison's definition of philosophy, which is lacking with Roberts, is the clear emphasis on how critical philosophy functions where faith is absent from consideration. In fact, as Morrison astutely notes, "Once the legitimacy and the power of critical philosophy and scientific method are established, a protracted methodological war erupts between religion and science, and a symposium of rebellion lectures against uncritical faith and against the theistic idea of god."[36]

Since philosophy addresses our basic assumptions and presuppositions, then those that undergird faith claims are just as well open to critical review. Faith claims, from the philosophical standpoint, do not have the power of self-justification. Philosopher Alfred North Whitehead astutely points out the following:

The philosophic attitude is a resolute attempt to enlarge the understanding of the scope of application of every notion which enters into our caring thought. The philosophic attempt takes every word, and every phrase, in the verbal expression of thought, and asked, what does it mean? It refuses to be satisfied by the conventional presupposition that every sensible person knows the answer. As soon as you rest satisfied with primitive ideas, with your permanent presuppositions, you have ceased to be a philosopher.[37]

In another context, yet, often one may hear Christians argue for *justification by faith alone*, which implies that faith is not only a necessary condition but also a sufficient one for legitimate standing as Christian devotee in the community of faithful believers. One's ethical conduct (in Christian parlance, "works") in the world is secondary to faith in God/Jesus and thus salvation is entirely determined by the measure of one's faith.

From the standpoint of Christianity, the relationship of philosophy to religion is often viewed as founded on a principle of mutual exclusion. This is particularly due to the overriding principle which animates philosophy, that is, reason. With respect to African American culture, the Christian influence concerning faith as a pivotal norm has decidedly shaped how a great number of Black Christians view the world.

Roy D. Morrison finds that faith is an inadequate source critically engaging the world in addition to assessing how a given worldview may function as culturally oppressive structures of thought. He states, "In so far as the total constellation of guidance systems in a culture constitutes a worldview . . . a viable corrective for its sins must be sought in another philosophy, not merely in faith."[38] It follows, for Morrison, that the Christian worldview based as it is on faith, thus restricts the development of establishing a culture of critical discourse.

Philosophy, however, emerges precisely from such a cultural framework and this is why Morrison recommends it as a viable corrective. On the basis of faith, rather than reason, the human encounter with nature takes the form of supernaturalism, wherein *anthropomorphism* and creationism are surrogates for naturalist explanations of reality. The extension of human attributes to supernatural beings is called "anthropomorphism." Anthropomorphism/creationism as an explanation of nature's origins subsequently helps *simplify* the workings of nature, especially for those not privy to the scientific conception of reality. From the perspective of creationism, we can simply imagine that nature was created just as we might create an artifact through human ingenuity. Before the advancement of scientific understanding, such creationist explanations gave comfort to our human curiosity about nature. The notion of creation, the concepts of heaven and hell, or the idea that the earth was flat and subsequently was also the center of the universe was ultimately refuted by the advancement of the materialist (scientific) explanations of nature.[39]

Undeniably, for most African American Christians their belief in the existence of God is established on faith and not reason. Generally, Black Christians argue that the limits of human reason mandate the necessity for faith in God's existence. The Christian notion of human finitude encompasses restrictions on the capability of reasonably comprehending the nature of God's existence. African American philosopher James B. Carter succinctly argues the point about the absolute character of God and the limitations on human thought:

> As inventions are but materialized ideas, it should not require argument to compel the acceptance of the statement that Ideas are the great civilizers— "the metaphysical notions," the machines in the mind—the "wheels in the head." . . . The difference between God's materialization of His original idea and man's manifestation of his is so vast as to admit of no proper comparison except that the latter may be rightly considered somewhat as a faint attempt at repetitions of the former.[40]

Carter's position has its basis in a very long tradition in African American religious culture. For instance, several decades later, Black theologian Major Jones makes the similar point about how faith compares with the limits of human reason. He argues,

> The divine unreality becomes the reality of God when a *community of faith* responds to the reality of divine unreality. Because God is not direct in his approach to human beings-because God is silent and hides himself-God is sometimes presumed to be nonexistent. Absolute proof of God's existence is *beyond the scope of mere human reason.*[41] (Italics added)

The various proofs on the existence of God such as the cosmological, ontological, and teleological forms, all depend on rational argumentation and thus significantly compose what remains as a crucial part of the philosophy of religion. In Western philosophy, we discern that Augustine, Aristotle, Aquinas, Anselm, Descartes, and Kant, among others, address how such proofs offer feasible means for philosophical deliberations, particularly concerning how (or how not) one can rationally approach the God concept. Unquestionably, energetic debates over the philosophical viability of these proofs steadfastly continue among contemporary scholars.[42]

Since Jones presumes that "absolute proof of God's existence is beyond the scope of mere human reason," it follows that philosophy is an inadequate tool for comprehending the existence of God. Transparently, Jones thinks that faith rectifies what are the limits on human reason. Hence, Jones conveys an antithetical position from what we earlier gathered from Morrison. The key point of contention centers on the epistemological grounding of faith and reason. In Jones's estimation, God as a matter of principle is unknowable, thus, his proposal reduces to a form of *skepticism*. Religious skepticism upholds that in principle God is unknowable. In short, Jones's claim is that there is no *rational justification* for belief in God.

Furthermore, he states, "Black theology knows that what God does for us in faith is greater than what God does for us in knowledge."[43] Consequently, he leaves us with *fideism* as the only basis for believing in God. By fideism, it is meant that faith is a sufficient condition for the justification of belief in God. However, this form of justification stands without rational demonstration; that is, there are no reasonable grounds for faith. Faith reduces to essentially a choice based on blind commitment.

By faith, one justifiably chooses to believe in God, albeit, without supporting rational principles. This results in the God concept being effectively removed from history that is, how we comprehend history as an empirical inquiry. Essentially, God cannot be grounded on historical evidence, because rational principles give way to faith claims. Biblical theology falls short of the mark with regard to historically justified belief. Theologian and historian Van A. Harvey notes the following:

> Only when the question "What really happened" was consistently and radically posed, did it become clear how much of what was previously accepted as fact was, in truth, fiction; how so many long-entrusted witnesses were actually credulous spinners of tales and legends. Indeed, it can be argued, all reliable history rest on some such distinction as whether or not something actually happened; "whether it happened in the way it is told or in some other way."[44]

The putative biblical witnesses were not historians, instead they were myth makers giving expression to theological claims. The song, "It Ain't Necessarily So," from the musical *Porgy and Bess* is a popular expression of Harvey's thesis on biblical history. When resorting to biblical literalism, the great probability is that history goes by the wayside as faith overrides reason. This critical note about biblical texts as historical source material is equally applicable to the New Testament and its treatment of the life of Jesus as both human and the Son of God.[45]

Christian belief and Jesus Christ: The matter of historical confirmation contra faith

African American theologian Howard Thurman recommends that the following is the methodological starting point for understanding the historical Jesus: "I am asking you to approach the life of Jesus stripped bare of much that is metaphysical and theological and mystical. Let us begin with the simple fact that Jesus of Nazareth was a Palestinian Jew."[46] Evidently, Thurman's recommendation directs us on a different path than the Christian conventional notion of faith. If we remove the Christian conceptions of the metaphysical, theological, and mystical, when deliberating on the historical Jesus, then this would drastically transform the scenario on biblical study recommended by Brad Braxton, Major Jones, and J. Deotis Roberts. For much that is involved with the Christian principle of faith entails precisely its metaphysical, theological, and mystical dimensions.

For many Christians, the principal belief—among Christianity's founding beliefs—is one's faith in Jesus as the Son of God. This cardinal belief functions as the underpinning for human salvation from mortal sin and earthly degradation. For some Black Christians, the Jesus of faith also has historical presence. In other words, what we know about Jesus from biblical texts is not only founded on articles of faith—because such texts are theologically true—but also true in the sense of how one understands actual historical events and persons.

In short, the biblical Jesus, founded on faith, is a real historical figure. Clearly this is a significant departure from Thurman's recommended methodology. Nevertheless, the idea that the two conceptions on Jesus are compatible is straightforwardly a rejection of the historical critical method. For illustration, African American theologian James H. Cone steadfastly declares,

> Since I contend that Jesus of the Gospels cannot be separated from the "real" Jesus and have discussed the reason for this conclusion elsewhere, there is no need here to enter into the critical discussion about the old and new quests for the historical Jesus. The text of the New Testament serves not only as a theological check on what we theologians are committed to do with Jesus; but it also serves as a *historical* check against contemporary historians.[47]

Cone's last point, "it [the New Testament] also serves as a *historical* check against contemporary historians," is an assertion that buttresses the idea that biblical texts contain more than support of theological truths, which derive from articles of faith. For Cone, the New Testament de facto serves as a history book, which means that belief in Jesus as the Son of God is more than a matter of faith. The grounds supporting the presence of a real, historical Jesus, along with Jesus as divine entity both can be established by reference to the New Testament. Furthermore, the New Testament confirms that the historical Jesus is congruent with the Jesus of faith.

Now we must confront the philosophical question, what is the substance of Cone's contention that "Jesus of the Gospels cannot be separated from the 'real' Jesus." Cone's claim is that the Jesus of the Gospels—with all of its mythic/supernatural elements—is actually quite consistent with a real, historical person. Then, Cone's presumption allows for the empirical verification of divine actions and events, that is, matters that are actually supernatural in character, which in fact stand outside of human and natural history. In summary, Cone thinks that we need not demarcate the mythic portrayal of Jesus from the process of historical verification. We discover that Cone chooses to ignore the epistemological divide between the *faith of theology* and the *facts of history* (which are rationally supported).[48]

Furthermore, Cone argues that the historical Jesus is not confined to the ancient past. The historic presence of Jesus has immediate significance today. Since the historical entrance of Jesus onto the world scene ushered in a new stage of history, accordingly, there will arise a new age of liberation from oppression. The historical Jesus—as the Son of God—continues to influence our present-day world. The new age of liberation is on the contemporary horizon. Cone remarks,

> The Bible, it is important to note, does not consist of units of infallible truths about God or Jesus. Rather, it tells the story of God's will to redeem humankind from sin, death, and Satan. According to the New Testament witnesses, God's decisive act against these powers happened in Jesus life, death and resurrection.[49]

Cone continues to magnify how Jesus—as the Christ of salvation—is directly related to the secular aim of human liberation.

> Christ's salvation is liberation; there is no liberation without Christ. Both meanings are inherent in the statement that Jesus Christ is the ground of human liberation. Any statement that divorces salvation from liberation or makes human freedom independent of divine freedom must be rejected.[50]

Since God is present in Jesus and concurrently Jesus is present in human history, then Cone seeks to override the secular task of human liberation on the theological premise, "there is no liberation without Christ." This presumption clearly establishes that human efforts are Christ dependent and not a concern based on human self-determination. Obviously, on Cone's analysis, the unification of human freedom with divine freedom explicitly rejects the primary line of demarcation between faith and reason. We cannot ignore that our *philosophical* point of departure rest on the assumption that faith is antithetical to reason. The discipline of history—as with philosophy— mandates that its research methodology adhere to rational principles as expressed by concrete empirical procedures that guide its investigation.[51]

In sum, historical research is not founded on articles of faith; hence, if the New Testament as history book presumption has legitimacy, it must come under the scrutiny of the same procedural rules that govern what conventionally applies to any history text. It is transparent that supernatural events as matters of historical causation are not open to empirical verification. In Western philosophy, David Hume notably arises as one of the chief proponents of this viewpoint. Hume argues that empirical methods of verification cannot confirm supernatural beliefs. In turn, there are no source materials that the historian can review for such supernatural explanations that have historical merit. We must now proceed, according to this dictum, for our judgment on Cone's proposition.[52]

While Cone identifies the Jesus of faith with the historical Jesus, the fact remains that Jesus reportedly lived over two-thousand years ago. It seems that given this fact, belief in Jesus as an agent of liberation for today, actually mandates that faith override any historical justification. Rational historical inquiry clearly demonstrates that Jesus is dead and cannot have an impact on those living in the world, let alone come back and completely change it for the better. Conclusively, there is no historical (rational) basis or empirical evidence that can justify the Christian belief in the resurrection of Jesus.[53]

At root, what we discern is that Cone provides us with nothing more than a faith claim. Cone's argument for the identity of the historical Jesus with the faith-based Son of God notion cannot meet the test of rational scrutiny. This is why most Christian theologians make the demarcation between faith and reason as the pivotal factor for grounding theological claims. Braxton keenly makes this point: "When contemporary communities of faith assert the Bible is inspired they are making a historical and theological claim that is rooted in faith."[54]

Christian faith encompasses believing that it is within the power of Jesus to eradicate all forms of human oppression and misery. Moreover, faith is the lynchpin of the Christian belief system and, subsequently, reason must be subordinated to it. Claims about returning to life from death and more generally acts exceeding the laws of nature cannot be established on rational grounds. Belief in the resurrection of Jesus Christ is patently an article of faith and not a rational conclusion based on scientific evidence.

Therefore, Paul declares that this belief in the resurrection of Christ is the cornerstone of the Christian edifice. Without it there can be no belief system known as Christianity nor can one claim to be truly Christian. Hence, not by reason but rather by faith does Christianity establish its theological foundation. From the standpoint of history, rational reflection contra faithful obedience signals why philosophy was often viewed as a threat to religious orthodoxy.

Paul states, "Beware lest any man spoil you through philosophy and vain deceit, after the tradition of men, after the rudiments of the world, and not after Christ" (Colossians 2:8 KJV). Paul's warning about philosophy spoiling the Christian faithful was not lost on a number of Christian theologians beginning with Tertullian.[55] Since it appears we have a relation of mutual exclusion regarding philosophy and religion, how can we make sense of the import attached to the philosophy of religion? In what manner can reason come to bear on the meaning of religion? Therefore, let us now return to this key concept—philosophy of religion.

The philosophy of religion contra religious philosophy

Mapping the contours of the philosophy of religion as an academic discipline comprises more than relating philosophy—in some arbitrary manner—to religion. The precise specification of the relation between the two terms is requisite. For instance, it is crucially important to note, the *philosophy of religion* substantially differs from *religious philosophy*. Apart from the obvious terminological appearances, the corresponding disciplinary outcomes are more than simply hairsplitting over lexicon. At this interval, the immediate question for our consideration becomes, what framework suitably renders how and why the philosophy of religion differs from religious philosophy? The answer, in part, rests on the fact that the faith/reason divide is actually commensurate with the distinction holding between religious philosophy and the philosophy of religion, respectively.

The driving force behind religious philosophy develops from how philosophy undergirds theological claims, which subsequently give expression to one's commitment to articles of faith. In contrast, the philosophy of religion critically evaluates theological claims and keenly assesses the logical grounds for the justification of faith. The reader must keep such conceptual distinctions in mind as we progress through the chapter. We start our inquiry by first inspecting the nature of religious philosophy. Black philosopher Rudolph V. Vanterpool succinctly captures the motivating impulse of religious philosophy vis-à-vis the intricacies of Christian philosophy. Vanterpool unequivocally announces,

> I deem it incumbent upon me as a scholar who identifies himself with the Christian philosophical tradition to maintain a clear hermeneutical focus that preserves the inviolable principle of the inerrancy of biblical truths. Hence, I must suspend the temptation to let the full scope of my rational dispositions freely take over the complex task of theological investigation when interpreting what is exactly that God is teaching us in particular contexts. This approach requires us to place ultimate credibility in whatever the Bible declares derives directly from the mind of the Supreme Being, Lord over all there is.[56]

As Christian philosopher, Vanterpool's conception of religious philosophy is committed to philosophical insights illuminating what amounts to Christian articles of faith. His conception of Christian philosophy is transparently quite different than our notion of the philosophy of religion. The very act of preserving "the inviolable principle of the inerrancy of biblical truths" speaks volumes concerning Vanterpool's overriding commitment to Christian theology. It should be transparent to the reader that Vanterpool—as Christian philosopher—stands in accord with our earlier observations on Brad Braxton and his recommendations for biblical interpretation, particularly the matter of how faith is steadfastly hegemonic.

Moreover, Vanterpool explicitly outlines how he finds it necessary to "suspend the temptation to let the full scope of my rational dispositions freely take over the complex task of theological investigation." He subordinates reason to faith, by willfully curtailing his own rational capacity. His position is in full alignment with Paul's admonition on philosophy. Vanterpool openly delineates how Christian philosophy departs from the critical inspection of theological claims, which is precisely our conception on the philosophy of religion.

However, some scholars—aligned with Christian philosophy—conflate the two approaches, namely, religious philosophy with philosophy of religion. Yet, if the philosophy of religion is rendered as synonymous with religious philosophy, the probability is that the philosophy of religion has been consigned to residing within the realm of theology. For example, *Christian philosophy*—as religious philosophy—presumes that the Christian worldview is the starting point for philosophical analysis or inquiry. L. Russ Bush in his book, *A Handbook for Christian Philosophy*, elaborates,

> Someone must seek and find the unity of God's truth both in the Word and in the world. Of all the *classical theological disciplines, the philosophy of religion is the most inter-disciplinary. . . .* A case could be made for the thesis that the greatest and most beneficial aspects of humanity's past have come from those who have seen the world in the greatest context—as a purposeful creation of holy, divine, infinite-personal intelligence. Such a context gives real (not illusory) purpose to human life. This worldview is fully elaborated in the Judeo-Christian Scriptures.[57] (Italics added)

Bush's God concept crucially rests on the basic notion of *divine purpose* as the foundation for the very purpose of human life. Consequently, the course of the history of nature and society is governed by an overriding purpose (*teleology*) and that purpose is God's reason for why things are as they are and we have no control over the course of history. At root, Bush contends that God as divine creator has "infinite-personal intelligence" thus possessing personal characteristics associated with the human persona. The idea that the world is a divine creation follows from creationism and the notion of such divine attributes as reason, results from anthropomorphism.

Let us examine some of the presuppositions of anthropomorphism and the creationism thesis. First, there is the presumption that nature is finite in character. Second is that finite nature in its origins is the outcome and product of an act of creation. The third assumption is that the creation of nature approximates human actions but in the grander manner and higher magnitude of super human-like creator. Fourth, since the origin of nature is much like that of human creation then we had to only look inwardly into how the activity of human creation is conducted. Fifth, we would discover (following four) that such supernatural creativity is based on analogies to human consciousness and reason. The sixth presumption of anthropomorphism is that with introspection into the human mind, we can obtain a finite glimpse into the infinite mind (or reason) of God. Lastly, it follows that if God's mind (logos) is the source of nature then reason governs the laws of nature and hence there is a reason (the rational basis) for all things and events.

In sketch, whatever rational means are employed to discover truth in the world, they must be consistent with so-called theological truth, which is established on articles of faith, such as the very belief in God. Nevertheless, on Bush's accounting, God is not the subject of philosophical inquiry; instead the Judeo-Christian God is the point of departure. On this theological opinion, Bush is in concert with Vanterpool as fellow Christian philosopher. Each seeks to illuminate God's presence by philosophical means.

Furthermore, Bush's notion of the philosophy of religion as constituting one of the classical theological disciplines most transparently sublimates the former within the realm of theology. We contend that rather than view the philosophy of religion, on Bush's presumption, what actually arises is *philosophical theology* or *religious philosophy*. Wherein the disciplinary focus is ancillary to philosophical theology, philosophical methods of analysis are employed to advance theological and faith claims.

Religious philosophy is equivalent with philosophical theology for Bush. Bush argues the very purpose of studying philosophy remains "in order to help us know what the questions are to which Christ is the answer. All truth is God's truth."[58] Clearly, in Bush's estimation, philosophy functions in the interest of theology; it has an instrumental purpose and does not challenge the basic theological presupposition that guides the process. The presumptions that God's word, that is, biblical Scriptures are consistent with the secular concerns of the world such as with scientific inquiry is known as "concordism." The proposition, "All truth is God's truth," serves as the foundation for "concordism." Tim Reddish remarks the following:

> Proponents of concordism naturally view Scripture as God's truth and therefore seek to harmonize the two together. One example is to interpret the days of Genesis as extended time periods (cf. geological eras) rather than literal 24 hours. This implies Scripture contains a scientific account of our origins, an assumption that concordism shares with creationism. Concordism seeks to take science and the Bible seriously, and tries to make Scriptures relevant for today's context.[59]

In a similar manner, Bush aims to show the relevance of philosophy respecting biblical Scripture. This view of philosophical tasks offers a metaphilosophy which is at base depended on biblical theology. Religious philosophies thereafter can only serve as instruments for providing the questions that Jesus has already answered. Still, the answers provided by Jesus via biblical Scripture are not subject to philosophical examination and critique.

Religious philosophy thus is restricted in both its substance and scope by way of *biblical theology*. By biblical theology, we mean that the grounding of theology is located on the merits of biblical texts. The key notion behind biblical theology is that God reveals himself via biblical text. Hence, biblical theology is synonymous with what Christian theologians describe as *Revealed theology*. *Revealed theology* is often contrasted with *Natural theology*. This contrast has particular importance for our assessment of African American theological thinking and its respective manifestation in religious cultural expression. African theologian James Amanze provides a useful synopsis on the distinctions between the two theological approaches.

> Generally speaking, theologians make a distinction between two types of theologies namely, natural theology ((*theologia naturalis*) and revealed theology ((*theologia revelata*). Natural theology is based on natural religion (sometimes known as the Book of Nature), in which people understand God through rationally observe nature. . . . Paratt notes the term "natural theology" is often used to designate the knowledge of God as Creator. Such knowledge is available to all human beings. . . . Revealed theology, on the other hand, is based on divine revelation as contain within the Bible. It notes that in the course of human history God revealed or manifested himself to the people of Israel, as recorded both in the Old and New Testaments.[60]

With respect to biblical or revealed theology, it is the most prevalent theological option within African American religious thinking. In concert with Hammon, Vanterpool, Cone, and Braxton, among others, Black theologian Thabiti Anyabwile conveys,

> The pages of scripture unveil the attributes of God—his wisdom, omnipotence, holiness, mercy, love, supremacy, sovereignty, justice, etc.—in sufficient clarity for human beings to know and relate to him with accuracy for their eternal redemption. In the Bible, one observed God's revealing himself in and through the history of his people. In the Bible, prophets and apostles spoke and wrote the very oracles of God as they heard "the word of the Lord" coming to them, interacting with angelic messengers, or receive visions directly from God.[61]

The viewpoint that a supernatural being (through a conscious act of creation) is responsible for the origins of nature or what is popularly known as "creationism" is a construction from mythology that seeks to explain how nature came into existence. Centered as it is on a super creator or maker, creationism actually extends the attribute of human agency to a supernatural being. Creationism is a form of superstition that stands opposed to a materialist (scientific) account of nature.

Black philosopher/theologian Charles Leander Hill argues that God precedes evolution. Speaking of God's identity,

> He is no God who is construed in terms of mere cosmic process or as the highest supervening level to appear in the scheme of the emergence of evolution. He is the living God who does things. For there we see him in action. Bringing things into existence.... The God of the Book is acknowledged to be a cosmic Person with cosmological significance.[62]

Indeed, biblical theology has a very strong influence in African American religious culture. A considerable number of Black theologians consider the Bible as the primary means, which God reveals himself to African Americans. Black theologian James Evans aptly illustrates this point:

> One cannot do theology in and for the African-American community without coming to terms with the influence of the Bible. It is necessary for the Bible to play an important, if not central, role in such theological discourse for it legitimately to be considered Christian theology. It is the primary, though not exclusive, conduit of the community's understanding of God's being and acts. It is the church's book in this sense, and it serves as a plumbline for the life and practice of the Christian community.[63]

Since religious philosophy is essentially framed around the merits of biblical theology then, clearly the philosophy of religion is fundamentally different. Subsequently, we contend that the very conceptual locus of philosophy is drastically at variance (in terms of concrete function) within the respective frameworks of religious philosophy and the philosophy of religion. While religious philosophy *advances theological claims*, we discern that the philosophy of religion *critically assesses theological claims*. This difference entails that a critical assessment on theological claims could very well lead to their rejection. However, religious philosophy in advancing theological claims is aimed at their affirmation. Vanderpool personifies this attitude, "This [religious philosophical] approach requires us to place ultimate credibility in whatever the Bible declares derives directly from the mind of the Supreme Being, Lord over all there is."

From our perspective, the philosophy of religion functions as the disciplinary lens on religion, rather than advocating any type of religious commitment or positing theological claims. Among theologians, Karl Barth stands in alignment with our position. Black theologian Noel Erskine succinctly captures Barth's perspective on the philosophy of religion.

Philosophy of religion may be the reflection of an individual in the solitude of his/her ivory tower. Or it may represent the attempt through reason and logic to reach God. This is the very opposite of the theological task and would call into question the ecclesiastical character of theology. . . . The theologian is accountable to the church and seeks truth that is already given in the birth of that community. If theology is regarded as a science like psychology and philosophy, we immediately highlight the human effort and in so doing we minimize the centrality of divine revelation.[64]

This chapter assumes the philosophical perspective (contra theology) with regard to how Christianity—as belief system—functions within the orbit of African American thought. In other words, without recommending any form of theological position, our deliberation seeks an alternative— philosophical—approach that allows for critical scrutiny without any religious allegiance.

The philosopher of religion—not to mention the reader of this text—need not hold to religious convictions as a matter of comprehending the subject matter under investigation. In sequence, the philosophical assessment of religion—respecting African American cultural life—is a critical inspection on its theological meaning and judgment on the sociopolitical nature of its impact.

It should be noted, however, religion presently continues to have a tremendous role in African American life and culture. It is frequently a molder and mirror of the African American experience. Black religious thought—from during slavery with Jupiter Hammon and Maria Stewart to the 1960s and beyond with Jamil Al-Amin (H. Rap Brown) and Malcolm X as proponents of Islam, along with Black Christian theologians such as James H. Cone and Katie G. Cannon, not to mention Prosperity Gospel advocates Creflo Dollar and T. D. Jakes, all merging into the twenty-first century—has been a source of inspiration as well as the foundation of ideological justification for oppression and exploitation.

Some have argued that the school of Prosperity Gospel is precisely a form of the exploitative use of Christianity. James Cone critically argues,

My job as a theologian is to tell Fred Price and T. D. Jakes that they cannot really be true to the gospel of Jesus if they preach a message of prosperity that contradicts it. I would say what they are preaching is very interesting and meaningful to people at some other level, but it is not meaningful at the true gospel level.[65]

Though Cone directs his attention at Prosperity Gospel advocates, philosopher/theologian William R. Jones (Figure 19) presents a more generalized criterion for evaluating any given Black (Christian) theological

Figure 19 William R. Jones (1933–2012).

position, respecting oppression and exploitation. The key question is centering on whether or not the interests of oppression and exploitation are facilitated by means of theological methodology. Although many Black theologians are intent on serving the interests of African American liberation, such intentions do not of necessity result in meeting this objective. Indeed, the practical results may be antithetical to such intentions; what Jones designates as "antithetical fit in praxis verification." Jones effectively argues,

> A consistent application of antithetical fit in praxis verification does not force one to conclude that the black church, black theology, or Christianity are incompatible with a theology of liberation. Rather, what is necessitated is a specific approach and method for theologizing that entails a total and comprehensive examination; each theological and moral imperative must be regarded—provisionally—as a carrier of oppression's virus. . . . Each one of our most cherished beliefs, every element of the creed and canon, must be ruthlessly probed and tested according to the praxis verification test question: what supports Black liberation?[66]

Jones's method of "antithetical fit in praxis verification" is not an a priori dismissal of Black Christian theology; instead it is the employment of a philosophical approach that facilitates the assessment of such theological allegiances. This method calls into question any theological position with respect to its adequacy for establishing how the aims of Black liberation, rather than oppression, transpires as a concrete result. The intention of the theologian does not in itself ground what are the sufficient conditions of the claims tendered regarding liberation.

In concert with the earlier remarks of Roy D. Morrison and Alfred North Whitehead concerning the objectives ancillary with philosophical thinking, Jones makes it crystal clear that "each one of our most cherished beliefs, every element of the creed and canon, must be ruthlessly probed and tested according to the praxis verification." Accordingly, the objective of overturning oppression and corresponding obligation to the principle of Black liberation is not a matter relying on articles of faith. In summation, Jones offers a philosophical assessment of theological claims. Hence, Jones's philosophical method amounts to offering critical inspection without regard to the intended position on which the Black theologian may stand.

Notes

1. Albert J. Raboteau, *Slave Religions: The "Invisible Institution" in the Antebellum South* (New York: Oxford University Press, 2004), 5.
2. See Kwame Nkrumah, *Consciencism: Philosophy and Ideology for Decolonization and Development with Particular Reference to the African Revolution* (New York: Monthly Review Press, 1970); V. I. Lenin, "Socialism and Religion," in *Collected Works*, Vol. 10 (Moscow: Progress Publishers, 1965), 83–87; V. I. Lenin, "The Attitude of the Workers' Party to Religion," in *Collected Works*, Vol. 15 (Moscow: Progress Publishers, 1973), 402–13; Lucy Parsons, "The Negro: Let Him Leave Politics to the Politician and Prayers to the Preacher," in Gale Ahrens, ed. *Lucy Parsons: Freedom, Equality and Solidarity, Writings & Speeches, 1878–1937* (Chicago: Charles H. Kerr, 2003), 54–56.
3. Karl Marx, "Introduction, Contribution to the Critique of Hegel's *Philosophy of Right*," in *Collected Works of Karl Marx and Frederick Engels*, Vol. 3 (New York: International Publishers, 1975), 175.
4. Angela Davis, "Unfinished Lecture on Liberation—II," in Leonard Harris, ed., *Philosophy Born of Struggle: Anthology of Afro-American Philosophy From 1917* (Dubuque: Kendall/Hunt Publishing, 1983), 135.
5. Read David Eller, "The Cultures of Christianities," in John W. Loftus, ed., *The Christian Delusion* (Amherst: Prometheus Books, 2010), 25–46.
6. Roy D. Morrison, "Black Philosophy: An Instrument for Cultural and Religious Liberation," *The Journal of Religious Thought* 33(1) (1976), 12. Also see Roy D. Morrison, "Black Enlightenment: The Issues of Pluralism, Priorities, and Empirical Correlation," *Journal of the American Academy of Religion* 46(2) (June 1978), 217–40. Also consult, Valarie Tarico, "Christian Belief Through the Lens of Cognitive Science," in John W. Loftus, ed., *The Christian Delusion* (Amherst: Prometheus Books, 2010), 47–64.

7. Jason Long, "The Malleability of the Human Mind," in John W. Loftus, ed., *The Christian Delusion* (Amherst: Prometheus Books, 2010), 66.

8. Gilbert Haven Jones, *Education in Theory and Practice* (Boston: The Gorham Press, 1919), 18.

9. George Yancy, "Gilbert Haven Jones as an Early Black Philosopher and Educator," in *APA Newsletter on Philosophy and the Black Experience* 2(2) (Spring 2003); Robert Munro, "Gilbert Haven Jones (1881–1966)," *BlackPast.org Remembered & Reclaimed*, http://www.blackpast.org/aah/jones-gilbert-haven-1883-1966

10. The first to document Jones's role in psychology was Dr. Robert V. Guthrie. Read, Robert V. Guthrie, *Even the Rat Was White a Historical View of Psychology* (Boston: Allyson and Bacon, 2004), 163.

11. William R. Woodward, *Hermann Lotze* (New York: Cambridge University Press, 2015), 426. See note 49.

12. Rufus Burrow Jr., "The Personalism of John Wesley Edward Bowen," *The Journal of Negro History* 82(2) (Spring 1997), 244. Also consult, "Bowen, John Wesley Edward Sr.," in Larry G. Murphy, J. Gordon Melton, Gary L. Ward, eds., *Encyclopedia of African American Religions* (New York: Routledge, 2011), 105–06.

13. Burrow Jr., "The Personalism of John Wesley Edward Bowen," 245.

14. On Bowen work in the psychology of religion, see J. W. E. Bowen, "A Psychological Principle in Revelation," *The Methodist Review* 7(5) (September 1891), 727–39. On Personalism, consult Rufus Barrow, "Afrikan American Contributions to Personalism," *Encounter* 60(2) (Spring 1999), 145–68; and also Willis J. King, "Personalism and Race," in Edgar S. Brightman, *Personalism in Theology* (Boston: Boston University Press, 1943), 204–24. For Martin Luther King, read Rufus Burrow Jr., *God and Human Dignity: The Personalism, Theology, and Ethics of Martin Luther King, Jr.* (Notre Dame, IN: Notre Dame Press, 2006).

15. Consult, "Francis Monroe Hammond, Professional and Personal Data," along with "A Presentation on the Life, Academic Works & Personality of Seton Hall University's First African-American Professor, Dr. Francis Monroe Hammond," all in the Hammond Collection. For our sources on Dr. Hammond, the authors thank Dr. Alan Delozier, Director of Archives and Special Collections, Walsh Library, Seton Hall University.

16. On Tarde's contributions to these various fields of study and his debates with Durkheim, see the "Introduction to Gabriel Tarde," in *Gabriel Tarde on Communication and Social Influence: Selected Papers* (Chicago: University of Chicago Press, 2010).

17. On this latter issue of Hammond's academic qualification, consult the correspondence of Francis M. Hammond to Beatrice LeCraft, June 1, 1954, in the Francis M. Hammond Collection, Seton Hall University.

On psychiatry of religion see, the correspondence, "Henry E. Kagan to Dr. Francis Hammond, December, 1953." Also consult, "Francis Monroe Hammond, Professional and Personal Data," along with "A Presentation on the Life, Academic Works & Personality of Seton Hall University's First African-American Professor, Dr. Francis Monroe Hammond," all in the Hammond Collection.

18. Roy D. Morrison, "Albert Einstein: The Methodological Unity Underlying Science and Religion," *Zygon* 14(3) (September 1979), 256.

19. Michael Joseph Brown, *What They Don't Tell You: A Survivor's Guide To Biblical Studies* (Louisville: Westminster John Knox Press, 2000), 2.

20. Anthony Pinn, ed., *Moral Evil and Redemptive Suffering: A History of Theodicy in the African-American Religious Thought* (Gainesville: University Press of Florida, 2002), 33. Margaret Brucia, "The African American Poet, Jupiter Hammon: A Home-Born Slave and His Classical Name," *International Journal of Classical Tradition* 7(4) (2001), 515–22. Sondra O'Neale, *Jupiter Hammon and the Biblical Beginnings of African-American Literature* (Metuchen: Scarecrow Press, 1993).

21. Anthony Pinn, *Moral Evil and Redemptive Suffering* (Tallahassee: University Press of Florida, 2002), 27–28.

22. William R. Jones, *Is God a White Racist? A Preamble to Black Theology* (Boston: Beacon Press, 1998); and Stephen C. Ferguson II, "Teaching Hurricane Katrina: Understanding Divine Racism and Theodicy" *American Philosophical Association Newsletter on Philosophy and the Black Experience* 7(1) (Fall 2007), 2. Patrick Rael, "Black Theodicy: African Americans and Nationalism in the Antebellum North," *The North Star* 3(2) (Spring 2000), 1–24.

23. See James W. Cornman, Keith Lehrer, and George Sotiros Pappas, *Philosophical Problems and Arguments: An Introduction* (Indianapolis: Hackett Publishing Company, 1992), 7.

24. Cornman et al., *Philosophical Problems and Arguments*, 8. Also consult, James B. Freeman, *Acceptable Premises: An Epistemic Approach to an Informal Logic Problem* (Cambridge: Cambridge University Press, 2005).

25. Brad R. Braxton, *No Longer Slaves: Galatians and the African American Experience* (Collegeville: The Liturgical Press, 2002), 35.

26. Howard Stone and James Duke, *How to Think Theologically* (Minneapolis: Fortress Press, 1996), 1.

27. David Law, *The Historical Critical Method: A Guide for the Perplexed* (London: Continuum International Publishing, 2012).

28. Edward Krentz, *The Historical Critical Method* (Philadelphia: Fortress Press, 1975), 48. Also read, Christian Hartlich, "Historical-Critical Method in its Application to Statements Concerning Events in the Holy Scriptures," *The Journal of Higher Criticism* 2(2) (Fall 1995), 122–39; Van A. Harvey,

The Historian and the Believer: The Morality of Historical Knowledge and Christian Belief (Urbana: University of Illinois Press, 1996); James Riley Strange, "Defining Judaism in its Classical Age: What is at Stake in the Academic Study of Religion" *The Journal of Higher Criticism* 6 (2) (Fall 1999), 175–85.

29. For scholarly treatments of the history of biblical texts, see Bart D. Ehrman and Zlatko Plese, eds., *The Other Gospels: Accounts of Jesus from Outside the New Testament* (New York: Oxford University Press, 2014); Lee Martin McDonald and James A. Sanders, eds., *The Canon Debate* (Grand Rapids: Baker Academic, 2002); Philip Jenkins, *Jesus Wars* (New York: HarperCollins Publishers, 2010); Bart D. Ehrman, *Lost Christianities: The Battles for Scripture and the Faiths We Never Knew* (New York: Oxford University Press, 2003).

30. Braxton, *No Longer Slaves*, 33.

31. Ibid., 35.

32. For an illustration of the historical critical method within African American religious culture see, Willis Jefferson King, *The Book of Habakkuk from the Standpoint of Literary and Historical Criticism* (Doctoral Dissertation, Boston University, 1921). Consult, the entry on "King, Willis Jefferson," in Larry G. Murphy, J. Gordon Melton, Gary L. Ward, eds., *Encyclopedia of African American Religions* (New York: Routledge, 2011), 432–33.

33. J. Deotis Roberts, "Black Consciousness in Theological Perspective," in James H. Cone and Gayraud Wilmore, eds., *Black Theology: A Documentary History* (Maryknoll: Orbis, 1993), 101.

34. Roy D. Morrison, "Albert Einstein: The Methodological Unity Underlying Science and Religion," 256.

35. Morrison, "Albert Einstein," 256.

36. Ibid., 258.

37. Alfred North Whitehead, *Modes of Thought* (New York: The Free Press, 1966), 171–72.

38. Roy D. Morrison, "Black Philosophy: An Instrument for Cultural and Religious Liberation," 12.

39. For an early defense of creationism by African American scholar see Edward A. Clarke, "Evolution," *The A. M. E. Church Review* 15(3) (January 1899), 729–34. For critical treatments of creationism vis-à-vis theory of evolution, see Andrew J. Petto and Laurie R. Godfrey. *Scientists Confront Creationism Intelligent Design and Beyond* (New York: W. W. Norton & Co., 2007); and John Bellamy Foster, Brett Clark, and Richard York, *Critique of Intelligent Design Materialism versus Creationism from Antiquity to the Present* (New York: Monthly Review Press, 2008).

40. Carter, "Wanted-An Idea," 736.

41. Major Jones, *The Color of God* (Macon: Mercer University Press, 1990), 26.
42. Yujin Nagasawa, *The Existence of God: A Philosophical Introduction* (New York: Routledge, 2011); Matthew Levering, *Proofs of God: Classical Arguments from Tertullian to Barth* (Grand Rapids: Baker Academic, 2016); Michael F. Palmer, *The Question of God: An Introduction and Sourcebook* (New York: Routledge, 2001). Also for a critical treatment on the viability of proofs for God's existence, read Michael Martin, *Atheism: A Philosophical Justification* (Philadelphia: Temple University Press, 1990).
43. Major Jones, *The Color of God*, 26.
44. Van A. Harvey, *The Historian and the Believer: The Morality of Historical Knowledge and Christian Belief* (Urbana: University of Illinois Press, 1996), 4.
45. For a critique of biblical literalism, see Conrad Hyers, "Biblical Literalism: Constricting the Cosmic Dance," *Christian Century* (August 4–11, 1982), 823–27. Consult, Mario Liverani, "The Chronology of Biblical Fairy-Tale," in Philip R. Davies and Diana V. Edelman, eds., *The Historian and the Bible: Essays in Honour of Lester L. Grabbe* (New York: T&T Clark International, 2010), 73–88. Criticism of how the Gospel texts render Jesus as a divine entity include Bart D. Ehrman, *How Jesus Became God: The Exultation of a Jewish Preacher from Galilee* (New York: HarperCollins, 2014); Helmut Köster, *From Jesus to the Gospels: Interpreting the New Testament in its Context* (Minneapolis: Fortress Press, 2007); and Robert M. Price, *The Incredible Shrinking Son of Man: How Reliable Is the Gospel Tradition?* (Amherst: Prometheus Books, 2003).
46. Howard Thurman, "The Significance of Jesus I: Jesus the Man of Insight (September 12, 1937)," in Howard Thurman and Walter E. Fluker, *The Papers of Howard Washington Thurman* (Columbia: University of South Carolina Press, 2009), 47.
47. James H. Cone, "Biblical Revelation and Social Existence," in *Black Theology: A Documentary History*, 175. For a critical treatment on the epistemological implications concerning biblical historical research, read "Knowledge, Fact, and Belief," in Hector Avalos, *The End of Biblical Studies* (Amherst: Prometheus Books, 2007), 113–15.
48. On this topic, read Leroy T. Howe, "Is History of Theological Problem?," *Journal of Religious Thought* 26(3) (1969), 81–99; and E. P. Sanders, *The Historical Figure of Jesus* (New York: Penguin Publishing Group, 1994).
49. James H. Cone, *God of the Oppressed* (New York: Seabury Press, 1975), 110.
50. Cone, *God of the Oppressed*, 141.
51. Ernst Breisach, *Historiography: Ancient, Medieval, and Modern* (Chicago: University of Chicago Press, 2007); and John Van Seters, *In Search of History: Historiography in the Ancient World and the Origins of Biblical History* (New Haven: Yale University Press, 1987).

52. Consult Section 10, "Of Miracles," in David Hume, *An Enquiry Concerning Human Understanding*, ed. Eric Steinberg (Indianapolis: Hackett Publishing Co., 1993). Also see Robert J. Fogelin, *A Defense of Hume on Miracles* (Princeton: Princeton University Press, 2003); Geza Vermes, *The Changing Faces of Jesus* (New York: Penguin Putnam Inc., 2000); Bart Ehrman, *Jesus: Apocalyptic Prophet of the New Millennium* (New York: Oxford University, 2001); and Craig A Evans, "The Misplaced Jesus: Interpreting Jesus in a Judaic Context," in Bruce Chilton, Craig A. Evans and Jacob Neusner, eds., *The Missing Jesus: Rabbinic Judaism and the New Testament* (Leiden: Brill Academic Publishers, 2002).

53. Robert Greg Caven, "Is There Sufficient Historical Evidence to Establish the Resurrection of Jesus?," in Robert M. Price, ed., *The Empty Tomb: Jesus Beyond the Grave* (Amherst: Prometheus Books, 2005), 19–42. Geza Vermes, *The Resurrection: History and Myth* (New York: Doubleday, 2008).

54. Braxton, *No Longer Slaves*, 34.

55. For a detailed discussion on Paul's admonition, see chapter 1 of John H. McClendon III, *Philosophy of Religion and the African American Experience: Conversations with My Christian Friends* (Leiden: Brill/Rodopi, 2017).

56. Rudolph V. Vanterpool, *Thus Spoke the Preacher: Solomon's Cosmic Gaze from Under the Sun* (Pittsburgh: Dorrance Publishing Company, 2017), viii.

57. L. Russ Bush, *A Handbook for Christian Philosophy* (Grand Rapids: Zondervan Publishing House, 1991), 9–10.

58. Bush, *A Handbook for Christian Philosophy*, 29.

59. Tim Reddish, *Science and Christianity: Foundations and Frameworks for Moving Forward in Faith* (Eugene: Wipf & Stock, 2016), 80.

60. James N. Amanze, "Introduction to Christian Theology: It's Tasks and Methods," in James N. Amanze, Fidelis Nkomazana, and Obed N. Kealotswe, eds., *Biblical Studies, Theology, Religion and Philosophy: An Introduction for African Universities* (Eldoret: Zapf Chancery, 2019), 141–42.

61. Thabiti Anyabwile, *The Decline of African American Theology* (Downers Grove: IVP Academic, 2007), 25–26.

62. Charles Leander Hill, *The Evangel in Ebony* (Boston: Meador Publishing Co., 1960), 37–38; Franz S. Klein, "Supernaturalism and Historical Study: An Account of the Resurrection of Jesus Christ from the Dead," *Quodlibet Journal* 7(2) (April–June 2005), http://www.Quodlibet.net.

63. James Evans, *We Have Been Believers: An African-American Systematic Theology* (Minneapolis, Minnesota: Fortress Press, 1992), 43; Vincent L. Wimbush, ed., *African Americans and the Bible* (New York: Continuum, 2001); and Cane Hope Felder, ed., *Stony the Road We Trod: African*

American Biblical Interpretation (Minneapolis, Minnesota: Fortress Press, 1991).

64. Noel Erskine, *King Among the Theologians* (Cleveland, Ohio: The Pilgrim Press, 1994), 68.

65. Cone is quoted in the following electronic article: David Bedsole, "Prosperity Gospel," *Punk Israel*, 2008, http://punkisrael.typepad.com/punkisrael/2008/06/prosperity-gospel.html (accessed November 27, 2010). Also read, Debra J. Mumford, "Prosperity Gospel and African American Prophetic Preaching," *Review and Expositor: International Baptist Journal* 109(3) (August 2012), 365–85; Eric Z. M. Gbote and Selaelo T. Kgatla, "Prosperity Gospel: A Missiological Assessment," *HTS Theological Studies* 70(1) (August 2014), 1–10 and Erik Peay, "The High Cost of the Slave Auction Block: The Prosperity Gospel in the African American Church," *Reformed Blacks of America*, 2010, http://www.reformedblacksofamerica.org/blog1/index.php?itemid=417 (accessed November 23, 2010).

66. William R. Jones, Is *God a White Racist?: A Preamble to Black Theology* (Boston: Beacon Press, 1998), 210.

Glossary of Key Terms

Aesthetics is the study of beauty, and of related concepts such as the sublime, the tragic, the ugly, and the humorous. It can involve the study of the values, tastes, attitudes, and standards involved in our experience of and judgments about things made by humans or found in nature that we consider beautiful.

Agnosticism is the belief (a) that we cannot have knowledge of God, and (b) that it is impossible to prove that God exists or does not exist. The term was first used by the British natural scientist Thomas Huxley.

Anti-Foundationalism is a philosophical position which rejects foundationalism, that is, it rejects the need to ground philosophy. Anti-foundationalist philosophers are often accused of being nihilists or moral relativists because their position cannot claim any objective ground on which to base itself. Anti-foundationalism rejects metaphysical categories such as truth. Noted anti-foundationalist philosophers include Richard Rorty and Stanley Fish.

Atheism is the belief that gods do not, or God does not, exist.

Axiology is the philosophical study of the nature of values.

Contractarianism can refer either to a view in political philosophy on the legitimacy of political authority or the ethical theory concerning the origin, or legitimate content, of moral norms. Both positions were developed from the concept of a social contract, the idea that the people give up some rights to a government and/or other authority in order to receive, or jointly preserve, social order.

Correlative categories are categories whose defining feature is the condition of mutual dependence. In other words, you cannot have one category without the other.

Creationism is an idealist doctrine holding that the matter, the various forms of life, and the world were brought into being by a single act of creation, usually in the way described in the book of Genesis in the Bible. Science provides proof of the complete unsoundness of creationism.

Deduction refers to the process of inference statements (premises) in which a necessarily true conclusion is arrived at by rules of logic. It is contrasted to induction.

Dialectics can refer to (a) the art of debate by means of questions and answers, associated with Socrates; (b) the art of classifying concepts, dividing things into genera and species; or (c) the view that nature, society, and thought are in a process of motion, change, and development.

Dialectical idealism is a school of thought associated with African American philosophers in the nineteenth and early twentieth centuries which argued that the catalyst for all motion, change, and development (laws of motion) rested in immaterial entities such as ideas, consciousness, or the human soul.

Dualism is any philosophical view that insists on the existence of two independent, separable, irreducible, unique realms. It is a prominent feature of the philosophies of Rene Descartes and Immanuel Kant. It is usually contrasted with monism.

Empiricism is the view that experience (what is observed, immediately given in sensation) is the sole source of knowledge. It is contrasted with rationalism.

Epistemology is the branch of philosophy which studies the origin, nature, and veracity of knowledge.

Existentialism is an irrationalist school of thought in philosophy which focuses on the nature of individual existence in an unfathomable universe and the plight of the individual who must assume ultimate responsibility for acts of free will without any certain knowledge of what is right or wrong or good or bad.

Essence is the meaning of a given thing, that which is in itself, in contradistinction from all other things and in contrast to the states of a thing changing under the influence of various circumstances. It can be contrasted with appearance or existence.

Foundationalism is the view in epistemology that beliefs can be justified based on basic or foundational beliefs (beliefs that give justificatory support to other beliefs). These basic beliefs are said to be self-justifying or self-evident, and do not need to be justified by other beliefs.

Idealism is the philosophical position that holds that nonmaterial things such as consciousness, ideas, values, culture, as well as ideal entities such as minds, spirits, and souls constitute the fundamental basis of reality. In terms of social analysis, idealism emphasizes the primary (if not absolute) role of consciousness, ideas, values, myths, and culture, in their connection to social relations and practices, for understanding social reality.

Induction is a form of nondeductive reasoning in which the conclusion expresses something that goes beyond what is said in the premises; the conclusion does not follow with logical necessity from the premises. It is contrasted with deduction or deductive reasoning.

Marxism is the political, economic, and social theory of Karl Marx, including the belief that class struggle is a major force in history, historic importance of the working class and that there should eventually be a society in which the dominant feature is public ownership of the means of production, distribution, and exchange. Marxism applies the principles of dialectical and historical materialism in an analysis of the functioning and development of nature, society, and thought.

Materialism is the philosophical position that holds that material things (such as matter and social institutions) constitute the fundamental basis of reality. In terms of social analysis, materialism emphasizes the primary role of social institutions and/or social relations for understanding social reality. Material conditions have to be the starting point for explaining the origin, nature, and developments in social reality.

Mechanistic materialism is the view that the universe is a machine and can be completely explained in terms of the effects of the mechanical operation of its parts upon one another. All phenomena are the outcome of the mechanical motions of matter.

Metaphilosophy (sometimes called philosophy of philosophy) is the study of the subject and matter, methods and aims of philosophy.

Metaphysics is generally considered to be the study of the nature of being. It is treated as synonymous with ontology.

Monism is the theory that all things in the universe can be explained in terms of the activity of one fundamental constituent (God, matter, mind, energy, Platonic Form).

Monogenisim is the theory that humans are all descended from a single pair of ancestors.

Natural theology is theology or knowledge of God based on observed facts and experience apart from divine revelation.

Objective idealism is the metaphysical view that takes as the basis of reality a personal or impersonal spirit, a kind of super-individual mind (e.g., Hegel's Absolute Spirit). It postulates that there is only one perceiver, and that this perceiver is one with that which is perceived. It accepts common sense realism (the view that independent material objects exist), but rejects naturalism (the view that the mind and spiritual values have emerged from material things). Plato is regarded as one of the earliest representatives of objective idealism.

Ontology is the branch of philosophy that deals with the order and structure of reality in the broadest sense possible, using categories such as being/becoming, actuality/potentiality, real/apparent, change, time, existence/nonexistence, essence, necessity, being-as-being, self-dependency, self-sufficiency, and ground.

Personalism is a philosophical perspective in which characteristics possessed by the person and personality are the keys to understanding the universe and all things in it.

Philosophical behaviorism argues that consciousness or mind is no more than surrogate language for human behavior, wherein behavior is the resulting conditioned reflex to environmental influences. Behaviorism and its auxiliary notion of conditioned reflex effectively remove social consciousness from the equation on the complexity of social existence. Subsequently, philosophical behaviorism is a form of mechanistic materialism.

Polygenism is the doctrine or belief that the existing human races have evolved from two or more distinct ancestral types.

Racism is not just an attitude or belief (social consciousness) there exist superior and inferior races. More importantly it is behavior (social practices) and institutions (social relations) which lend material support to such beliefs by the actual suppression of the supposed inferior group (race).

Rationalism is the philosophical approach that emphasizes reason as the primary source of knowledge, prior or superior to, and independent of, sense perceptions.

Religious philosophy is also known as philosophical theology. Philosophical methods of analysis are employed to advance theological and faith claims.

Subjective idealism is the view that the knower and the thing known do not have independent existence; all knowledge is knowledge of our conscious states and not of any external (objective) world.

Substance is that which is the underlying ground (support, substratum) of all phenomena.

Teleology is the study of phenomena exhibiting order, design, purposes, ends, or goals.

Theodicy is an attempt to vindicate the goodness and justice of God in ordaining or allowing moral and natural evil and human suffering.

Vitalism is the belief that the activities of living organisms are due to a vital force or vital principle that is different from other physical forces in the universe.

Voluntarism is the metaphysical belief that the will is the primary and dominant factor in all human experience and in all the processes of the universe.

Select Bibliography

"Memorial Minutes: Robert C. Williams, 1935–1987," *Proceedings and Addresses of the American Philosophical Association* 61(2) (November, 1987), 385.

James P. Allen, *Genesis in Egypt: The Philosophy of Ancient Egyptian Creation Accounts* (New Haven: Yale University Press, 1988).

Norm R. Allen, *The Black Humanist Experience: An Alternative to Religion* (Amherst: Prometheus Books, 2003).

Anita L. Allen, "Novel Thought: An African American Woman Philosopher at Mid-Career," *American Philosophical Association Newsletter on Feminism and Philosophy* 9(2) (Spring, 2010), 3–5.

Louis Althusser, *Lenin and Philosophy and Other Essays* (New York: Monthly Review Press, 1971).

Thabiti Anyabwile, *The Decline of African American Theology* (Downers Grove, Illinois: IVP Academic, 2007).

R. B. Atwood, H. S. Smith, and Catherine O. Vaughan, "Negro Teachers in Northern Colleges and Universities in the United States," *The Journal of Negro Education* 18(4) (Autumn, 1949), 559–67.

Hector Avalos, *The End of Biblical Studies* (Amherst: Prometheus Books, 2007).

Thomas Nelson Baker, "Ideals, Part 1," *Alexander's Magazine* (September, 1906), 23–29.

Thomas Nelson Baker, "Ideals, Part 2," *Alexander's Magazine* (October, 1906), 37–42.

Donald R. Barbera, *Black and Not Baptist: Nonbelief and Freethought in the Black Community* (New York: iUniverse, 2003).

James B. Barnes, "Alain Locke and the Sense of African Ancestry," in *Alain Locke: Reflections on a Modern Renaissance Man*. Edited by Russell J. Linnemann (Baton Rouge: Louisiana State University Press, 1982), 100–08.

Allison Blakely, "Richard T. Greener and the 'Talented Tenth's' Dilemma," *The Journal of Negro History* 59(4) (October, 1974), 305–21.

Gilbert A. Belles, "The College Faculty, the Negro Scholar, and Rosenwald Fund," *The Journal of Negro History* 54(4) (October, 1969), 383–92.

J. W. E. Bowen, "A Psychological Principle of Revelation," *The Methodist Review* 7(5) (September, 1891), 727–39.

Brad R. Braxton, *No Longer Slaves: Galatians and the African American Experience* (Collegeville: The Liturgical Press, 2002).

Michael Joseph Brown, *What They Don't Tell You: A Survivor's Guide to Biblical Studies* (Louisville: Westminster John Knox Press, 2000).

Robert T. Browne, *The Mystery of Space* (New York: E. P. Dutton & Co., 1919).

Margaret Brucia, "The African American Poet, Jupiter Hammon: A Home-Born Slave and His Classical Name," *International Journal of Classical Tradition* 7(4) (2001), 515–22.

Rufus Burrow, "The Personalism of John Wesley Edward Bowen," *The Journal of Negro History* 82(2) (Spring, 1997), 244–56.

Rufus Burrow, "Afrikan American Contributions to Personalism," *Encounter* 60(2) (Spring, 1999), 145–68.

James B. Carter, "Wanted: An Idea," *African Methodist Episcopal Church Review* 15(3) (January, 1899), 734–745.

Reynolds Chaddock, *Uncompromising Activist: Richard Greener, First Black Graduate of Harvard College* (Baltimore: Johns Hopkins University Press, 2017).

Edward A. Clarke, "Evolution," *American Methodist Episcopal Church Review* 15(3) (January, 1899), 729–33.

Winson R. Coleman, "Knowledge and Freedom in the Political Philosophy of Plato," *Ethics* 71(1) (October, 1960), 41–45.

James H. Cone, *God of the Oppressed* (New York: Seabury Press, 1975).

James H. Cone and Gayraud Wilmore, eds., *Black Theology: A Documentary History* (Maryknoll: Orbis, 1993).

Joyce Mitchell Cook, "On the Nature and Nurture of Intelligence," *The Philosophical Forum* 9(2–3) (1977–78), 289–302.

Anna Julia Cooper, "The Ethics of the Negro Question," in *The Voice of Anna Julia Cooper*. Edited by Charles Lemert and Esme Bhan (Lanham: Rowman & Littlefield Publishers, Inc., 1998), 206–15.

Angela Y. Davis, "Unfinished Lecture on Liberation—II," in *Philosophy Born of Struggle: Anthology of Afro-American Philosophy from 1917*. Edited by Leonard Harris (Dubuque, Iowa: Kendall/Hunt Pub. Co., 1983), 130–36.

W. E. B. Du Bois, "Criteria of Negro Art," *The Crisis* 32(6) (October, 1926), 290–97.

W. E. B. Du Bois, "The Souls of White Folk," in *W.E.B. Du Bois: A Reader*. Edited by David Levering Lewis (New York: Henry Holt and Company, 1995), 453–65.

Berkeley B. Eddins, *Appraising Theories of History* (Cincinnati: Ehling, 1980).

James Evans, *We Have Been Believers: An African-American Systematic Theology* (Minneapolis, Minnesota: Fortress Press, 1992).

Stephen C. Ferguson II, "Teaching Hurricane Katrina: Understanding Divine Racism and Theodicy," *American Philosophical Association Newsletter on Philosophy and the Black Experience* 7(1) (Fall, 2007), 1–5.

Stephen C. Ferguson II, "On the Occasion of William R. Jones's Death: Remembering the Feuerbachian Tradition in African-American Social Thought," *American Philosophical Association Newsletter on Philosophy and the Black Experience* 12(2) (Spring, 2013), 14–19.

Stephen C. Ferguson II, "Understanding the Legacy of Dr. Wayman Bernard McLaughlin: On the Problem of Interpretation in the History of African American Philosophy," *American Philosophical Association Newsletter on Philosophy and the Black Experience* 13(2) (2014), 2–11.

Stephen C. Ferguson II, *Philosophy of African American Studies: Nothing Left of Blackness* (New York: Palgrave Macmillan, 2015).

Robert Fikes, Jr., "The Triumph of Robert T. Browne: The Mystery of Space," *American Philosophical Association Newsletter on Philosophy and the Black Experience* 6(2) (Spring, 2006), 10–13.

Juan M. Floyd-Thomas, *The Origins of Black Humanism in America: Reverend Ethelred Brown and the Unitarian Church* (New York: Palgrave Macmillan, 2008).

William T. Fontaine, "Philosophical Implications of the Biology of Dr. Ernest E. Just," *The Journal of Negro History* 24 (July, 1939), 281–90.

William T. Fontaine, "The Mind and Thought of the Negro of the United States as Revealed in Imaginative Literature, 1876–1940," *Southern University Bulletin* 28 (March, 1942), 5–50.

William T. Fontaine, "The Means-End Relation and Its Significance for Cross-Cultural Ethical Agreement," *Philosophy of Science* 25(3) (July, 1958), 157–62.

William T. Fontaine, "Toward a Philosophy of the American Negro Literature," *Présence Africaine* 24–25 (1959), 164–76.

E. Franklin Frazier, "The Failure of the Negro Intellectual," *Negro Digest* 11(4) (February, 1962), 52–66.

Charles A. Frye, "Einstein and African Religion and Philosophy: The Hermetic Parallel," in *Einstein and the Humanities*. Edited by Dennis P. Ryan (New York: Greenwood Press, 1987), 59–70.

Albert S. Foley, *Dream of an Outcaste: Patrick F. Healy* (Tuscaloosa: Portals Press, 1989).

Kevin K. Gaines, *Uplifting the Race: Black Leadership, Politics, and Culture in the Twentieth Century* (Chapel Hill, North Carolina: University of North Carolina Press, 1996).

Addison Gayle, Jr., ed., *The Black Aesthetic* (Garden City: Doubleday, 1972).

Cornelius L. Golightly, "Race, Values, and Guilt," *Social Forces* 26(2) (December, 1947), 125–39.

Cornelius L. Golightly, "Value as a Scientific Concept," *The Journal of Philosophy* 53(7) (1956), 233–45.

Richard T. Greener, "The Intellectual Position of the Negro," *The National Quarterly Review* (July, 1880), 168–89.

Richard T. Greener, "The White Problem," in *Blacks at Harvard: A Documentary History of African-American Experience at Harvard and Radcliffe*. Edited by Werner Sollors, Caldwell Titcomb, and Thomas A. Underwood (New York: New York University Press, 1993), 42–56.

Robert V. Guthrie, *Even the Rat Was White a Historical View of Psychology* (Boston: Allyson and Bacon, 2004).

Hubert H. Harrison, *A Hubert Harrison Reader*. Edited by Jeffrey Babcock Perry (Middletown, Connecticut: Wesleyan University Press, 2001).

Charles Leander Hill, "American Democracy," *The Negro Journal of Religion* 6(2) (March, 1940), 9.

Charles Leander Hill, *The Loci Communes of Philip Melanchthon* (Boston: Meador Publishing Co., 1944).

Charles Leander Hill, *A Short History of Modern Philosophy: From the Renaissance to Hegel* (Boston: Meador Publishing Co., 1951).

Charles Leander Hill, "William Ladd, the Black Philosopher from Guinea: A Critical Analysis of His Dissertation on Apathy," *The A.M.E. Church Review* 72(186) (1955), 20–36.

Charles Leander Hill, *The Evangel in Ebony* (Boston: Meador Publishing Co., 1960).

Eugene Clay Holmes, "Negro in Recent American Literature," in *American Writers' Congress*. Edited by Henry Hart (New York: International Publishers, 1935), 145–53.

Eugene Clay Holmes, "The Main Philosophical Considerations of Space and Time," *American Journal of Physics* 18(59) (December, 1950), 564–65.

Eugene Clay Holmes, "A General Theory of the Freedom Cause of the Negro People," in *Afro-American Philosophies: Selected Readings from Jupiter Hammon to Eugene C. Holmes*. Edited by Percy E. Johnston (Upper Montclair: Montclair State College Press, 1970), 18–36.

Langston Hughes, "The Negro Artist and the Racial Mountain," in *The Collected Works of Langston Hughes: Essays on Art, Race, Politics and World Affairs* (Columbia, Missouri: University of Missouri Press, 2002), 31–36.

Sikivu Hutchinson, *Moral Combat: Black Atheists, Gender Politics, and the Values Wars* (Los Angeles: Infidel Books, 2011).

George G. M. James, *The Stolen Legacy* (New York: Philosophical Library, 1954).

Henry T. Johnson, "Philosophy Religiously Valued," *The A.M.E. Church Review* 7(4) (April, 1891), 421–24.

Henry T. Johnson, *The Negro Tried and Triumphant, or, Thoughts Stirred by Race Conflict* (Philadelphia: A.M.E. Publishing House, 1895).

Henry T. Johnson, *The Black Man's Burden* (Philadelphia: Privately Printed, 1899).

William D. Johnson, "Philosophy," in *Afro-American Encyclopedia*. Edited by James T. Haley (Nashville, Tennessee: Haley and Florida, 1895), 284–91.

Charles Johnson, *I Call Myself an Artist: Writings by and about Charles Johnson*. Edited by Rudolph P. Byrd (Bloomington: Indiana University Press, 1999).

Abby A. Johnson and Ronald N. Johnson, *Propaganda and Aesthetics: The Literary Politics of African-American Magazines in the Twentieth Century* (Amherst: University of Massachusetts Press, 1991).

Percy E. Johnston, ed., *Afro-American Philosophies: Selected Readings from Jupiter Hammon to Eugene C. Holmes* (Upper Montclair: Montclair State College Press, 1970).

Gilbert Haven Jones, *Education in Theory and Practice* (Boston: The Gorham Press, 1919).

William R. Jones, "Crisis in Philosophy: The Black Presence' Report of the Subcommittee on the Participation of Blacks in Philosophy," *Proceedings and Addresses of the American Philosophical Association* 47 (1973–1974), 118–25.

William R. Jones, "The Legitimacy and Necessity of Black Philosophy: Some Preliminary Considerations," *The Philosophical Forum* 9(2–3) (Winter–Spring, 1977–78), 149–60.

William R. Jones, "Religious Humanism: Its Problems and Prospects in Black Religion and Culture," *Journal of Interdenominational Theological Center* 7(2) (1980), 175–80.

William R. Jones, "Liberation Strategies in Black Theology: Mao, Martin, or Malcolm?" in *Philosophy Born of Struggle: Anthology of Afro-American Philosophy from 1917*. Edited by Leonard Harris (Dubuque: Kendall/Hunt, 1983), 229–41.

Major Jones, *The Color of God* (Macon: Mercer University Press, 1990).

William R. Jones, *Is God a White Racist?: A Preamble to Black Theology* (Boston: Beacon Press, 1998).

D. J. Jordan, "The Philosophy of Progress," *The A.M.E. Church Review* 10(1) (July, 1893), 111–28.

George D. Kelsey, "The Racist Search for Self," *The Journal of Religious Ethics* 6(1) (Fall, 1978), 240–56.

J. Kershaw, "Evolution: Its Darwinian and Jordanic Theories Compared," *The A.M.E. Church Review* 14(4) (April, 1898), 429–35.

Willis J. King, "Personalism and Race," in *Personalism in Theology*. Edited by Edgar S. Brightman (Boston: Boston University Press, 1943), 204–24.

Edward Krentz, *The Historical Critical Method* (Philadelphia: Fortress Press, 1975).

Bruce Kuklick, Black *Philosopher, White Academy: The Career of William Fontaine* (Philadelphia: University of Pennsylvania Press, 2008).

Michael Lackey, *African American Atheists and Political Liberation* (Gainesville: University Press of Florida, 2007).

David Levering Lewis, *W. E. B. Du Bois, 1868–1919: Biography of a Race* (New York: Henry Holt and Company, 1993).

Alain Locke, "Values and Imperatives," in *American Philosophy, Today and Tomorrow.* Edited by Sidney Hook and Horace M. Kallen(New York: Lee Furman, 1935), 313–36.

Alain Locke, *The Negro and His Music* (Washington, DC: Associates in Negro Folk Education, 1936).

Alain Locke, "Cultural Relativism and Ideological Peace," in *The Philosophy of Alain Locke: Harlem Renaissance and Beyond.* Edited by Leonard Harris (Philadelphia: Temple, 2010), 67–78.

John W. Loftus, ed., *The Christian Delusion* (Amherst: Prometheus Books, 2010).

Ernest Mason, "Black Art and the Configurations of Experience: The Philosophy of the Black Aesthetic," *CLA Journal* 27(1) (1983).

Portia Maultsby, "Africanism in African American Music," in *Africanism in American Culture.* Edited by Joseph E. Holloway (Bloomington: Indiana University Press, 1990).

John H. McClendon III, "The Afro-American Philosopher and the Philosophy of the Black Experience: A Bibliographical Essay on a Neglected Topic in Both Philosophy and Black Studies," *Sage Race Relations Abstracts* 7(4) (November, 1982), 1–51.

John H. McClendon III, "Eugene C. Holmes: A Commentary on a Black Marxist Philosophy," *Philosophy Born of Struggle: Anthology of Afro-American Philosophy from 1917.* Edited by Leonard Harris (Dubuque: Kendall/Hunt, 1983), 37–50.

John H. McClendon III, "Black and White Contra Left and Right? The Dialectics of Ideological Critique in African American Studies," *American Philosophical Association Newsletter on Philosophy and the Black Experience* 2(1) (Fall, 2002), 47–56.

John H. McClendon III, "My Tribute to a Teacher, Mentor, Philosopher and Friend: Dr. Francis A. Thomas (March 16, 1913 to September 17, 2001)," *American Philosophical Association Newsletter on Philosophy and the Black Experience* 3(1) (Fall, 2003), 36–37.

John H. McClendon III, "Introduction to Drs. Anton Wilhelm Amo and Charles Leander Hill," *American Philosophical Association Newsletter on Philosophy and the Black Experience* 2(2) (Spring, 2003), 42–44.

John H. McClendon III, "Charles Leander Hill: Philosopher and Theologian," *The A.M.E. Church Review* 119(390) (April–June, 2003), 81–105.

John H. McClendon III, "Jazz, African American Nationality, and the Myth of the Nation-State," *Socialism and Democracy* 18(2) (July/December, 2004), 21–36.

John H. McClendon III, "African or American? A Dialectical Analysis of Jazz Music," in *The African Presence in Black America*. Edited by Jacob U. Gordon (New Jersey: Africa World Press, 2004), 85–114.

John H. McClendon III, "Dr. Richard Ishmael McKinney: Historical Summation on the Life of a Pioneering African American Philosopher," *American Philosophical Association Newsletter on Philosophy and the Black Experience* 5(2) (Spring, 2006), 1–4.

John H. McClendon III, "Richard B. Moore, Radical Politics and the Afro-American History Movement: The Formation of a Revolutionary Tradition in African American Intellectual Culture," *Afro-Americans in New York Life and History* 30 (July, 2006), 7–46.

John H. McClendon III, "On the Politics of Professional Philosophy: The Plight of the African-American Philosopher," in *Reframing the Practice of Philosophy Bodies of Color, Bodies of Knowledge*. Edited by George Yancy (Albany: SUNY Press, 2012), 121–45.

John H. McClendon III, "Nkrumah's *Consciencism*: Philosophical Materialism and the Issue of Atheism Revisited," *Journal of African Philosophy* 4 (2012), 29–52.

John H. McClendon III, "Dr. William Ronald Jones (July 17, 1933–July 13, 2012): On the Legacy of the Late 'Dean' of Contemporary African American Philosophers," *American Philosophical Association Newsletter on Philosophy and the Black Experience* 12(2) (Spring, 2013), 21–29.

John H. McClendon III, *Philosophy of Religion and the African American Experience: Conversations with My Christian Friends* (Leiden: Brill/Rodopi, 2017).

John H. McClendon III and Stephen C. Ferguson II, *Beyond the White Shadow: Philosophy, Sports, and the African American Experience* (Dubuque: Kendall Hunt Publishing Company, 2012).

John H. McClendon III and Stephen C. Ferguson II, "On the Dialectical Evolution of Malcolm X's Anti-Capitalist Critique: Interrogating His Political Philosophy of Black Nationalism," in *Malcolm X: From Political Eschatology to Religious Revolutionary*. Edited by Dustin J. Byrd and Seyed Javad Miri (Leiden: Brill, 2016), 37–90.

Howard McGary and Bill E. Lawson, *Between Slavery and Freedom: Philosophy and American Slavery* (Bloomington: Indiana University Press, 1995).

Wayman B. McLaughlin, "Symbolism and Mysticism in the Spirituals," *Phylon* 24(1) (1963), 69–77.

Richard I. McKinney, "Existential Ethics and the Protest Movement," *Journal of Religious Thought* 22(2) (1965–66), 108–09.

James Montmarquet and William Hardy, eds., *Reflections: An Anthology of African-American Philosophy* (Belmont, Massachusetts: Wadsworth Publishing, 2000).

Roy D. Morrison II, "Black Philosophy: An Instrument for Cultural and Religious Liberation," *The Journal of Religious Thought* 33(1) (1976), 11–24.

Roy D. Morrison II, "Black Enlightenment: The Issues of Pluralism, Priorities, and Empirical Correlation," *Journal of the American Academy of Religion* 46(2) (June, 1978), 217–40.

Roy D. Morrison II, "Albert Einstein: The Methodological Unity Underlying Science and Religion," *Zygon* 14(3) (September, 1979), 255–66.

Roy D. Morrison II, "Christian Culture and South Africa: Racism, Philosophy and Theology," *The A.M.E. Zion Quarterly Review* 98(1) (April, 1986), 2–11.

Wilson J. Moses, *Alexander Crummell: A Study of Civilization and Discontent* (New York: Oxford University Press, 1989).

Albert Mosley, "On the Aesthetics of Black Music," *The Journal of Aesthetic Education* 35(3) (Autumn, 2001), 94–98.

Albert Mosley, "The Moral Significance of the Music of Black Atlantic," *Philosophy East and West* 57(3) (July, 2007), 345–56.

Alfred Moss, *The American Negro Academy* (Baton Rouge: Louisiana State University Press, 1981).

Sondra O'Neale, *Jupiter Hammon and the Biblical Beginnings of African-American Literature* (Metuchen: Scarecrow Press, 1993).

James O'Toole, *Passing for White: Race, Religion, and the Healy Family, 1820–1920* (Amherst: University of Massachusetts Press, 2002).

Théophile Obenga, *African Philosophy during the Period of the Pharaohs, 2800–330 B.C.* (London: Karnak House, 2000).

Henry Olela, *From Ancient Africa to Ancient Greece: An Introduction to the History of Philosophy* (Atlanta: The Select Publishing Corporation, 1981).

Innocent C. Onyewuenyi, "Traditional African Aesthetics: A Philosophical Perspective," in *African Philosophy*. Edited by Albert Mosley (Englewood: Prentice Hall, 1996), 421–27.

Jeffrey B. Perry, *Hubert Harrison: The Voice of Harlem Radicalism, 1883–1918* (New York: Columbia University Press, 2009).

Rufus L. Perry, *Sketch of Philosophical Systems* (Privately Printed, 1918?).

Anthony B. Pinn, ed., *By These Hands: A Documentary History of African American Humanism* (New York: NYU Press, 2001).

Anthony B. Pinn, ed., *Moral Evil and Redemptive Suffering: A History of Theodicy in the African-American Religious Thought* (Gainesville: University Press of Florida, 2002).

Roosevelt Porter, "Some Peculiarities about Musical Aesthetic Qualities," *The Review of Metaphysics* 48(3) (March, 1995), 483–509.

Joseph C. Price, "The Value of Soul," in *Afro-American Encyclopedia*. Edited by James T. Haley (Nashville, Tennessee: Haley and Florida, 1895), 518–26.

Jerome R. Riley, *The Philosophy of Negro Suffrage* (Washington, DC: Privately Printed, 1897).

Max Roach, "Jazz," in *Freedomways Reader*. Edited by Esther Cooper Jackson (Boulder: Westview Press, 2000), 173–76.

Paul Robeson, *Here I Stand* (Boston, Massachusetts: Beacon Press, 1971).

Paul Robeson, *Paul Robeson Speaks: Writings, Speeches, Interviews, 1918–1974*. Edited by Philip S. Foner (Secaucus, New Jersey: Citadel Press, 1982).

C. V. Roman, *A Knowledge of History Is Conducive for Racial Solidarity and Other Writings* (Nashville: Sunday School Union Print, 1911).

C. V. Roman, "Philosophical Musings in the By-Paths of Ethnology," *The A.M.E. Church Review* 28(1) (July, 1911), 446–47.

C. V. Roman, "Right Thinking the Chief Factor in the Advancement of a Race," *The A.M.E. Church Review* 28(2) (October, 1911), 567–81.

C. V. Roman, *American Civilization and the Negro* (Philadelphia: F. A. Davis Company, Publishers, 1921).

Jeffrey C. Stewart, *The New Negro: The Life of Alain Locke* (New York: Oxford University Press, 2018).

John Milton Smith, "A Critical Estimate of Plato's and Dewey's Educational Philosophy," *Educational Theory* 9(2) (April, 1959), 109–15.

A. B. Stidum, "Originality in Individual and in Race Development," *The A.M.E. Church Review* 7(4) (April, 1891), 408–12.

C. R. Stockton, "The Integration of Cambridge: Alexander Crummell as Undergraduate, 1849–1853," *Integrated Education* (Winter, 1979), 15–19.

Askia Muhammad Touré, "Jihad: Toward a Black National Credo," *Negro Digest* 17(9) (July, 1969), 10–17.

J. R. Van Pelt, "John Wesley Edward Bowen," *The Journal of Negro History* 19(2) (April, 1934), 217–22.

Rudolph V. Vanterpool, *Thus Spoke the Preacher: Solomon's Cosmic Gaze from Under the Sun* (Pittsburgh: Dorrance Publishing Company, 2017).

Forrest Oran Wiggins, "Ethics and Economics," *Phylon* 6(2) (Second Quarter, 1945), 154–62.

Robert C. Williams, "Afro-American Folklore as a Philosophical Source," *Journal of the West Virginia Philosophical Society* (Fall, 1976), 1–6.

Kwasi Wiredu, *Cultural Universals and Particulars: An African Perspective* (Bloomington, Indiana: Indiana University Press, 1996).

Carter G. Woodson, *The Mis-Education of the Negro* (Trenton: Africa World Press, 1998).

George Yancy, ed., *African-American Philosophers: 17 Conversations* (New York: Routledge, 1998).

George Yancy, "History: On the Power of Black Aesthetic Ideals: Thomas Nelson Baker as Preacher and Philosopher," *The A.M.E. Church Review* 117(384) (October–December, 2001), 50–67.

George Yancy, "Gilbert Haven Jones as an Early Black Philosopher and Educator," *American Philosophical Association Newsletter on Philosophy and the Black Experience* 2(2) (Spring, 2003), 42–48.

George Yancy, "Situated Black Women's Voices in/on the Profession of Philosophy," *Hypatia* 23(2) (2008), 155–59.

Shamoon Zamir, *Dark Voices: W. E. B. Du Bois and American Thought, 1888–1903* (Chicago: University of Chicago Press, 1995).

Index